THE TIMES WERE

STRANGE AND STIRRING

THE TIMES WERE
STRANGE AND STIRRING

Methodist Preachers and the

Crisis of Emancipation

———

Reginald F. Hildebrand

Duke University Press *Durham and London* 1995

© 1995 Duke University Press
All rights reserved
Printed in the United States
of America on acid-free paper ∞
Library of Congress Cataloging-in-Publication Data
appear on the last printed page of this book.

This book is dedicated with respect, gratitude, and love, to those of my forebears who were, and are, ministers of the African Methodist Episcopal Church. They all were born in South Carolina. The most senior was a slave there. All of them were products of, and contributors to, the tradition that began with the events described in the following pages.

The Reverend Couthman F. Brogden, great-grandfather
The Reverend Richard E. Brogden, granduncle
The Reverend Arnette C. Brogden, granduncle
The Reverend Benjamin F. Hildebrand, grandfather
The Reverend Christopher C. Burgess, uncle
Bishop Richard Allen Hildebrand, uncle
The Reverend Walter L. Hildebrand, uncle
and most especially this book is dedicated to my father
The Reverend Henry A. Hildebrand

Foolish talk, all of this, you say, of course; and that is because no American now believes in his religion. Its facts are mere symbolism; its revelation vague generalities; its ethics a matter of carefully balanced gain. But to most of the four million black folk emancipated by civil war, God was real. They knew Him. They had met Him personally in many a wild orgy of religious frenzy, or in the black stillness of the night. His plan for them was clear; they were to suffer and be degraded, and then afterwards by Divine edict, raised to manhood and power; and so on January 1, 1863, He made them free.

The magnificent trumpet tones of Hebrew Scripture, transmuted and oddly changed, became a strange new gospel. All that was Beauty, all that was Love, all that was Truth, stood on top of these mad mornings and sang with the stars. A great human sob shrieked in the wind, and tossed its tears upon the sea,—free, free, free.

—W. E. B. Du Bois, *Black Reconstruction*

CONTENTS

ACKNOWLEDGMENTS

Years ago, when I was a young man with fire in my eyes, a song in my heart, and hair on my head, I began this book. During the course of its completion, I have accumulated many debts, only a few of which can be acknowledged here. Librarians and archivists are the essential, unsung collaborators for every work of history. I had the good fortune to be able to avail myself of the assistance, advice, and patience of many of them, including the following: Andrew Simons, Amistad Research Center; Louise Marie Rountree, Carnegie Library, Livingstone College; Cassandra M. Norman and Carrie K. Thompson, Collins-Callaway Library, Paine College; Mary-Louise Mussel and Louise L. Queen, Commission on Archives and History of the United Methodist Church; Edith Fredericks, Manning Library, Clafflin College; William R. Erwin Jr., Perkins Library, Duke University; and Lee B. Dalzell and Allison O'Grady, Sawyer Library, Williams College.

As is the case with many first works, this book began as a dissertation. I decided to enter the graduate program at Princeton, primarily to work with James M. McPherson, who actually did become my thesis advisor. At the time, I did not fully realize how good and how important that decision was, but subsequently, I have often congratulated myself for my keen insight. I trust that, in time, some measure of Professor McPherson's thoughtful scholarship, good writing, and integrity will be reflected in my own work and career. I made the transition from thesis student to author under the knowledgeable, supportive supervision of Lawrence J. Malley, editor par excellence and former director of Duke University Press. While at Duke, Larry strove to create an "author-friendly" publishing house, and I can attest that he succeeded. After his departure from Duke, this project fell into the capable hands of Rachel Toor, who skillfully saw it through to completion. I am also indebted to William Keech of the University of North Carolina at Chapel Hill, who brought this manuscript to the attention of Duke Press, and to Raymond Gavins of Duke University, who also helped this book find a publisher and offered a few words of brotherly support and encouragement when they were needed.

Beginning in January 1991, I had the opportunity to spend an indispensable eighteen months of research and writing in the pleasant environment of the University of North Carolina at Chapel Hill as a Carolina Scholar with UNC's Minority Postdoctoral Fellowship Program, which was then superbly administered by Mary Sue Coleman, dean of research. Dean Coleman's assistance, support, and encouragement were extraordinary. Along the way, several other persons also went significantly above and beyond the call of duty as friends and colleagues to make sure that this book and its author kept moving ahead. A few of them are Donald G. Mathews of UNC, Colin A. Palmer of the City University of New York, Lillie Johnson Edwards of Drew University, and Charles B. Dew and Shanti M. Singham of Williams College. Each one knows how they helped me, and I will not forget.

I also benefited greatly from the valuable criticism, information, and sound advice that was generously provided to me by a long list of sterling colleagues including Allen B. Ballard, Joan L. Bryant, Randall K. Burkett, Kenneth M. Coleman, Dennis C. Dickerson, Jualynne Dodson, Katherine L. Dvorak, William B. Gravely, Warren M. Jenkins, C. Eric Lincoln, James H. Moorhead, Ralph E. Morrow, Nell Irvin Painter, Albert J. Raboteau, Edwin S. Redkey, David L. Smith, Preston H. Smith, George B. Tindall, Joel Williamson, and David W. Wills. In addition, Franz Burnet-Gocht undertook the formidable task of copy-editing what turned out to be a primitive version of this manuscript. Only a few of my errors could have managed to escape his ruthless pencil and keen judgment. The work done by historians requires extended periods of solitude, but none of us can get by without a little help from our friends.

Finally, I am happy to acknowledge the contributions of Ebony Chatman, R. Todd Bunch, and Martin Burkett, three energetic, resourceful, and capable research assistants who worked with me while they were undergraduates at Williams College. I expect that each of them will accomplish a great deal of great value during the course of their careers.

As one final gesture of gratitude, I absolve all of the aforementioned people of any responsibility for the shortcomings of this book. They did their best, and I did the rest.

INTRODUCTION

This is a book about emancipation and about the ways in which some Methodist preachers tried to shape the world that began when slavery ended. For most antebellum blacks, freedom had existed only in hopes and prayers and in a dimly remembered past in another land. But, in due course, the earth moved, Pharaoh yielded, and there came the supreme moment. They did not all hear about it at the same time, and they did not all experience it in the same way, but for each slave there was the moment of emancipation, the discrete point in life's journey when slavery ended and freedom began. There is very little likelihood that we could ever grasp how it felt when "the big freedom" came.

W. E. B. Du Bois tried to enter that moment in *The Souls of Black Folk* when he wrote:

> Few men ever worshipped freedom with half such unquestioning faith as did the American Negro for two centuries. To him, so far as he thought and dreamed, slavery was indeed the sum of all villainies, the cause of all sorrow, the root of all prejudice; Emancipation was the key to a promised land of sweeter beauty than ever stretched before the eyes of wearied Israelites. In song and exhortation swelled one refrain—Liberty; in his tears and curses the God he implored had Freedom in his right hand. At last it came, . . . suddenly, fearfully, like a dream. With one wild carnival of blood and passion came the message in his own plaintive cadences:
> Shout, O Children!
> Shout, you're free
> For God has bought your liberty.[1]

In the 1930s, an ex-slave from Mississippi named Hamp Santee looked back over his life and recalled the day of Jubilee. The interviewer who heard Mr. Santee's remembrances chose to record the old man's words in the following manner:

> At surrender I kin remember de niggers wuz all so happey. Dey jes rung bells, blowed horns and shouted like deys crazy. Den dey all bought a brand new rope, and cut hit up into little pieces and dey gives every nigger a piece of hit to keep and say, dat when ever dey look at de rope dey remembers dat dey is free from bondage.[2]

The transcriber's pirouette between anthropological accuracy and ethnocentric condescension cannot obscure the poignant brilliance of Santee's story, or the clarity with which it reveals the power of one community's first encounter with freedom.

Ira Berlin's magisterial, multivolume documentary history of emancipation, as well as recent works by William Cohen, Seymour Drescher and Frank McGlynn, Russell Duncan, Robert F. Engs, Barbara Jeanne Fields, Eric Foner, Leon Litwack, Edward Magdol, Jay R. Mandle, Clarence L. Mohr, and others, have signaled the fact that scholars have begun to focus on emancipation as a period and a process in and of itself, and no longer regard it merely as the event that preceded Reconstruction.[3] To underscore that shift in historiographical emphasis, it is useful to make a distinction between emancipationists and Reconstructionists: *emancipationists* were primarily concerned with securing and expanding the fruits of freedom; *Reconstructionists* were primarily concerned with reuniting the nation on an enduring basis. Sometimes the efforts and the objectives of emancipationists and Reconstructionists coincided; sometimes they ran on separate tracks. At other times, they were in direct conflict with each other. Emancipationists were black and white, northern and southern. This work is primarily a study of the actions and aspirations of emancipationists.

The emancipation of black southerners was both conventional and radical. It was conventional in the sense that, in their quest for freedom, the freedpeople did not try to alter the commonly held understandings of what that term meant. They did not challenge the fundamental political, social, or economic ideals of the American republic. Southern blacks wanted to direct their own lives: they wanted to have secure families, to be educated, to own property, to be protected by the law, and to participate in the political process. In short, their aspirations were very traditional. On the other hand, emancipation was radical in the sense that it challenged the omnipresent, multifaceted ideology of white supremacy which posited that blacks should be subordinate to whites in all areas of life. Some emancipationists tried to finesse that ideology by allowing freedom to be mediated through white paternalism. Others insisted on confronting the ideology head-on through a kind of black nationalism. Still others believed that the ideology of white supremacy could be transcended, and they tried to construct a new social order in which color would play no significant part.

Emancipationists were an eclectic set of true believers. Among the strategies and goals that they pursued were the following: accommodationism, moral reform, black nationalism, civil rights legislation, integration, migration, emigration, Pan-Africanism, economic self-help, federal intervention, electoral politics, and uplift through education. Booker T. Washington, W. E. B. Du Bois, Marcus Garvey, Adam Clayton Powell Jr., Malcolm X, and Martin Luther King Jr. all could have found their precursors among the emancipationists. In fact, all of those leaders spent all of their careers trying to achieve the goals that had seemed so close at hand when freedom was still new. The apparent similarities with ideas and leaders from subsequent time periods are interesting, but the aim of this study is to understand the extraordinarily complex phenomenon of emancipation in its own context and on its own terms. As I will attempt to show, the period of emancipation was unique.

This essay uses religious denominations as vehicles for exploring some of the dimensions of emancipation and as the means for developing a new typology of some of the ways in which emancipation was approached. To some degree, I am seeking some new information from institutions that have already received a great deal of scholarly attention, of a sort. Traditionally, monographs on emancipation and Reconstruction have both acknowledged and neglected the significance of the black church. Such studies almost always include a chapter on the church, explaining that blacks left white religious organizations to form churches of their own, which then became centers of social organization and served as staging grounds for political activities in which clergymen played prominent leadership roles. Generally, those monographs also point out that black worship was emotional. After making those almost obligatory and predictable general observations about the significance of the church, most studies quickly move on to explore other topics in much greater depth, and, I believe, with far greater seriousness.[4]

Two of the most thoughtful, comprehensive, and important recent books on this period help substantiate the foregoing assessment of the literature on emancipation. In his impressive and thoughtful study called *Reconstruction,* Eric Foner focuses on "the centrality of the black experience" during that period.

He points out that "religious convictions profoundly affected the way blacks understood the momentous events around them." Yet, Foner devotes only eight of the over six-hundred pages of his text to an examination of the role played by the black church.[5] Few works have even come close to the thoroughness of Leon Litwack's landmark study of the aftermath of slavery, *Been in the Storm So Long*. Yet, Litwack devotes only one half of one chapter of his book to the black church.[6] The few works that do focus on the role of the freedpeople's religious institutions have made important contributions to our understanding of emancipation, but they have their own shortcomings. For example, the best monographs on the history of Methodist denominations during emancipation and Reconstruction have tended to focus on intense denominational rivalries and cutthroat competition for new members.[7] Those institutional rivalries were indeed important parts of the drama of the postwar years, but the history of the black church during that period cannot be properly understood outside the context of the impassioned search to find the meanings of freedom. The missionaries to the freedpeople were engaged in much more than competition for members. They were key players in a battle of ideas. They had deep convictions about how the future of the freedpeople should unfold, and more than a few of them paid for their convictions with their lives. To date, the best and most ambitious general study of the black church during the period of emancipation and Reconstruction is William E. Montgomery's, *Under Their Own Vine and Fig Tree*, which was published in 1993.[8]

FREEDOM. The word was surely sweet, but what did it mean? Emancipation had merely determined that blacks would no longer be slaves. It said nothing about what they would become. Before the war, the Supreme Court had ruled that free blacks were not entitled to the same legal rights as whites, and the Black Codes enacted right after the war seemed to confirm that view. Was there any reason to assume that freedom would mean more for blacks after emancipation than it had meant for the mostly marginalized antebellum free blacks? How, from the rubble of slavery, could blacks fashion an instructive image of what it could mean to be free and black?

At the moment of emancipation, the freedpeople began a long, frustrating, and sometimes painful process of finding answers to those questions. Many other players in the drama of emancipation tried to promulgate answers of their own. Officers of the Union army, the Freedmen's Bureau, President Andrew Johnson, the moderate Republicans, the radical Republicans, the courts, southern state governments, white landowners, and the Ku Klux Klan were among the forces who had strong ideas about how freedom should be defined and about where the freedpeople should fit within the new national order.

At the outset, former slaves with neither the ballot nor the bullet, forty acres nor a mule, were put in the position of having to wrest freedom from the grip of all those powerful, conflicting forces. For the freedpeople, the passage from slavery to freedom was treacherous and unpredictable. In making that passage they had to develop their own points of reference; they had to develop a vision of who they were and of what they could become; they had to find ways to give institutionalized expression to their concepts of freedom. The church was one of the few areas in which blacks were relatively free to define an aspect of freedom in ways that made sense to them. This essay will examine some of the ways in which Methodism attempted to play a role in that process.

The African Methodist Episcopal Church (A.M.E.) the African Methodist Episcopal Zion Church (A.M.E. Zion), the Colored Methodist Episcopal Church (C.M.E.), the Methodist Episcopal Church (M.E.), and the Methodist Episcopal Church, South (M.E. South) each offered southern blacks working models of what freedom could mean. Each denomination promoted a distinctive set of social values, and each pursued its own approach to racial issues. E. Franklin Frazier argued that Christianity made it possible for slaves to make sense of the world they entered after the trauma of the middle passage displaced them from the social and cultural moorings that had defined life in Africa. Albert J. Raboteau has shown the key role that religion played in helping slaves sustain themselves as they passed through the vicissitudes of existence in chattel slavery.[9] Similarly, it is the thesis of this study that religious denominations played an important role in helping the freedpeople make sense of the world they entered after the happy trauma of emancipation.

I will attempt to define some of the ways in which freedom was perceived and pursued at a unique moment in American, African-American, and Methodist history. During this period, the nation's political, legal, and economic institutions were focused on two tasks: one was determining on what bases the states would once again be united; the other was defining what freedom would mean for nearly four million black southerners. It should not be surprising that religious institutions also concerned themselves with the latter task; it was the paramount social issue of the immediate postwar era. When former slaves made a religious affiliation, they were not just choosing a church and a preacher; they were also engaged in the process of redefining themselves as free people. Selecting a religious affiliation was just as significant as selecting a surname or deciding where to live and work.[10] To a large degree, the freedpeople bequeathed their religious identities to their descendants, just as surely as they bequeathed their names.

This study explores the ideas and the ideals of missionaries of the several branches of the Methodist family. There was a time when Methodists were one, but they fell apart, largely because of different ideas about race. Both African Methodist denominations declared their independence from the Methodist Episcopal Church in the early 1800s because blacks had been denied equality and authority. The Methodist Episcopal Church, South, broke away from the national denomination in 1844 because southerners could no longer tolerate the antislavery positions of their northern coreligionists. From 1844 until the Civil War, the slave states and the slave quarters were the exclusive dominions of the M.E. Church, South.

Beginning in 1863, the missionaries of every branch of Methodism had free access to the souls of nearly four million black southerners. Methodists of every stripe pursued those souls with zeal and fervor. No important theological issues separated one branch of Methodism from another, nor did the race of the missionary personnel distinguish one denomination from another because all of the denominations recruited and made use of southern black preachers. The battle between Methodisms was waged largely over different interpretations of the meaning of freedom. This essay explains what those differences were and why the missionaries adhered to them with such fidelity. This work is not intended to be a chronicle of the spread of Methodism among southern blacks; rather, it is an exploration of how Methodist missionaries responded to the crisis of emancipation.

This work has a single theme. It should not be read as if it were three traditional denominational histories under one cover. As has been noted earlier, the major objective of this study is to interpret the emancipatory social gospels of Methodist preachers in order to develop a typology of three of the ways in which freedom was approached and understood. Consequently, the book is divided into three distinct sections, each of which could be read as a separate essay. Each was written and structured to reflect a different set of dynamics. Part 1 deals with the efforts of some black and white southerners to establish a new paternalism that could define the parameters of race relations after slavery no longer served that purpose. Part 2 deals with the actions and attitudes of northern black missionaries from African Methodist denominations who attempted to promote a kind of evangelical black nationalism. Those northern blacks advocated what I have referred to here as the Gospel of Freedom. Part 3 deals with the struggles of integrationist missionaries of the Methodist Episcopal Church who believed that dismantling the racial caste system was the logical and necessary successor to the fight against slavery. By no means, however, is the typology that will be developed in the following pages intended to imply that there were only three ways of understanding the elusive and complex concept of freedom, even among Methodist missionaries.

Because of the somewhat unorthodox organization of this book, perhaps I should offer a few additional words of explanation, or apology, which I hope will serve as a kind of "readers' guide." Each of the three sections offers a different interpretation of the significance of the same time period and a different perspective on the meaning of similar events. Because all of the sections deal with the same chronological period, they do overlap, but I have made an effort to keep actual repetition to a minimum. One major figure, named James Lynch, appears in more than one part of this study because he moved from one denomination to another. I have tried to explain the motivations for his switch as fully as possible in order to highlight the significance of the distinction between the ways in which the different denominations approached the challenge of freedom. This study invites the reader to enter three distinct mindsets and three conflicting denominational cultures. Although they could stand apart, the significance of each of the three sections is derived, in part, from contrasting it with the other two. It is hoped that the reader will find what could be whimsically referred to as a "triographic" approach (as opposed to monographic) to be an interesting and useful way of investigating one complex historical theme.

The period of emancipation began when the first black refugee fled to Union lines and was declared to be "contraband of war." For all intents and purposes, affirmative federal involvement in the process of emancipation ended about a decade and a half later when the "Compromise of 1877" resulted in the withdrawal of military support from what remained of a remarkable, though seriously flawed, experiment in biracial democracy.[11] To paraphrase a literary cliche, emancipation/Reconstruction was the most promising of times and the most disappointing of times. During no other period in American history were idealism and depravity so exaggerated, so widespread, and so intermingled. The greatest beneficiaries of the period were the four million black southerners who had been chattel property; the greatest victims of the period were those same black southerners. For a wonderful and cruel moment, they were teased with the prospect of becoming citizens of the United States. Ultimately, their government found that maintaining their freedom was too difficult and too costly. Fortunately, the task of defining freedom was not left entirely in the hands of politicians. As might be expected, preachers had a great deal to say on the subject, and the freedpeople, who had little control over the vagaries of government policies, could decide where they would go to church and who would be their preachers. As has already been indicated, those decisions were fraught with significance.

This study focuses on Methodist ministers who preached to the freedpeople and on the factors that influenced the way those preachers saw the world. The preacher was the leader whose job it was to preside over life's rites of passage and to plumb their meaning. Baptisms, marriages, conversions, deaths, funerals—the preacher gave those moments context and explained their significance to the community. The preacher issued admonitions about values and about the responsibilities that members of the community had to God, to humanity in general, and especially to their downtrodden race. The preacher offered lyrical meditations on the powerful imponderables that could strike without warning or reason, reminding the prideful of their vulnerability and of the fragility of life—imponderables such as illness, violent storms, and white people. The words of the preacher provided consolation, inspiration, and meaning.[12] No truly momentous occurrence could pass without a few words from the community's spiritual leader, and emancipation was the most momentous occurrence that black folk had ever experienced.

Politics and political parties brought forth a wholly new category of leadership and a largely new cadre of leaders, but as important as politicians were, they could not displace preachers as the primary dispensers of meaning. The preachers served as precinct captains and ward heelers for the process of emancipation. They were authentic leaders whose survival and success depended on the effectiveness of their relationships with their parishioners. The state legislature, the county courthouse, and the local credit agency/general store were all locations that came to have tremendous impact on the lives of the freedpeople, but southern black churches—independent of white oversight—were also products of this era. The churches became bulwarks for communities in the midst of transition and reformation, and it was to the church that many people came for healing and hope and to seek the wisdom and strength they needed to live with life's powerful imponderables. On a day-to-day basis, even nonchurchgoers probably knew a lot more about the ideas and actions of local ministers than they did about the machinations of legislators at the state capital, although the emphases of many of the studies of this period might suggest just the opposite. It should be kept in mind that preachers and missionaries began to exert their influence even before the war was over, but the freedpeople weren't even permitted to register to vote until the process of emancipation was already two years old in most of the South, and in a few places even older than that. Certainly, no less attention should be given to politics (much important work has yet to be done on that subject), but our understanding of emancipation would be enhanced by having more serious, creative, and resourceful scholarly attention focused on religion, preachers, and the church.

I end this introduction with a few caveats. First, this essay examines a moment in the history of five religious denominations in order to answer some secular questions about the ways in which the process of emancipation took place in the southern United States. This study does not discuss the spiritual dimension of religious organizations, even though I am well aware of the great significance of that dimension for the people who are the protagonists of this story. If I were a theologian, this would be a different kind of book. Second, this book focuses on the views of influential preachers for the reasons explained earlier, but that does not imply a disregard for the views of the laity. Obviously, a study based on the members' perspectives on the issues dealt with here would be of enormous value. Unfortunately, membership lists from this time period have not yet been found in sufficient numbers and of sufficient quality to make it possible to mount a sound comparative analysis. Third, in my two chapters on Colored Methodism I offer an interpretation of the founding of the Colored Methodist Church which departs from some of the traditional accounts of that event, and for that reason it may draw some criticism from colleagues for whom I have a great deal of respect.[13] Nevertheless, I believe that my interpretation is firmly grounded in the primary sources.

Finally, a thoughtful colleague pointed out to me that writing about the black church while leaving out the Baptists is a little like writing about American politics and leaving out the Democrats—and, of course, he was right. Nevertheless, I believe that there are some sound methodological reasons for the one-denominational approach taken here. By limiting this study to Methodism, I have controlled for differences based on theology and/or polity. This allows me to keep the focus on the differences that developed primarily because of divergent understandings of the meaning of freedom. In addition, because of its centralized administrative structure, denomination-wide policies are more clearly discernable for Methodists than for the more decentralized Baptists. Furthermore, as Donald G. Mathews has observed, the policies of the Methodist church generally have been good reflectors of social and political developments in this country. Readers interested in how the Baptists dealt with the challenge of freedom should consult the relevant chapters of *Frustrated Fellowship: The Black Baptist Quest for Social Power* by James M. Washington.

In addition, J. Carleton Hayden and Joe M. Richardson have done important work on the southern missions of the Episcopal and Congregational churches, respectively.[14]

Despite the limitations and the inevitable errors of my own exposition, I hope that the reader will find the actions and the ideas of Methodist emancipationists to be as engrossing and as instructive as I have.

METHODIST DENOMINATIONS
REFERRED TO IN THIS BOOK

African Methodist Episcopal Church (A.M.E.) An independent denomination founded by blacks in the North and border states as a protest against racial discrimination in the Methodist Episcopal Church. The A.M.E. Church held its inaugural General Conference in 1816 at Bethel Church in Philadelphia. Richard Allen was chosen to be the first bishop of the A.M.E. Church. In addition to being a Methodist minister, Allen was also one of the founders of a black mutual aid society called the Free African Society of Philadelphia. Allen also served as president of the first National Negro Convention, which took place in 1831 and was held at Bethel A.M.E. Church in Philadelphia. Allen's activism helped establish the values and objectives of the A.M.E. social gospel.

African Methodist Episcopal Zion Church (A.M.E. Zion) An independent denomination founded by blacks in the North in 1822 as a protest against racial discrimination in the Methodist Episcopal Church and because of dissatisfaction with the A.M.E. alternative.[1] James Varick became the first superintendent of the denomination at its inaugural conference, which took place at Zion Church in New York City. In 1848 the new denomination officially adopted the name by which it is now known; before then it was called the A.M.E. Church, just like its Philadelphia-based sister denomination.

Colored Methodist Episcopal Church in America (C.M.E.) An independent denomination founded in 1870 in Jackson, Tennessee, by southern blacks with the assistance of the Methodist Episcopal Church, South. The founding of the

C.M.E. Church represented both an assertion of black independence from white evangelical oversight and an attempt to retain some of the traditions of antebellum paternalism. The C.M.E. Church was also a black southern alternative to African Methodism and Northern Methodism.

Methodist Episcopal Church (M.E.), or Northern Methodist John and Charles Wesley brought Methodism to North America from England in the 1730s. The first General Conference of the Methodist Episcopal Church took place in Baltimore in 1784. Initially, the M.E. Church took strong positions in opposition to slavery. The denomination modified its antislavery policies in order to survive in the South and have access to slaves, although antislavery sentiment remained strong in the North. Because the M.E. Church was the original source of all Methodism in North America it is sometimes referred to as the "Mother Church."

Methodist Episcopal Church, South (M.E. Church, South), or Southern Methodist In 1844, the General Conference of the M.E. Church directed Bishop James O. Andrew of Georgia to desist from the exercise of his office until he was no longer in possession of slaves. Methodists from the South protested against that action by withdrawing from the M.E. Church and forming the Methodist Episcopal Church, South. Although the decision to found a separate denomination was made in 1844, the first General Conference of the M.E. Church, South, did not convene until 1846.

The most comprehensive single volume on the history of black Methodism is *Dark Salvation: The Story of Methodism as It Developed among Blacks in America* by Harry V. Richardson.

THE TIMES WERE
STRANGE AND STIRRING

PART I

SOUTHERN METHODISM AND
COLORED METHODISM
"BLEST BE THE TIE THAT BINDS"

Blest be the tie that binds
Our hearts in Christian love.
The fellowship of kindred minds
Is like to that above.

When we are called to part,
It gives us inward pain;
But we shall be joined in heart,
And hope to meet again.

—*The Methodist Hymnal*

1

SOUTHERN METHODIST PATERNALISM,

OLD AND NEW

The members of the Colored Methodist Episcopal Church were subjected to a great deal of disparagement. Some of the harshest came from the leaders of other black Methodist denominations. During Reconstruction, some blacks regarded Colored Methodists as evangelical pariahs, who had an unseemly attachment to the past at a time when the fulfillment of the promise of freedom seemed to belong to the future. Yet, in 1873, after only three years of existence, the denomination claimed nearly 68,000 members, and its 635 preachers held forth from pulpits throughout the South.[1] To understand the significance of Colored Methodism, it is useful to review some of the factors that brought the C.M.E. Church into being.

The relationship between blacks and Southern Methodism was intimate and longstanding by the time of emancipation. In the years before it achieved respectability, many whites dismissed Methodism as a refuge for the refuse of society. The denomination also labored under the suspicion that there were antislavery embers smoldering somewhere in the core of its social gospel. As a consequence, it was in part by default that blacks came to swell Methodist ranks. In 1826, blacks made up about forty percent of the membership in South Carolina and Georgia, and in some local areas black Methodists vastly outnumbered their white coreligionists. It was with considerable pride that a minister who had preached to slaves observed: "It cannot be refuted that from the earliest appearance of Methodism in the South, the negro shared largely in the labor and care of her ministry." Southern Methodists took a special interest in carrying the gospel to slaves on plantations: the slave population represented a huge, inviting mission field on southern soil. White Southern Methodists believed that God had caused the salvation of blacks to be entrusted to their hands. Reverend William Martin expressed a sentiment that was shared by many of the missionaries to slaves when he recalled: "It was a great work, a momentous work, a special one for the South."[2]

Of course, the spread of Christianity among antebellum black southerners did not require white missionaries or membership in white churches, any more than the transmission of spirituals required white choir directors, but this study is concerned with the official Methodist mission to plantations and its legacy. Reverend William Capers is generally credited with establishing ongoing missions to slaves on plantations in 1829, although individual efforts by Methodist preachers, black as well as white, preceded that date. In a sense, the officially recognized Methodist mission to slaves was called into being by Charles Cotesworth Pinckney, who was an Episcopalian. Pinckney asked Capers to send missionaries to his plantation on the Santee River in South Carolina. He had been favorably impressed by the influence that a Methodist overseer had on the slaves of a fellow planter in Georgia. Pinckney was joined in his request by two other owners of large plantations, neither of whom were Methodists. The endorsement of those influential planters gave an important fillip to the missionary enterprise. Under Capers's supervision, the plantation missions grew rapidly. Between 1829 and 1844, the mission project grew from two missionaries with little financial support, working with 417 slaves on three plantations; to seventy-one missionaries with a budget of $22,377, serving sixty-eight mission stations with a total of 21,063 members.[3]

In 1844, slaveholding by a southern bishop, under some extenuating circumstances, exacerbated already existing tensions within Methodism and split the denomination into separate northern and southern bodies. The southern church became known as the Methodist Episcopal Church, South, also called Southern Methodism. Having completely divorced itself from the antislavery sentiments of its northern coreligionists, Southern Methodism became even more acceptable to slave owners, and the mission to slaves continued its rapid expansion under strictly southern auspices. By 1861, there were 327 missionaries in the field, serving 329 missions with 66,559 members, supported by a budget of $86,359.20. According to William P. Harrison, the historian of the plantation mission, on the eve of the Civil War, Methodist missionaries were active in an area that "extended from the Potomac to the Gulf of Mexico, and from the Atlantic seaboard to the Mississippi and beyond."[4]

Southern Methodists held their missionaries in high esteem. In the estimation of Capers's biographer, the labors of some of those men evoked "the heroic spirit of the ancient faith." It is not likely that the record of the missionaries' travail is free from romanticization, but it is clear that some of them did encounter insalubrious conditions, isolation from other whites, meager remuneration, and long, hard hours of demanding work. The rice-growing regions of South Carolina were considered to be particularly hazardous for missionaries. By working in the swampy environment that the slaves were forced to inhabit, white Methodists exposed themselves to "billious fever," "the dread pestilence," and "deadly miasmatic exhalations." As one missionary remembered: "It was no holiday time."[5]

Ministering to the slave quarters also had its own unique rewards. Some missionaries were deeply touched by the willingness with which slaves drew from their own meager resources to contribute to the support of "their" preacher. As exemplars of evangelical paternalism, white Southern Methodists were particularly gratified by expressions of gratitude and affection from their black charges. In 1859, Reverend J. A. Clement, who served as a missionary in Alabama, wrote a letter to the *Southern Advocate* in which he asked: "Mr. Editor, did you ever preach to negroes? Do you not recognize the hearty Amen, the impressive shake of the hand? And then that 'Thankee massa, for dat sarmon. You told me sumpin I dint know afore.'" Mission historian Harrison concluded that, despite the hardships, "many" preachers sought plantation duty because of the "peculiar unction" that was bestowed upon the missionaries who served the "sable children of Africa."[6]

Most of the Southern Methodists who answered the call to serve as plantation missionaries were sincerely committed to the slaves' salvation and spiritual welfare. It is too easy to draw their motives into question because the subordination of blacks and the justification of slaveholding were such integral parts of their ministry. For the most part, they were not being hypocritical; they simply believed that the Bible mandated both salvation and slavery. As Donald G. Mathews observed in his thoughtful and perceptive study, *Religion in the Old South:* "The Gospel of love could sometimes be mistaken as a means instead of an end; the conversion of slaves became the means of saving the South."[7]

On the other hand, the spiritual sincerity of the missionaries did not mitigate the impact of their equally sincere efforts to maintain the social order of which slavery was a part. Under Capers's supervision, the Southern Methodist mission to slaves won the confidence of slave owners by demonstrating that the business of saving souls would not produce troublesome disciplinary by-products. The missionaries subjected their captive congregations to homilies on hard work, honesty, chastity, fidelity, and responsibility. They preached the whole canon of middle-class virtues and obligations, without the promise of middle-class respectability or social mobility. In 1836, Capers explained: "Our missionaries inculcate the duties of servants to their masters, as we find those duties stated in the Scriptures. They inculcate the performance of them as indispensably important. We hold that a Christian slave must be submissive, faithful and obedient."[8] The most radical of the Southern Methodists only attempted to make slavery a less brutal institution, and hence a stronger one, better able to withstand the fulminations of northern abolitionists.

By the early 1830s, experience and observation had convinced plantation owners that the missionaries were safe on the issue of slavery. Southern Methodists took great pride in the large number of prominent patrons who endorsed, encouraged, and financed their efforts. In addition to Charles Cotesworth Pinckney, luminaries such as Robert Barnwell Rhett and Wade Hampton also made Methodism a part of the culture of their slaves. The planters, many of whom were not Methodists themselves, believed that they got a handsome secular return for their investment in missions.[9]

Over the decades, Southern Methodism invested time, money, and manpower into the construction of a social order in which slavery and the gospel functioned together, smoothly and symbiotically. Its missionaries overcame the initial suspicions of slaveholders and withstood the denunciations of those Northern Methodists who were opposed to slavery. The church believed that it had kept faith with its evangelical responsibilities by bringing thousands of slaves into the light. White Southern Methodists were proud of the accomplishments of their denomination. They were confident that God would continue to smile upon their efforts and bring them even greater success in the future. Then, the war came and things fell apart.

Reverend Francis Asbury Mood was pastor of the Colored Mission Church organized in Charleston during the war. Reverend Mood viewed the war from the perspective of the missionaries.[10] He recalled the Union bombardment of Charleston in this way: "Trinity Church was soon compassed by shells and its pastor left the city. One of the first shells that fell—penetrated the tomb of Rev. John Honour in Trinity cemetery, the first missionary to the Negroes in Carolina, exploded and literally tore it to atoms."[11]

Reverend Mood's recollection could be apocryphal, but it accurately conveys the impact of the war on plantation missions. The reverend recalled with regret that territory gained for the Union was territory lost for the missions. It was difficult for the denomination to function effectively in occupied territory. The planters who had lent their support to the missions lacked authority. The denomination's finances dried up.[12] Slavery was demolished. Perhaps the most disorienting development of all was that far, far too many of the black beneficiaries of the evangelical concern of Southern Methodism abandoned the denomination and embraced the glad tidings of aggressive emissaries of black and white Methodist denominations from the North.

In 1860, the Methodist Episcopal Church, South, claimed a total of 207,776 black members. By 1866, only 78,742 of that number remained, and the exodus of former slaves showed no signs of abating. During that same time period, the South Carolina Conference of the Church, which had given birth to the mission to slaves, lost a staggering sixty-seven percent of its black membership; 33,384 black South Carolinians chose to leave the paternal care of Southern Methodism. The North Carolina Conference lost sixty-two percent of its black members, and the Tennessee Conference lost forty-five percent. During the final winter of the war, the Mississippi Conference reported that its missions to slaves along the Mississippi River had been "completely broken up, with perhaps one or two exceptions." [13] Southern Methodist missionaries would have to try to make some sense out of what had happened to them and then decide what, if anything, they could do to redeem the situation.

Could it be that the troubles that befell the South were produced by the "terrible swift sword" of a deity angered by the immorality of slavery? There is no reason to believe that the outcome of the war, or the exodus of black Methodists, caused the missionaries to question the support their denomination had given to slavery.[14] Military defeat had little impact on scripturally based beliefs. As Southern Methodists saw things, enslavement, particularly the enslavement of the descendants of Ham, was a biblically sound social practice. The Apostle Paul had not been an abolitionist. Even if Providence had decreed that the time for slavery had come to an end, it had not decreed that the institution had ever been sinful, or that those who supported it had been misguided in their interpretation of divine will.

Why, then, would the Lord have caused the South to drink from such a bitter cup? True believers could not leave the question unanswered. Toward the end of the war, Methodist ministers in Georgia reaffirmed their belief that slavery was the instrument that God had chosen to place Africans "under the Christian tutelage of Anglo-Saxon Protestants," but their equanimity was not complete. The clergymen wondered whether southern evangelicals had done enough to bring salvation to the souls that had been entrusted to their stewardship. Perhaps they had not measured up to the task of making slavery a truly Christian institution. "If we had been faithful to this high trust," the Georgians conjectured, "God might have turned aside the red waves of war." [15]

In any event, suffering could be redemptive, and it was not necessarily a sign of God's displeasure. An editorial that appeared in the *Southern Christian Advocate* in January 1865 reminded its readers that "the foundations of Israel's greatness were laid in the sufferings undergone in Egypt." Even though the Jews had been conquered, they remained "God's elect people" and they preserved their "national distinctiveness." The *Advocate* offered a comforting homily to those southerners who were dismayed by the course of the war: "If we would be a great and good people, we must be formed to greatness and goodness by God's own hand, in God's own way." [16]

The resolve of southern evangelicals had not been broken. "Though cast down, we are not destroyed," the Missionary Society of the South Carolina Conference asserted in November 1865. Of course, there were some expressions of resentment and bitterness, but, for the most part, the missionaries pledged to continue to put forth their best efforts on behalf of their former charges. They concluded that many of the freedpeople who left the denomination did so simply because they had become intoxicated by their new freedom and had allowed themselves to be beguiled by northern interlopers. The Missionary Society advised that the circumstances required patience: "The people we have long served may yet discover that old friends are the best friends, and we can afford to abide God's time, and calmly await the result." The Georgia Conference also met in November 1865 and resolved to maintain its mission work even though many blacks had "unwisely and ungraciously" severed their ties with Southern Methodism and succumbed to the influence of "evil counselors." During the year after the defeat of the Confederacy, every state conference in the denomination resolved to continue to work with blacks,[17] but the message of the membership figures was clear. Southern Methodist mission work had suffered a defeat that was just as devastating as the one experienced by the secular South.

Nevertheless, the basic assumptions that had shaped the mission to slaves did survive the war pretty much intact. White Southern Methodists continued to believe that their objectives in regard to the black population were correct and sanctioned by God. They did not dissemble when they professed a desire to keep blacks in the Methodist Episcopal Church, South. They had strong religious, psychological, and social reasons for wanting to retain the membership of former slaves. Religious consistency and the evangelical imperative required that the missionaries not let emancipation lessen their zeal for redeeming black souls. If a denomination that took great pride in its concern for the spiritual welfare of slaves took no interest in the salvation of freedpeople, it would leave itself open to the charge of hypocrisy. It would seem as though the missionaries had been commissioned by slave owners and not by God. Southern Methodists were not inclined to play into the hands of northerners who accused them of having been no more than overseers in clergymen's clothing.

Evangelical paternalists also had a psychological investment in the missions that they did not want to lose because of the war. The missionaries believed that God had selected southern whites to be the guardians of his African children. Divine Providence set apart white evangelicals to be emissaries of the gospel to those who were most in need of its influence. The mission to slaves made southern churchmen chosen people. It provided reassuring evidence of their own sanctification and gave special purpose and luster to southern religion. The mission to slaves was the most distinctive element of the religious identity of the South. It was a distinction that whites would not yield willingly.

In addition, southern evangelicals had a social agenda that they wanted to carry over into Reconstruction. Before the war, the institution of slavery had defined how the races were to relate to each other. The church assisted slavery in carrying out that conservative social function. The missionaries tried to teach slaves to understand and appreciate the place God had ordained for them to occupy in the social and economic order of the South. From the evangelical perspective, blacks, like white women, were not quite adult. They could avoid calamity only if they confined themselves to their appropriate spheres of activity and recognized the authority that white men had over their lives.[18]

Within the context of slavery, evangelicals labored to help slaves resist inappropriate aspirations. With the destruction of slavery, they felt an even more urgent need to exert the restraining influence of religion over the black population. The war had let northern, radical serpents loose in the garden. Unless conservative churchmen stood watch at the boundaries of the appropriate spheres, anarchy would overwhelm the well-ordered society that they had helped construct. The evangelical assessment of where blacks should fit in the postwar South was expressed succinctly by a Methodist from Lenoir, North Carolina, who urged the readers of the *Southern Christian Advocate* to do all they could "to make what was the happiest and best class of slaves in the world to be the happiest and best class of peasants."[19]

Some Southern Methodists hoped that education would buttress religion in upholding the traditional social order. They argued that if conducted by trustworthy southern whites, education could refine and restrain the black population. It would equip former slaves with the tools and the attitudes they needed to function productively and without friction, within their proper sphere.[20]

In April 1866, a Methodist from Thomaston, Georgia, asserted: "The work of instructing the negro is our work." The Georgian tried to make a case for establishing schools for blacks:

> By teaching the poor class (thrown from comfortable homes into the world without food, shelter, clothing or medicine, exposed to all temptations, corruption and train of evils that their *quasi* friends have brought them to) are we not protecting ourselves, protecting society? Are we not thus preparing the colored people to make faithful industrious laborers? [21]

In spite of support from the bishops and other leaders of the denomination, the concept of black education remained alien and alarming to most white Methodists. Proponents of education made a strong effort to convince southerners that there was no shame or danger in teaching the freedpeople, but they had little success. Even when it was presented in terms of self-interest and as a way to counter the meddling of northern teachers, instruction for former slaves seemed unnecessary and unnatural, and any white who was brazen enough to engage in such an unnatural activity risked social ostracism. In June 1866, Reverend James E. Evans, who was a staunch supporter of black education, conceded: "In many places the southern people were not fully prepared for this work. It was not reasonably to be expected that they should be. It takes time to adjust the thoughts of the mind and the feelings of the heart." [22] Then by default, religion would have to serve as the main cultural support for the traditional order.

The first postwar General Conference of the Methodist Episcopal Church, South, convened in New Orleans in spring 1866 to set policy for the denomination as a whole. One of the items on the agenda was formulating a new policy toward blacks that would be effective in a world without slavery. The new policy would also have to be appropriate for a competitive environment in which the souls of black southerners would have to be saved from Northern Methodism as well as from the devil, although from the point of view of many Southern Methodists, the distinction between the two was slight.

It had become clear that the kind of control the missionaries appeared to have had over slaves was a thing of the past. If the denomination was to influence the beliefs and behavior of the freedpeople, it would have to do so indirectly. It could not stem the desire of newly emancipated blacks to be free from white control. Secular freedpeople refused to be religious slaves. It appeared that the great majority of them would seek churches in which they could be full and equal members. It was also clear that however much white Methodists wanted to retain their black membership, southern evangelicals would not countenance the anarchy of racial equality within their denomination. They were committed to preserving a traditional, paternalistic social order in which blacks were relegated to a subordinate sphere. The delegates to the General Conference of 1866 had to devise a policy that would allow blacks to function as free adults, but not as the equals of whites.

So, in response to pressure exerted by blacks and in an effort to deal with the crisis posed by postwar conditions, the General Conference launched a plan to organize a separate black denomination, which was unofficially referred to as the Colored Methodist Episcopal Church, South. Reverend James Evans served as chairman of the committee that drafted the plan. He explained its intent: "It is proposed by this plan to provide for our colored membership, an independent track, running parallel with the whites."[23] Colored Methodism was planned to be a conservative, southern alternative to radical northern denominations. It was designed to concede the freedpeople's independence and keep them within the ethos of the M.E. Church, South. It provided southern evangelicals with a way to contain the black challenge to white paternalism. In effect, it was a last-ditch effort to prevent the mission to slaves from joining the Confederacy as a lost cause.

For the most part, white Methodists received the new policy toward blacks with enthusiasm. The editor of the *Southern Christian Advocate* strongly endorsed the proposal to establish a Colored Methodist denomination:

> Intelligence has reached this place of the action of the General Conference, establishing the relations of our colored membership. Beyond all question, it is the greatest and best thing that that body has yet accomplished. We are glad for the honor of our Church that it was accomplished by a unanimous vote.[24]

The editor was pleased that the denomination had granted blacks "equal church privileges" in a way that also provided for "a happy and prudent separation" of the races.[25]

During the four years following the adjournment of the General Conference, Southern Methodist clergymen carried out the plan to establish Colored Methodism. They methodically went about the business of creating the component parts of the new organization by ordaining black clergymen, organizing black congregations, transferring control of church property, and setting up the local and state administrative units called District and Annual Conferences.[26]

About two months after the close of the General Conference, Southern Methodist bishop William M. Wightman was in Starkville, Mississippi, explaining and promoting the new policy. Bishop Wightman urged "immediate zealous action" to rescue blacks from the "clutches" of denominations whose true aim was "swallowing up the M.E. Church, South." The white preachers of the Starkville District responded to the bishop's directive by pledging "to immediately put in operation and carry out the plan of the General Conference."[27]

Bishop Robert Paine gave Reverend Thomas Taylor responsibility for organizing Colored Methodism in the Memphis area. Reverend Taylor received no remuneration for his efforts, although he did accept traveling expenses when they were offered. Bishop Paine explained that Taylor was merely "carrying out his life-long care and sympathy for the black man." By June 1867, Reverend Taylor had organized ten black churches. The bishop praised the "great work" Taylor had done and urged other white Methodists to "assist him in his noble efforts to benefit the colored people." In 1869, the delegates to the North Carolina Annual Conference lauded the efforts that had been made to bring Colored Methodism into being and offered this cheery assessment of how things stood in their state: "We are persuaded . . . that there is a desire, on the part of many of the colored people, to return to us and secure our sympathy and aid."[28]

The organizers of the new denomination were faced with the major challenge of rapidly finding a sizable number of preachers capable of taking charge of neophyte congregations and building them for the future. Fear and hostility following the Nat Turner slave revolt in 1831 caused southern states to curtail or severely limit the activities of black preachers, slave and free. In any case, the number of black clergymen who had been ordained or licensed before the war was minute, and almost none of that very small number had any experience with church administration or any firsthand knowledge of how a denomination functioned beyond the local level. Slave communities did produce individuals who knew the Bible and could preach effectively. Those persons were acknowledged to be religious leaders, even though they had not been accorded official denominational recognition as such. It was largely from the ranks of those unordained and unlettered veterans of the slave quarters that the first generation of Colored Methodist ministers was drawn.[29]

For a brief period, Southern Methodists did try to gain access to the services of a cadre of experienced, ordained black ministers through an ill-conceived alliance with the African Methodist Episcopal (A.M.E.) denomination. The A.M.E. Church was a northern, independent, black denomination that had been founded in 1816. Following emancipation, it dispatched missionaries to the South to proselytize the freedpeople. Representatives of African Methodism encouraged Southern Methodists to regard their denomination as an ally in the effort to block the inroads of white Methodists from the North. In 1866, the southerners agreed not to interfere with the black Southern Methodist congregations who chose to affiliate with the A.M.E. Church. They hoped that in time African Methodism and Colored Methodism would merge, but that hope turned out to be a delusion. It soon became apparent that A.M.E. preachers did not have much interest in preserving the traditional social order of the South. They certainly had no interest in maintaining a subordinate sphere for blacks. Furthermore, they were knee-deep in politics.[30] Losing members to African Methodists was less painful than losing them to Yankee Methodists, but only slightly so.

Chastened by that unpleasant experience, Southern Methodists concluded that the only prudent course was to concentrate on their plan to create a new denomination in their own image and to entrust the leadership of the new organization to black preachers imbued with the values of the Southern Methodist Church. They sought preachers such as Reverend Emmanuel Hamit of Galveston, Texas, who was reported to be " 'Southern' in his feelings," and Reverend James Smith of Tallahassee, Florida, who had the sterling credential of being "a firm supporter and unwavering member of our Church." A very optimistic white admirer of Reverend Smith predicted that under the influence of preachers of his caliber and sentiments "the larger part, if not the whole of the colored people will return to our Church, leaving the political preachers without flocks."[31]

In some areas, Southern Methodist bishops reported finding a surprisingly high level of literacy among the men they brought into the Colored Methodist ministry. Bishop Holland McTyeire found that of the twenty-five preachers he organized into the Kentucky Colored Conference in 1868, twenty-two could read and eighteen could read and write. In the same year, Bishop Robert Paine reported that "nearly all" of the preachers who composed the Memphis Colored Conference could read and "more than half" could write. The bishop averred that the few who could neither read nor write were "old, well-tried and of most approved character."[32]

In fall 1868, Bishop George F. Pierce assessed what progress had been made in organizing Colored Methodism. At that time, the bishop was reported to be "much gratified, and quite confident of the success of this movement, as conservative in its influence upon all the interests, religious and social, of the southern people, both white and colored." A few months later, Bishop Pierce predicted: "In two years, a colored Bishop will find things made ready to his own hands."[33]

The still-developing denomination secured a means of communication in the form of the *Christian Index,* a newspaper that began publication in October 1869 under the editorship of Reverend Samuel Watson, a white preacher who had done mission work among blacks. Reverend Watson's first editorial was called "An Appeal to the White in Behalf of the Colored People." The "Appeal" began by pointing out that blacks were going to be a permanent part of the population of the South. The only thing at issue was whether they would become "a blessing or a curse." Emancipation had removed blacks from the protective care and direction of whites and left them vulnerable to the "wicked devices" of northern radicals who "seduced" them from their "best and only real friends." As a consequence, the freedpeople had become like sheep without a shepherd and their temporal and spiritual welfare was at peril.[34]

Reverend Watson contended that many blacks were beginning to see the error of their ways, and more than ever they needed the guidance of strong, steady, southern, white hands. "This is emphatically our work," he exhorted. "By us only can they be saved." The editor urged his fellow southerners to try to overlook the desertions and disappointments of recent years and remember the bonds of happier times. Both self-interest and Christian duty required that they take blacks "by the hand and lead them safely over the dangerous paths along which they are now moving so unsteadily."[35]

By the end of 1870, there were about 40,000 Colored Methodists; only a remnant of the original black membership still chose to remain in the Methodist Episcopal Church, South. Preachers in Alabama, Georgia, Kentucky, Mississippi, and Tennessee had been organized into annual conferences, and initial steps had been taken to organize conferences in Arkansas, South Carolina, and Texas. On 16 December of that year, Bishops Paine and McTyeire convened the first General Conference of the Colored Methodist Episcopal Church in Jackson, Tennessee. The inaugural meeting of the new denomination culminated with the elections of Reverends William A. Miles and Richard H. Vanderhorst as the first bishops of Colored Methodism.[36]

After the white bishops transferred control and responsibility for the new denomination to their black counterparts, they made some appropriate parting remarks. Bishop Paine evoked the heritage of the mission to slaves. "Our missionaries," he recalled, "are buried on the rice and cotton and sugar plantations, who went preaching the Gospel to your fathers and to you while slaves." Both bishops promised that whites would not attempt to impose their will on the fledgling denomination. Both of them also pledged that the advice and assistance of Southern Methodism would always be at the disposal of Colored Methodism. As Bishop Paine put it: "Can a mother forget her children?" Finally, Bishop McTyeire concluded his remarks with this admonition: "Yours is exactly on the model of the Old Ship. See that you sail as nearly on her track as you can."[37]

2

COLORED METHODISM AND
THE NEW PATERNALISM

" 'Democrats,' 'bootlicks' and 'white folks' niggers.' " Bishop Lucius H. Holsey remembered the ways that many blacks, particularly African Methodists, referred to the members of the Colored Methodist Episcopal Church. Holsey and two other men were elected bishops in 1873, following the death of Richard Vanderhorst and the continued growth of Colored Methodism. Bishop Holsey was certain that his denomination was misunderstood. He was also sure that his black evangelical antagonists were misguided in their approach to race advancement.[1]

Colored Methodists could not have been surprised that a large part of the black population greeted the emergence of their new denomination with displeasure. Colored Methodism was an anomaly. It appeared a year and a half after ratification of the Fourteenth Amendment guaranteed blacks full citizenship, and less than a year after ratification of the Fifteenth Amendment made clear that the freedpeople were entitled to the vote. The keys to full citizenship, independence, equality, education, and power all appeared to be held by northern hands. Yet, Colored Methodists spoke of southern whites with warmth and affection and of northerners, white and black, with disdain.

They chose to belong to a denomination that grew out of the proslavery heritage of Southern Methodism, and by doing so they rejected membership in the Northern Methodist Church, in spite of that denomination's antislavery history and its missionaries' egalitarian pronouncements. Colored Methodists also rejected association with the racially assertive African Methodist denominations. They appeared to be swimming against the tide of history and out of the mainstream of their race. Bishop Holsey spoke for all of the early leaders of the c.m.e. Church when he observed: "In the seventies and eighties I was very much slandered, persecuted, and rejected by my own race and people."[2]

Under such circumstances, what sort of person would be drawn to a position of Colored Methodist leadership? During the first two and one-half years of its existence, the following five ministers were elected by their colleagues to serve as bishops of the denomination: William H. Miles, Richard H. Vanderhorst, Joseph A. Beebe, Lucius H. Holsey, and Isaac Lane. Those five men shaped the denomination's policies during its formative years, and they became the most visible symbols of Colored Methodism. What were the factors in their backgrounds that might help explain why they chose to affiliate with the c.m.e. Church and why Colored Methodists would select them to be their standard-bearers?

At the time of Lee's surrender, the ages of those five men ranged from twenty-four for Holsey, the junior member of the group, to fifty-three for Vanderhorst, the eldest. Miles, Beebe, and Lane were all in their thirties. The first five bishops of Colored Methodism were all born as slaves. It was not until 1914 that the denomination elevated a free-born person to that office. Beebe and Vanderhorst were able to purchase their freedom while they were young men, but Miles, Lane, and Holsey remained slaves until they were freed by the war.[3]

In fact, Holsey declined to leave his master even after emancipation, electing instead to remain in service to Colonel Richard M. Johnston of Georgia for an additional year. The colonel, who was a planter and also a professor at Franklin College in Athens, was Holsey's third master. His first owner, James Holsey, was also his father. The elder Holsey was never married. As his son delicately put it, he "mingled" with his female slaves. Bishop Holsey described his father as "a gentleman of classical education, dignified in appearance and manner of life."[4]

During his career as a slave, Holsey was spared the rigors of field labor. At various times, he was a house servant, gardener, body servant, and carriage driver. In 1862, while he was still a slave, he married Harriet Anne Turner, the personal servant of the daughter of Bishop George F. Pierce of the Southern Methodist Church. Bishop Pierce himself officiated at the fairly elaborate wedding ceremony that was arranged by his family and held in his home. Lucius Holsey looked back on his life in slavery without bitterness or regret. "I have no complaint against American slavery," he wrote. "It was a blessing in disguise to me and to many. It has made the Negro race what it could not have been in its native land."[5]

Like Holsey, Isaac Lane was the son of his master. Lane was born in 1834 in Madison County, Tennessee, about five miles from the town of Jackson. He remembered his father, Cullen Lane, as a "Methodist of the purest type" and characterized him as "a good, true man, faithful to God and his obligations." Years after emancipation, Lane proudly recalled how his father had spurned an opportunity to sell him for a substantial profit. Cullen Lane also earned his son's admiration by purchasing Isaac's wife and children after their master left Tennessee for Arkansas. But, of course, being a slave was not the same as being a son. Lane, who was a field slave, recalled "dark and bitter days" on his father's farm. Unlike Holsey, he saw no positive value in slavery. He denounced it as "the greatest and foulest crime of the nation."[6] Being both property and progeny, the future bishops must have had very complex feelings about their lineages. They were, quite literally, possessed by their inheritance.

The *Southern Christian Advocate* described Richard Vanderhorst as "a pure specimen of a black man." Initially, he was the slave of a Huguenot family from which he took his name. He then passed into the possession of two elderly ladies in Charleston, Elizabeth and Judith Wragg, who employed him as a personal servant. One of his duties was accompanying his owners to the Methodist Church, carrying their hymnbooks and Bibles. The Misses Wragg gave Vanderhorst permission to serve as an apprentice to a free black carpenter and to use the skills that he acquired to earn the price of his freedom. Joseph Beebe was also a craftsman. He was born in Fayetteville, North Carolina, in 1832. While he was a slave, Beebe worked as a boot maker, and, like Vanderhorst, he was permitted to use his craftsmanship to earn his freedom. Beebe succeeded in becoming his own master around 1859.[7]

William Miles had a singular history as a slave, although the details are sketchy. Miles was born in Kentucky in 1828. He was legally manumitted by the will of his late owner, Mary Miles, in 1854, but remained a de facto bondsman until 1864, presumably not by choice. In 1871, a correspondent for the *Raleigh Christian Advocate* wrote that he heard Bishop Miles "make allusion in a feeling manner to the kindness which he had received at the hands of his former mistress." Although Miles's parentage is uncertain, a writer for the *Trenton [Tennessee] Gazette* described him as being "not a black man, but a bright mulatto."[8]

The first five leaders of Colored Methodism all experienced spiritual awakenings under the aegis of the Southern Methodist Church. They associated Southern Methodism with the liberating power of the gospel and gave no indication that they viewed white missionaries as parts of the slavocracy's apparatus of control. Those who felt the call to preach while still slaves sought to have their calling officially sanctioned by white Methodist officials. There is no reason to believe that identification with the church of their masters caused them any discomfort.

Methodist missionaries made regular visits to the farm on which Isaac Lane was enslaved. His father made sure that "his people" would have access to the gospel: prayer meetings were regular Saturday night occurrences in the slave quarters. When he was twenty-one, Lane underwent a conversion experience. Over forty years after the event he recalled, with clarity, the morning of 11 September 1854, when he "was made happy in a Savior's love." Shortly thereafter, Lane joined the Methodist congregation in Jackson, of which his father was a charter member. Only a few months later he felt the call to preach, but he was troubled by his calling. For a time, he could neither accept it nor reject it. In an effort to resolve this very personal spiritual crisis, Lane sought the counsel of his earthly father and master. Cullen Lane advised his son to seek the aid of a white clergyman of his acquaintance. As it turned out, that minister only added to Isaac's inner turmoil by telling him that he did not believe that blacks should preach. The troubled slave then turned to an "old colored preacher" who assured him that the Lord knew how to conduct his own business and that if his calling was real, there was no need for him to be concerned about the outcome.[9]

Thus reassured, Lane sought a license to preach. The church in Jackson decided against raising a slave to the level of a licensed preacher, but it did allow Lane to become an exhorter, which was the lowest rank in the hierarchy of Methodist clergy. The partial rebuff did not diminish Lane's gratitude for the official recognition white Methodists had accorded his calling. "They did not refuse me," he explained; "indeed, they held out a hand of help and encouragement." Lane believed he enjoyed the support and respect of his white coreligionists, and he regarded the pastor of his church as a "personal friend." Clearly, he could not have pursued his calling at all without at least the acquiescence of his master.[10]

As an exhorter, Lane had frequent opportunities to preach to blacks, although opposition to black clergymen remained strong and became even more intense after the war heightened apprehensions concerning their ability to galvanize discontent among slaves. On at least one occasion, arsonists burned down a church after its pastor allowed the slave exhorter to use its pulpit.[11]

Reverend Lane, who was hardly an incendiary, gave white evangelicals much credit for continuing to encourage his preaching under such circumstances:

But my white brethren upheld me. And not only the Methodists, but Christians of other denominations. One good old Presbyterian brother said to me after I had preached in his church: "Brother Lane, keep on preaching to your people, and we will keep on building churches until the trumpet blows. Let them burn down. We will build and you shall preach."[12]

After serving as an exhorter for nearly a decade, Reverend Lane was granted his long-sought-after preacher's license in May 1866, about a month after Southern Methodism decided to establish a separate black denomination.[13]

William H. Miles had greater success in overcoming Southern Methodism's reluctance to grant licenses to black preachers. Miles became a church member after his conversion in 1855. Two years later, he secured a license to preach. In 1859, Southern Methodist bishop James O. Andrew ordained Reverend Miles, elevating him to the status of deacon, the next rank in the clerical hierarchy.[14] As an ordained deacon, the black clergyman had the authority to officiate at weddings and baptisms. He could also assist senior ministers during communion services. Even after taking into account his quasi-free status, the rapid progress of Reverend Miles's career was remarkable. After the war, Miles moved to Ohio and became a member of the A.M.E. Zion denomination, but in less than three years he had returned to his native Kentucky, reaffiliated with Southern Methodism, and helped organize a Colored Conference in the Bluegrass state.[15]

The white minister who wrote the introduction to Lucius Holsey's autobiography accurately described him as "a faithful product of the missionary zeal" of Southern Methodism. Holsey acknowledged that the initial catalyst for his conversion was a free black preacher named Henry M. Turner, but he gave most of the credit to W. A. Parks, the white preacher in charge of the Colored Mission in Athens, Georgia. Holsey pointed out that many slaves like himself were delivered from the "bondage of sin" through the efforts of "noble white men who, like Brother Parks, toiled faithfully for the redemption of their souls." Like Reverends Lane and Miles, Holsey felt the call to preach shortly after his conversion, but he declined to challenge antebellum opposition to black preachers. Instead, he bided his time until February 1868, a full decade later. At that time, he was examined and approved for licensing by his wife's former owner, Bishop George Pierce.[16]

Joseph A. Beebe recalled having had "constant opportunity of hearing the Gospel preached" both as a slave and then later as a free black in antebellum North Carolina. He gave Southern Methodist ministers credit for bringing about his "spiritual change" and for sparking his desire to become a preacher. Obtaining a license to preach appeared to be beyond his reach until after the war, when the African Methodist Episcopal Zion Church offered him the opportunity to become an ordained clergyman. Reverend Beebe remained in that denomination until the year after the C.M.E. Church was founded. He then joined the new denomination and quickly became one of its most influential leaders.[17]

Richard Vanderhorst was first exposed to Southern Methodism while ac- companying his owners to church in Charleston. A free black exhorter named Samson Dunmore also had a great influence on his religious development— so much so that Vanderhorst himself became an exhorter. When the African Methodist Episcopal denomination established itself in Charleston in 1865, Vanderhorst seized the opportunity to become an ordained clergyman, but his career as an African Methodist was brief. In 1869, he accepted an invitation to become a Colored Methodist minister.[18]

None of the first five Colored Methodist bishops were formally educated, but they all achieved literacy through their own efforts. Holsey recounted how as a slave he studied pages torn from a spelling book as he discharged his daily duties and then continued his studies by the light of a fireplace at night. Bishop Lane also learned to read and write while still a slave, but his explanation of how he managed to do so did not extend beyond a cryptic "I had to learn the best I could."[19]

The men Colored Methodists chose to lead their denomination were south- erners by choice as well as by circumstance. After buying their freedom, both Richard Vanderhorst and Joseph Beebe chose to remain in the Carolinas, where they had been slaves. At the war's end, William Miles spent two years in Ohio before deciding to return to his native Kentucky in 1867. None of these men claimed to have ever considered fleeing to freedom in the North while they were slaves.[20]

In sum, the leaders of Colored Methodism were self-educated former slaves who took pride in their Southern Methodist heritage. Their lives in slavery appear to have been less onerous than those of most of their peers. They had not been runaways or harborers of runaways. They did not flee to Union lines or wear the Union uniform. They did not become agents of the Freedmen's Bureau, delegates to state constitutional conventions, or members of state legis- latures. None of them were scions of prominent free black families. Save for their being preachers, they had none of the characteristics generally associated with black leadership during Reconstruction. Yet, they were the leaders chosen by an organization of southern blacks which was formed during the upheavals of Reconstruction and which claimed a membership of nearly 68,000 by 1873.

Although they did not fit the general profile of black leadership, these men were purposeful, disciplined, and ambitious. In a society that mandated black ignorance, servility, and dependence, they achieved literacy, became skilled artisans, purchased freedom, and obtained licenses and even ordination from a major white denomination. The leaders of Colored Methodism had mastered the intricacies of southern racial diplomacy. They knew how to negotiate space for their ambitions when conditions allowed. When conditions were unfavorable, they knew how to wait patiently. Their lives before the war demonstrated what could be accomplished within the slavocracy with the support or compliance of influential whites. Conversely, their achievements seemed to demonstrate the pointlessness of launching frontal assaults on racial boundaries and white sensibilities.

The leaders of Colored Methodism were exemplars of a mind-set that was shared by a significant minority of the southern black population. This minority of black traditionalists had made their peace with the white South. Traditionalists certainly did not pine for the return of slavery, but otherwise they were comfortable with southern values and customs, and they shared the religious beliefs of white evangelicals. Traditionalist blacks were unsettled and perhaps even threatened by the alien ideas and impatient people who descended upon them from the North. They had no desire to launch out into uncharted waters with untested friends. Over the years, they had developed strategies for living in an environment that was dominated by southern whites. These freedpeople saw relationships between white and black southerners as cords of stability in a world that had become tumultuous and unpredictable.

Traditionalists believed that ties to the white South were essential, but they did not want to revive the kind of paternalism that had bound slaves to masters. They wanted paternalism, but at a distance. This new kind of paternalism was exemplified by the relationship that developed between Southern Methodism and Colored Methodism. After the war, the leaders of the movement to establish a separate black denomination made clear that they were no longer satisfied with being dependent wards of Southern Methodism. When their denomination was being established, Colored Methodists did not establish any official connection with the Southern Methodist Church, even though the General Conference of the white denomination had stated that it wanted such a relationship. Some black petitioners insisted on being governed by black bishops. Colored Methodists also rejected the name by which their denomination had been known while it was being organized: the Colored M.E. Church, South. Instead, they adopted the name Colored M.E. Church in America. One historian of Colored Methodism points out that the advocacy of those positions was "of singular importance" because it showed "the assumption of initiative, which heretofore had rested solely with the white group."[21] Perhaps because they were the objects of vituperative derision from other blacks, Colored Methodists strained to demonstrate that their denomination was an independent organization and not merely the black auxiliary of a Confederate church.

On the other hand, Colored Methodists had no intention of ending their relationship with southern whites; they just wanted to renegotiate its terms. It was, after all, at least in part at the insistence of blacks that white Methodists assumed responsibility for supervising the formation of the Colored Methodist denomination. White bishops presided over the first sessions of the first General Conference; they ordained the first Colored Methodist bishops; they set the new denomination in motion. Shortly after becoming a bishop at that first General Conference in 1870, Richard H. Vanderhorst turned to his white counterparts and said, "Brothers, say not good bye, that is a hard word. Say it not. We love you and thank you for all you have done for us. But you must not leave us—never." [22]

Bishop Holsey interpreted the outcome of that inaugural General Conference in this way: "In 1870, we were 'set up' as a distinct and independent branch of the great Methodist family by and under the authority of the Methodist Episcopal Church, South." Lest there be any misunderstanding about the implications of Colored Methodist independence, he explained further: "In no sense does this 'setting up' business destroy, neither was it intended to destroy, the religious inter-racial relations that had obtained in days of old." Neither emancipation, the dislocations of war, the turmoil of Reconstruction, or denominational independence could disturb "the old landmarks of love and esteem." [23]

Bishop Holsey insisted that the essentials of the relationship between white evangelical paternalists and the Colored Methodist remnant of the mission to slaves remained unchanged. Nevertheless, it was true that Southern Methodists could no longer work through the institution of slavery in order to have direct personal impact and control over the religious development of blacks. The new paternalism required that whites discharge their evangelical responsibilities more indirectly through black intermediaries and black institutions, and for that reason, many whites found the new paternalism to be less satisfying than the old—some found it to be a little alarming, as well. Be that as it may, Holsey persisted in urging white southerners to maintain their commitment to missions and to continue to make blacks the primary focus of that commitment. [24]

During the years when the blood of black Republicans was being shed to redeem the old South, black practitioners of the new paternalism assiduously cultivated good relations with southern whites and foreswore all political involvement. They based their positions on the prescient belief that, ultimately, the powers with which southern blacks would have to come to terms were not northern. Colored Methodists pursued a southern solution largely because that was their cultural orientation, but also because it simply seemed to make good sense.[25] Bishop Holsey explained the nonreligious reason why he became an unswerving, energetic champion of Colored Methodism:

> Not because I thought it to be the best church in itself, not because I thought it purer and better than other such organizations, but because I thought it to be the most fitted religious power to meet the peculiar conditions that exist in the Southern States. Harmony between the two races is what is needed. There can be no progress in the betterment of the people of color without peace and harmony.[26]

An early black organizer of the c.m.e. Church in Georgia proclaimed: "Wherever its banner floats, peace and charity prevail between white and colored people." During their frequent appearances before Southern Methodist bodies, representatives of Colored Methodism praised the heritage of the mission to slaves and made appeals for support for c.m.e. causes. In 1879, a white observer noted that during a conference of Colored Methodist ministers in Kentucky, Bishop Beebe "took occasion to state that the white people of the South had been generally very kind to the colored race. He took great pleasure in bearing testimony to this fact."[27]

The c.m.e. proscription against political activity was even more unequivocal than that of its Southern Methodist progenitor. At the denomination's first General Conference, legislation was passed which officially forbade the use of c.m.e. churches for any political purpose. Bishop Holsey explained that "as ministers of the Gospel, we make no stump speeches and fight no battles of the politicians." In 1871, a correspondent for the *Southern Christian Advocate* reported that Colored Methodists in Georgia had "not organized themselves into political leagues, governed by imported preachers or been instigated to general hostility to the whites by false stories of Ku-Klux outrages."[28]

The following year, the white pastor of the Southern Methodist church in Holly Springs, Mississippi, heard Bishop Miles preach two sermons. On one night, the bishop preached to blacks in the church basement; the next night he preached to whites in the "audience-room." The pastor reported that, despite charges to the contrary, the Colored Methodist bishop "never introduced the subject of politics, excepting to state that his Church was non-political." He also pointed out that Bishop Miles succeeded in organizing a Colored Methodist congregation in Holly Springs, "in spite of the lying and malicious opposition from the radical preachers and members in this town."[29] In one sense, the denomination's ostensible nonpolitical stance was itself an effective political maneuver that could be dismissed as transparent posturing—but it was also an expression of sincere religious belief. In the well-ordered world of evangelicals, politics had no business in religion. Each had its appropriate sphere. Colored Methodists did see themselves as defenders of the unadulterated Word of God.

Colored Methodists also had a distinctive approach to education. In fact, it is in education that the workings of the new paternalism can be seen most clearly. The first efforts to establish denominational schools were initiated by Bishop Miles in 1874 and 1875, but they bore no fruit. Funds from within the denomination were not sufficient to support his plans for establishing schools in Kentucky and Mississippi. Bishop Holsey tried to raise money to support Miles's projects, but he got the impression that Southern Methodists considered the plans "rather untimely and impracticable."[30] As was explained in the previous chapter, southern whites had little use for educational plans that had the potential to educate blacks out of their traditional subordinate position in the social and economic hierarchy of the South. In spite of those setbacks, Colored Methodists continued to try to navigate plans for establishing denominational schools through the shoals of white fears and prejudices. In the early 1880s, they succeeded in founding the two schools which are still the most prominent C.M.E. educational institutions: Lane College in Jackson, Tennessee, and Paine College in Augusta, Georgia.

Bishop Lane was the principal promoter and fund-raiser for the school that was to bear his name. The bishop's stated objectives did not include using education to lift blacks above their traditional place in the economic and social order of the South. He made clear that it was not his intention to try to educate the general black population. Contrary to the impressions of most observers, Bishop Lane asserted that most freedpeople had "but little love for education." He proposed establishing a school that would limit its focus to educating clergymen. Bishop Lane's plan materialized in fall 1882 as the C.M.E. High School. In 1886, Colored Methodist bishops sought the assistance of their Southern Methodist counterparts in finding a person to teach theology at the school. The Southern Methodists recommended one of their own ministers, Reverend T. F. Saunders, for the teaching position and for the presidency of what by then was known as Lane Institute. The white denomination paid Reverend Saunders's salary for the fifteen years that he directed the affairs of the black school.[31] His appointment established an enduring link between the M.E. Church, South, and the C.M.E. school.

Bishop Lucius Holsey was the driving force behind establishment of the institution that began as Paine Institute and in time became known as Paine

College. As early as 1869, Holsey had urged blacks to look to the white South for teachers and financial support for schools. Like Lane, Holsey made clear that his educational plans were not directed at the general population. Even as late as 1891, he contended that it was still too soon to try to educate "the masses." Bishop Holsey advocated schools for preachers and teachers. He wanted those professionals who would have a direct impact on shaping the values of the black South to have a distinctly southern education. He wanted them to emulate their white counterparts. The bishop described himself as "a perpetual and persistent advocate of the establishment of a school for the training of our preachers under the care and complete control of the M.E. Church, South, with teachers from the same place."[32] He proposed the kind of education that would produce effective agents of the new paternalism. Bishop Holsey expressed his educational philosophy and his hopes for Paine Institute in the following manner:

> It is great to educate, but it is still greater to impart the right kind of education, . . . Teachers and preachers are to give shape and tone to those sentiments, ideas, and actions which are to control and characterize the black man of tomorrow. Much depends upon what he conceives to be his relations and his duties representing himself and his brother in white. Conceive in him that the white man is his enemy, and then he becomes a jarring discord, . . . The Paine Institute is designed to counteract such tendencies.[33]

Perhaps it should be noted, at least in passing, that although the educational philosophy of Holsey and his denomination was limited and conservative, it should not be equated or confused with the industrial education programs associated with Hampton and Tuskegee Institutes. Aspiring teachers and preachers were taught the liberal arts at Paine College.[34]

In 1882, Bishop Holsey made another appeal to the Southern Methodist General Conference on behalf of C.M.E. education. This time he was successful. The white evangelicals responded by establishing the position of "Commissioner of Education in aid of the Colored Methodist Episcopal Church." The commissioner was to be appointed by the Southern Methodist bishops "in consultation with the bishops of the Colored Methodist Episcopal Church." The General Conference also established a board of trustees to exercise stewardship over an education fund that would be amassed from "subscriptions, contributions and bequests." The board was to be chaired by the commissioner and have as its members three Southern Methodists and three Colored Methodists.[35]

A few months after the conclusion of the General Conference, a delegation of Southern Methodists, led by Bishop Pierce, met with a delegation of Colored Methodists, led by Bishop Holsey. They met in Atlanta to carry out the conference's directives. At the time of the meeting, Bishops Pierce and Holsey had known each other for over two decades. Their relationship extended back to the days of slavery, when the white bishop had conducted and hosted Holsey's wedding ceremony. Bishop Pierce also licensed and ordained the young black clergyman and assigned him to his first church. In addition, Pierce participated in Holsey's ordination as bishop after he was elected to that office in 1873. The two men had reason to believe that they knew what they could expect from each other.[36]

The most significant outcome of the meeting was the decision to establish the Paine Institute. Paine did not actually open its doors until January 1884, and it did not become known as Paine College until 1903. The school was named in memory of the late senior bishop of Southern Methodism, Robert Paine, who had been one of the bishops presiding over the conclave that gave birth to Colored Methodism in 1870. Another important result of the meeting was the appointment of Southern Methodist cleric, James Evans, as commissioner of education. Reverend Evans had publicly supported education for blacks as early as 1866 and had been deeply involved in the events that led to establishment of the c.m.e. Church. Unfortunately, the education fund Evans administered fell far short of expectations; during the first fourteen years of the fund's existence, the commissioner was able to make outlays that totaled no more than $84,000, most of which went to Lane and Paine. During the twenty-year period between 1844 and 1864, Southern Methodists had invested $1,706,207 in their mission to plantation slaves. During the twenty years following the founding of Paine Institute, the denomination contributed a total of only about $160,000 to its efforts to educate southern blacks. The disappointing size of the fund was one indication that the new paternalism could not surmount the old prejudices. Bishop Pierce himself had serious misgivings about the propriety of educating blacks. Even beyond the issue of education, it was clear that the new paternalism did not stir the souls of white evangelicals, and among some Southern Methodists, compassion was devolving into contempt.[37]

But for Bishop Holsey, the lackluster financial support was only an unfortunate smudge on his grand design. For him, Paine Institute had a symbolic significance that was even greater than its educational value: it was the capstone of his interracial diplomacy; it was an institutional expression of the new paternalism. In a sense, it was a new incarnation of the mission to slaves.[38] As Holsey put it, Paine "tied the Colored Methodist Episcopal Church in America to the Methodist Episcopal Church, South, so that as conditions would allow, they would work together, or at least, along parallel lines, to evangelize and save our people for God and Christ."[39]

From its founding until 1971, all the presidents of Paine Institute, and then Paine College, were white Southern Methodists. During its first year of operation, its board of trustees had four black members and fifteen whites. Thirteen years later, an expanded board had nine black members and thirty-two whites. In 1888, Paine hired an alumnus, who had gone on to earn additional degrees from Brown University in Rhode Island, as its first black faculty member, prompting the angry resignation of one of the white teachers as a protest against "this revolutionary measure." That measure was repeated the following year when another black alumnus who did postgraduate work in New England was also added to the faculty. In 1890, Paine had 219 students, 35 of whom were studying theology.[40]

Paine Institute provided a sphere for interaction between blacks who were no longer slaves and whites who were no longer masters, or missionaries, but who were nonetheless unwilling to abandon some of the traditions and relationships that were forged during antebellum years. The educational institution, like the C.M.E. Church itself, was a product of that complex skein of southern attitudes and relationships which kept the races separate and bound them together. It demonstrated some of the possibilities and some of the limitations of the kind of approach to race relations that Booker T. Washington would raise to the level of art during a strikingly different period of southern history.[41] Traditionalism and the new paternalism helped a significant minority of the freedpeople bring order to the chaos of freedom, but there were other, stridently different philosophies competing for the allegiance of the black South.

PART 2

AFRICAN METHODISM
AND THE FREEDPEOPLE
"TO PROCLAIM LIBERTY
TO THE CAPTIVES"

The Spirit of the Lord God is upon me,
because the Lord has anointed me to bring
good news to the suffering and afflicted.
He has sent me to comfort the broken-hearted,
to announce liberty to captives
and to open the eyes of the blind.

—Isaiah 61:1, *The Living Bible*

3

AFRICAN METHODISTS SEEK
THEIR BRETHREN

On the morning of Monday, 15 May 1865, Bishop Daniel Alexander Payne stood in the pulpit of Zion Church on Calhoun Street in Charleston and convened the first session of the South Carolina Conference of the African Methodist Episcopal Church. As the frail and venerable bishop looked out into the crowded sanctuary, he saw the expectant faces of preachers who had recently emerged from bondage and of missionaries who had come from the North, all alive to the significance of the occasion.[1] But none of the clergy or onlookers could have felt the significance of that moment more keenly than Payne himself.

Thirty years before, Payne had fled from Charleston in despair. From 1829 until 1835 he had invested himself in building a school for black Charlestonians, but then Payne's academy was abolished by an act of the state legislature, and with it his hopes for uplifting his race in South Carolina. In his autobiography the future bishop confessed that for a time he was ready to "deny the existence of God, . . . for permitting one race to grind another to powder." Payne left the city where he had been born free twenty-four years before and headed north to Pennsylvania. He had been preceded on the trek north thirteen years earlier by Reverend Morris Brown, pastor of the short-lived African Methodist Church of Charleston. In 1822, Reverend Brown's church had been closed following the discovery that one of its members, a free black man named Denmark Vesey, had conspired to bring a violent end to slavery. Vesey was hanged, Reverend Brown had to flee, and African Methodism was banished from the South.[2]

So, when Bishop Payne stood in the pulpit of Zion Church on that Monday morning in the spring of 1865, he was reconnecting broken flows in personal and denominational history. He wrote of his emotion-laden homecoming in this way: "Yes, after thirty years to the day and the hour when the spirit of slavery forced me away from my native city, Charleston, S.C., I returned, led by the triumphant genius of freedom." Northerners and southerners, free and freed, came together in that church, offered thanks to their God, and proclaimed a new Gospel of Freedom. Serving as secretary of the conference and as chair of the committee on missions was James Lynch, a young protégé of Payne's from Baltimore. Reverend Lynch was born free in 1839 and was educated at the Kimball Union Academy in New Hampshire. Since the spring of 1863, Lynch had been doing mission work in South Carolina and Georgia. Reverend Richard Harvey Cain was another prominent member of the inaugural conference. Reverend Cain was a recent arrival from Brooklyn, New York, who landed in the South brimming with energy, enthusiasm, and ideas.[3] During the five days the conference was in session, Bishop Payne and Reverends Lynch and Cain frequently rose to give expression to some of the goals, values, and attitudes that came to define African Methodism in the South.

An account of the conference proceedings was published in the *Charleston News and Courier*. In that account, Reverend Cain was reported to have said that "God's providence had leveled the barriers, and rolled away tyranny's mountain—the pathway was cleared, lit up by the sunlight of liberty, and the presence of God." Cain's statement reflected the heady mood of those who had come to the South to witness the dawning of a new era. The atmosphere was supercharged. Freedom surged through it, igniting hopes, dispelling doubts. The day of Jubilee had come and the day of redemption was at hand. "The people have been praying for this day," Cain said, "and they were ready to fulfill that prophecy which says, 'Ethiopia shall soon stretch out her hands to God.'"[4]

African Methodists believed that their denomination was uniquely suited to serve as the vehicle for conveying southern blacks from the shadows of slavery into the "sunlight of liberty." Bishop Payne chastised freedpersons who opted to remain in churches that relegated members of their race to "negro pews." The bishop maintained that any black person who consented to such indignity "ignored half his own manhood." At one point in the conference, Cain rose to defend the A.M.E. Church from a charge circulated by some of its Methodist competitors implying that his denomination had come to minister to dark-complexioned freedpersons to the exclusion of mulattoes and whites. Cain characterized the rumor as "wicked and malicious and unwarranted," and he pointedly observed that "*ours* is a Church without distinction of color—accepting gladly all men who believe in Christ, and work for the elevation of our race." Bishop Payne supported Cain's comments and added that even though he loved and revered the Methodist Episcopal Church, that denomination had not permitted blacks and whites to worship as equals in the North, except in New England "where colored men were few in number."[5]

African Methodist missionaries preached a Gospel of Freedom that emphasized the need for former slaves to free themselves from the control of whites and become equal, independent, fully franchised citizens. African Methodists extolled the virtues and the power of education, even when schools were under the aegis of agencies other than their own denomination. For example, the South Carolina Conference unanimously adopted a resolution proposed by Reverend Lynch, praising northern religious and philanthropic organizations for undertaking the "glorious work" of educating the freedpeople. In his report for the Committee on Education, Reverend Cain gave a "statistical account" of the schools for freedpeople that had been established on military posts in the Department of South. He reported that the schools were well attended and that the students were making rapid progress. The conference also established a "Literary and Scientific Society" and heard a lecture on "The Unity of the Races," by Major Martin R. Delany, one of the few black officers in the Union army and the author of a book called *The Condition, Elevation, Emigration and Destiny of the Colored People in the United States*. The account of the proceedings published in the *Charleston News and Courier* concluded with the following observation: "Never was greater earnestness displayed by the colored race in the work of their development than at present in this city; and the most hopeful indications of a complete success of the freedmen of the race is apparent to all."[6]

The organization of the South Carolina Conference of the A.M.E. Church established what was then the southernmost outpost of an independent Methodist denomination that had been founded by free blacks in the North almost fifty years before. The African Methodist Episcopal denomination was organized in Bethel Church in Philadelphia in April 1816. Taking part in the inaugural meeting of the denomination were representatives from black churches in Maryland, Delaware, Pennsylvania, and New Jersey. During the decades preceding 1816, black Methodists had formed separate churches of their own in order to escape discrimination in white congregations. Subsequently, after much contention with the hierarchy of the M.E. Church over the control of those churches, blacks resolved to form their own denomination.[7]

One of the first actions of the new denomination was to select a bishop. The person ultimately elevated to that office was a former slave from Delaware named Richard Allen. As a young man, Allen bought his own freedom, became a preacher, and moved to Philadelphia where he held services for the black members of a predominantly white Methodist congregation. Reverend Allen and the other black members withdrew from that congregation after what they considered to be a particularly flagrant incident of discrimination. A few years later, Allen founded Bethel Church. For twenty-two years before the A.M.E. denomination was founded, Reverend Allen had served as pastor of Bethel, although his authority to do so was often contested by white officials of the Methodist Episcopal Church. It was Allen who issued the call for black Methodists to come to Philadelphia to bring the African Methodist Episcopal denomination into being.[8]

Richard Allen died in 1831 at the age of seventy-two, but his denomination continued to grow and develop. By the time the General Conference of 1860 convened, there were A.M.E. churches in Illinois, Indiana, California, and Canada. There were even a few A.M.E. churches in the slave states of Kentucky, Missouri, and Louisiana, although the denomination remained primarily a northeastern institution. The A.M.E. Church also published a weekly newspaper called the *Christian Recorder* and a quarterly journal called the *Repository of Religion and Literature*. By 1860, the denomination required the supervision of three bishops, one of whom was the scholarly refugee from the South, Daniel A. Payne. After Payne had left Charleston in 1835, he enrolled in a Lutheran seminary in Pennsylvania. In 1841, he entered the African Methodist ministry. The General Conference of 1848 made Reverend Payne the first official historian of the denomination, and in 1852 he was selected to be one of its bishops.[9]

In spring 1863, Bishop Payne presided over the session of Baltimore Annual Conference that launched the A.M.E. mission to the South. The conference took place in April, just four months after emancipation became one of the stated objectives of the Union war effort. For several months, subscribers to the *Christian Recorder* had been reading urgent appeals from organizations like the Contraband Relief Association and the Union Relief Association of Bethel Church, soliciting assistance for the thousands of black refugees who had escaped to find freedom in the relative security of the Union's capitol city.[10]

The *Christian Recorder* also urged eligible young men to fill the ranks of the 54th Massachusetts Regiment, the first regiment of colored troops to be organized in the North. The newspaper passed on assurances that the men of the 54th would have "all the rights of soldiers" and observed that the regiment was entrusted with the "hopes and responsibilities of a race." In late March, the *Recorder* carried the news that Bishop Payne had concluded negotiations with the Methodist Episcopal Church for the purchase of Wilberforce University in Ohio. In fact, the bishop had to delay the opening of the Baltimore conference for a week so that he could finalize plans for the acquisition of the first institution of higher learning to be owned and directed by blacks. One enthusiastic A.M.E. minister characterized the purchase of Wilberforce as "the greatest move that has ever been undertaken by the colored citizens in the United States of America."[11] The spring of 1863 was a spring of hope.

With those events as prologue, the Baltimore Annual Conference convened on April 23rd in Bethel Church on Saratoga Street. From the beginning of the proceedings, an enthusiasm for missionary enterprise was evident. Reverends James Lynch and Richard H. Cain were in attendance, as were the Reverends Henry McNeal Turner and William H. Hunter, both of whom would soon be commissioned as chaplains of colored regiments and would also serve as African Methodist missionaries to the freedpeople. Cain and Hunter delivered stirring addresses at a special meeting held to promote the cause of missions. In addition, Reverend C. C. Leigh, a white Methodist minister who worked with the National Freedmen's Relief Association, visited the conference and spoke of the great need for black missionaries in the South.[12]

But the most significant outcome of the Baltimore Conference was the appointment of two missionaries to carry African Methodism into the areas of South Carolina and Georgia that had been captured by the Union. James Lynch was the first person to volunteer for service in the South, and he was joined by Reverend J. D. S. Hall of the New York Conference. A few weeks earlier, Lynch had written an article for the *Christian Recorder* in which he urged the A.M.E. Church to commit itself to ministering to the spiritual and secular needs of the masses emerging from slavery. He wrote: "The Christian Colored Men and Women must rush to these our brethren, standing on the sea shore of freedom, saved from the wreck of slavery, but shivering with the cold blast of prejudice; naked with ignorance, and hungry for the bread of life."[13] Bishop Payne gave young Reverend Lynch the opportunity to act on his own dictum.

The next month Lynch and Hall left from New York harbor aboard the steamship that would take them to South Carolina. Seeing them off at the dock were Bishop Payne, R. H. Cain, and Lynch's father, the Reverend Benjamin Lynch. Mindful of posterity, Cain wrote a detailed account of the departure:

On Wednesday morning, May 20th, 1863 at twelve minutes before 12, Revs. James D. S. Hall, and James Lynch; the former of New York, the latter of the Baltimore Conference, sailed in the steamer Argo, for Port Royal, to begin the work of teaching, and planting the A.M.E. Church in the South. There is no event so pregnant of great results as this beginning.

Who shall tell what great good shall accrue to our race by this first great act of our church? [14]

Lynch's father and the others watched the ship until it went out of sight. Cain praised the missionaries and the families they left behind: "It is these kind of characters that will do something for their race. I shall never forget that hour while reason holds her sway, or memory has a place." Lynch and Hall arrived in Hilton Head, South Carolina, on May 23rd and began laying the foundation for what was to come.[15]

According to Clarence E. Walker's study of the A.M.E. Church during the Civil War and Reconstruction, a total of seventy-seven missionaries worked in the South between 1863 and 1870. One of that number went South even before the Baltimore Conference of 1863. Reverend George A. Rue of the New England Conference made an unsuccessful attempt to enter the South as early as summer 1862, even before the preliminary Emancipation Proclamation had been issued and about eight months before Lynch and Hall left New York. After the failure of his initial foray into the South, Reverend Rue returned to the mission field in spring 1865. This time he successfully established the A.M.E. Church in New Bern, North Carolina, which had been his hometown before he migrated to the North. Reverend Rue was one of those in attendance when Bishop Payne called the South Carolina Conference to order for the first time.[16]

Some African Methodists marched into the mission field wearing the uniform of the Union army. As chaplain/missionaries, William H. Hunter and Henry M. Turner functioned as though they had been commissioned both to free blacks from slavery and to recruit members for African Methodism. As soldiers and officers, the chaplains were dramatic symbols of the sudden empowerment of a marginalized race. As such, they were particularly well suited to represent the Gospel of Freedom and to provide former slaves with a new "theology" that affirmed and defined the new status of their race.

In February 1865, Chaplain Hunter's colored regiment occupied Wilmington, North Carolina. On the first Sunday after the city fell, the chaplain attempted to capture the eight hundred black members of Wilmington's Front Street Southern Methodist Church for African Methodism. The beleaguered white minister of the church recalled that on that Sunday, Chaplain Hunter "marched up the aisle and took the seat usually vacated for the pastor." The Southern Methodist minister understood what he was up against when Hunter rose to speak, "stretching himself to his full size and displaying to the best advantage for a profound impression his fine uniform."[17] Then the chaplain, who was a native of North Carolina, delivered what might be described as a sermonette from the Gospel of Freedom:

> My brethren and friends (Amen), I rise to address you, but I scarcely know what line of thought to pursue (hallelujah, Amen, etc.) . . . A few short years ago I left North Carolina a slave (hallelujah, oh, yes); I now return a man. (Amen). I have the honor to be a regular minister of the [African] Methodist Episcopal Church of the United States (glory to God, Amen) and also a regularly commissioned chaplain in the American Army. (Amen) [18]

After identifying with his audience and sharing in their celebration of freedom, Chaplain Hunter gave them a glimpse of what freedom could mean:

> I am proud to inform you that just three weeks ago today, as black a man as you ever saw, preached in the city of Washington to the Congress of the United States; and that a short time ago another colored man was admitted to the bar of the Supreme Court of the United States as a lawyer. (Long, loud and continued applause, beating on benches, etc.) One week ago you were all slaves; now you are all free. (Uproarious screamings). Thank God the armies of the Lord and of Gideon has [sic] triumphed and the Rebels have been driven back in confusion and scattered like chaff before the wind. (Amen! Hallelujah!) [19]

Reverend Hunter had marched up the aisle of the church, taken charge of its pulpit, and presented himself as an example of what it meant to be free. He gave voice to feelings that stirred within a congregation that had known freedom for less than a week. He gave hopeful blacks concrete examples of what their race could accomplish. Not long after that first Sunday of freedom, Reverend Hunter succeeded in persuading three-fourths of the black members of Front Street Church to leave Southern Methodism and become African Methodists.[20] The episode was repeated all over the South, wherever African Methodist missionaries engaged the aspirations of people who were in the process of transforming themselves from chattel into free men and women. Sometimes struggles over church property and denominational affiliations could be long, drawn-out, contentious affairs, but it should be kept in mind that, on some level, those struggles were also over the meaning of freedom.

Chaplain Henry M. Turner had high praise for Hunter. Turner once wrote that his "old friend and brother" was the kind of missionary who could "take a man from the very rubbish of slavery, and in a few hours infuse into him all the manhood and energy necessary for any purpose of life." He also commended Hunter for being a teacher, as well as a preacher and soldier. A few months after occupying Wilmington, Hunter's regiment was assigned to provost duty in Goldsboro, North Carolina. While there, Chaplain Hunter took possession of that city's Southern Methodist church. In addition to conducting religious services, Hunter also used the church building for a school where he and some of the men from his regiment taught nearly four hundred students. Commenting on his colleague's activities in Goldsboro, Turner wrote: "There are few men who take more pride in training children than Chaplain Hunter." [21]

Chaplain Turner himself was a committed educator, who made great efforts to ensure that the men in his regiment would become literate. As Turner's regiment marched through the Carolinas, he vigorously engaged in promoting the cause of African Methodism and preaching the Gospel of Freedom. Turner was a free-born native of South Carolina who migrated north. Before entering the army, he was the well-known pastor of a church in Washington, D.C. In early February 1865, Chaplain Turner preached to blacks in Smithville, North Carolina, weaving into his sermon the theme of "freedom, liberty, and justice to all men, irrespective of color." Perhaps in order to impress local blacks with how much things had changed since the onset of freedom, Turner chose the formerly forbidden setting of the county courthouse for a meeting in which he made a case for membership in the A.M.E. Church.[22]

A few months later, the editor of the *Christian Recorder* gleefully reported that Chaplain Turner had pushed on to another front. "He has gone into Raleigh, N.C., hoisted the flag of the A.M.E. Church, and taken in some four or five hundred members." The editor's ebullience was probably enhanced by the fact that he had several relatives in the newly liberated areas of the Tarheel State. "That is right, Bro. Turner!" he wrote. "May the good Lord continue to crown your efforts with success." When Turner passed through his own native state of South Carolina, he reported that blacks in Columbia had "thrown off the slave-yoke of Southern Methodism, and united with the A.M.E. Church, and are standing in the full vigor of their God-given rights." But Chaplain Turner's most impressive proselytizing took place in Georgia and continued even after he was mustered out of the army. Reverend Turner boasted of bringing several thousand black Georgians into the A.M.E. fold, and his bombast had a basis in fact.[23]

The keynote of the African Methodist mission to the freedpeople was sounded in fall 1864 by Reverend Alexander Wayman of Baltimore. On that occasion Reverend Wayman was in Norfolk to preach to a congregation that had expressed an interest in affiliating with the A.M.E. Church. Wayman chose as his text for that sermon a passage from the 37th chapter of the book of Genesis, "I come to seek my brethren." As he moved through the South, Reverend Wayman often returned to that text, and his sermon became well known among A.M.E. missionaries. In fact, several of them offered Wayman the ultimate compliment by attempting their own versions of it.[24]

Among them was Theophilus Gould Steward, a young preacher from Camden, New Jersey. Reverend Steward had not quite completed his first year at his first church when he was given a new assignment. In his memoirs of his ministry, Steward wrote: "On April 30, 1865, in the evening, I received a note from Bishop Payne to meet him in New York, prepared to embark for Charleston, S.C.; and by 8 o'clock next morning I was on the train." Reverend Steward and two other ministers accompanied Bishop Payne on his voyage to Charleston to organize the South Carolina Conference. During the conference the bishop assigned Steward the task of starting a mission church in the coastal town of Beaufort, South Carolina. Incidentally, but perhaps not inconsequently, in Beaufort the young missionary lived in the same boarding house as Major Martin R. Delany, the prominent advocate of black pride and independence.[25]

When the time came for his first sermon to the freedpeople, Reverend Steward chose "I come to seek my brethren" as his text. He was aware of Reverend Wayman's famous sermon, but decided that "no man can take out a patent right on any particular passage of God's book."[26] In the course of his sermon Steward said, "I have thought I could not better tell you my business than to quote this language of Joseph and claim it as my own—I seek my brethren. I come from New Jersey to South Carolina in search of, or hunting for, my brethren."[27]

As the missionary developed the main theme of his sermon, he evoked the heritage that bound educated northern free blacks like himself to southerners whose experience did not extend much beyond the watery rice fields where they had been enslaved:

Our fathers have passed through the fiery furnace of slavery and escaped to the North, where a nominal or partial freedom reigns; they have taught us in infancy to remember those in bonds as being bound with them; and from our churches, our firesides and our closets has gone up the petition: "Oh Lord, remember those that are bound down under hard task masters, our brethren in affliction! Break every yoke, snap in sunder every chain, and let the oppressed go free!"[28]

And then Reverend Steward sounded the high notes of the Gospel of Freedom: "God has heard; Glory to His name! Answered the prayers of His people, and so to speak, has come down to deliver them. The yoke is cast off, the chains are broken and we come in search of our brethren, the Freedmen."[29]

During the next three years, Steward was sent to four other mission stations in South Carolina and to one in Georgia. In addition, he taught school and tried to get a fledgling newspaper off the ground. Financial support he expected to receive from the American Missionary Association never came. His existence was difficult, and then got worse. He had bouts with fever and penury. At one point, necessity forced him to pawn his watch. Yet, for the most part, his enthusiasm for the work remained undiminished. In March 1867, he wrote a letter to the *Christian Recorder* in which he said, "Oh! I cannot express how dearly I love the work in this field." As a zealous A.M.E. partisan he reported on the denomination's successes in South Carolina: "our name is known and influence felt in nearly every part of the State, conferring religious freedom and responsibilities upon the people who join us." In 1874, two years after having been reassigned to a pulpit outside the South, Reverend Steward gave his second son the middle name Hunter, in honor of his "esteemed friend, Chaplain W. H. Hunter."[30]

Much of Steward's work as a missionary was done under the supervision of Reverend Richard Harvey Cain, the most influential A.M.E. cleric in the South Carolina Conference. Reverend Cain became the de facto bishop of the area because Bishop Payne was away much of the time supervising the Baltimore Conference and serving as president and chief fund-raiser for Wilberforce University. Henry M. Turner played a similar supervisory role in the Georgia Conference. Reverend Cain was born free in what was later to become the state of West Virginia. He attended Wilberforce when the school was still owned by the Methodist Episcopal Church. Cain came to Charleston in spring 1865, having left a leading A.M.E. church in Brooklyn to become a missionary at the age of forty. He did not consider his departure to be a sacrifice. Two years earlier he had wished Godspeed to the first A.M.E. missionaries as they departed from New York, and since then he had been possessed by a desire to take part in the momentous transformations taking place in the South. Cain grew increasingly weary of Brooklyn. "It is a charming thought," he wrote in June 1863, "to turn from the small-souled contentionists in our cities to the great and glorious work of instructing the freed-men in the great fields of South Carolina."[31]

Within a few months of his arrival in Charleston, Reverend Cain began construction of Emanuel, the church that was to become the flagship of African Methodism in South Carolina. The building was a symbol of the Gospel of Freedom. Cain commissioned Robert Vesey, son of the martyred freedom fighter, Denmark, to serve as architect of Emanuel. The church was prominently located on Calhoun Street, between Meeting and Elizabeth, and was large enough to seat 2,500 people. Cain boasted that every nail in the building was driven in by a black worker. The cornerstone was laid on 25 September 1865, and a Reverend E. J. Adams spoke for the occasion. According to Cain, Reverend Adams "looked truly like an African Prince, whose soul was fired by the love of his race." Perhaps with some exaggeration, Cain estimated that over three thousand people attended the ceremony. He reported that "houses, fences, porches, wagons and every means of getting a good view was resorted to by the people." The following spring, Cain sent Reverend Steward to organize another church in Charleston. That church was named in honor of the late Morris Brown, who had been Denmark Vesey's pastor before being forced to flee from Charleston to the North in 1822.[32]

Reverend Cain also threw himself into the work of organizing A.M.E. churches in rural areas. "We have visited many plantations and secluded spots," he wrote to the *Christian Recorder* in September 1866, "and we are constantly being sent for to labor in some new locality." In addition to his church activities, Cain was editor of a newspaper called the *South Carolina Leader*. He pushed himself and his colleagues to the point of exhaustion. On at least one occasion, he was temporarily forced to retreat from the field because of prostration due to overwork. According to the editor of the *Recorder,* Cain and Henry M. Turner were each responsible for bringing thousands of freedpeople into the A.M.E. Church, and the two were among the denomination's most effective missionaries in the South.[33]

The missionary efforts of Bishop Payne and Reverends Lynch, Hall, Rue, Hunter, Turner, Wayman, Steward, and Cain were paralleled by the activities of others in other parts of the South. For example, Bishop Jabez P. Campbell organized the Louisiana Conference in November 1865, only a few months after Payne inaugurated the South Carolina Conference. The primary objective of this volume, however, is not to provide a chronological account of the establishment of African Methodist churches and conferences in the South, but to examine the African Methodist meaning of freedom. The vital facts concerning the development of the denomination in the South have been carefully chronicled by Charles Spencer Smith in his compendium, *The History of the African Methodist Episcopal Church*, which was published in 1922. Smith points out that any list of missionary "trailblazers" should include "Bishop James A. Shorter, who led the forces in Tennessee, Texas, and Mississippi; Bishop J. P. Campbell, who led the forces in Arkansas; and Bishop J. M. Brown, who led the forces in Alabama," among others. In addition, a volume entitled

African Methodism in the South, or Twenty Five Years of Freedom was published by John Wesley Gaines in 1890, and shortly after the turn of the century, Revels A. Adams and Israel L. Butt wrote works on A.M.E. history in Mississippi and Virginia, respectively. A history of the A.M.E. Church in Florida by Charles Sumner Long appeared in 1939. Perhaps the most thoughtful, lucid, and engaging of the early state histories is H. T. Kealing's *History of African Methodism in Texas,* which was published in 1885.[34] In one amusing passage, Kealing reminds us that not all of the missionaries were human:

> He [a Texan missionary] had a horse called Old Charley, that insisted on stopping at every cabin where there were colored people, because he was accustomed to Elder Haywood stopping to talk to every one he met about African Methodism. If the elder refused to stop, Old Charley became refractory and showed strong symptoms of being given over to total depravity. No history of African Methodism would be complete that ignored Old Charley as a factor in the itinerant service.[35]

More seriously, the dynamics of missionary work cannot be fully understood without taking into account the significance of initiatives taken by black worshipers. Reverend A. Weston of Newberry, South Carolina, made that point in an essay he wrote on "How African Methodism Was Introduced in the Up Country":

> We were still wondering what we should do about a church, and, in 1866, we sent two sisters to Columbia, S.C., to seek us a pastor. . . . They started on their journey like heroes. They went to Rev. W. H. Brown, who was then pastor of Bethel A.M.E. Church, Columbia, S.C. . . . Then Brother Brown and his members presented to them Simon Miller. They accepted him and immediately returned to Newberry bringing Brother Miller with them and presented him to us as our pastor, and he was gladly received.[36]

That story not only illustrates the strategic importance of lay initiative, it also shows the authority that could be exercised by women members. Unfortunately, the story does not tell us why, or whether, those women deliberately set out to find an A.M.E. pastor. In any event, from his base in Newberry, Reverend Simon Miller directed the organization of several other A.M.E. churches in the surrounding countryside.[37]

The A.M.E. mission to the South was loosely structured. For the most part, the missionaries shared a common set of values and objectives, but their actions were not orchestrated by any single agency or governed by denomination-wide policies. The A.M.E. Church did have a body called the Parent Home and Foreign Missionary Society, which loosely coordinated efforts to raise money to support the work in the South, but the Society did not set policy on how, when, or where that work was to be conducted.[38] The effectiveness of the mission to the freedpeople depended on the energy and resourcefulness of individual bishops and missionaries in the field. Under the uncertain conditions existing in the postwar South, flexibility and the decentralization of authority may have been advantageous.

In addition to funds raised within the denomination in the North, Bishop Payne secured some financial support for African Methodist missionary work from the American Missionary Association, a strongly antislavery and nominally nonsectarian evangelical society founded in 1846. Payne's arrangement with the A.M.A. was fairly straightforward, but some of the denomination's other efforts to solicit support could serve as the basis for a Methodist version of the old adage about politics and bedfellows. In 1864, the corresponding secretary of the Missionary Society made an unsuccessful appeal to the Methodist Episcopal Church for financial assistance, even though the M.E. Church and the African M.E. Church were sometimes bitter rivals in the South and had a troubled history in the North. The African Methodists were sure that they had worked out an agreement. Understandably, the M.E. Church was far from sure about the wisdom of subsidizing a competitor, and so the matter was dropped.[39]

Even more perplexing was the philosophically convoluted alliance the A.M.E. Church attempted to forge with Southern Methodism in 1866. African Methodists hoped that such an alliance would give them control of the church buildings used by black Southern Methodist congregations, eliminating property as an ongoing source of contention with Southern Methodists and providing a competitive edge for the battle with Northern Methodists. For their own reasons, Southern Methodists also wanted the A.M.E. Church to be better able to help block the advance of the M.E. Church into the South. As it turned out, neither side fully understood the other's objectives, but soon it was evident to both denominations that the African Methodist vision of the future for free black citizens was profoundly incompatible with the expectations that white Southern Methodists had for erstwhile slaves, and so the alliance fizzled quickly, having produced little more than confusion and conflict.[40]

The A.M.E. Missionary Society did make efforts to support the work in the South. In May 1865, the Society's board of managers began a campaign to raise $10,000 from northern conferences during the ensuing year. That ambitious goal was made even more difficult to reach by the fact that the denomination was still paying for Wilberforce University. To make matters worse, the main building of the university had burned to the ground in April. Even without those special burdens, the hard fact was that northern black incomes simply were not sufficient to support a massive mission to millions of freedpeople. The members of the New England Conference concluded that local demands on their missionary funds were "so pressing" that they could not pledge a specific amount for the South, but they resolved to give all that they could "to help on the great and glorious work of human redemption."[41]

While presiding at the Baltimore Conference in spring 1866, Bishop Payne revealed his frustration at being unable to send more ministers with families into the southern work. "Are you going to force upon the bishops married men for the missionary fields?" Payne implored, abandoning the serene dignity for which he was known. "What are they going to do with them? There will be documents read in this house which will make you weep, if you have the hearts of men. I have seen our missionary agent weep over them as if his heart would break. We have work for them, but where are the means for their support?" On more than one occasion, Bishop Payne personally borrowed money or reached into his own pocket to meet the expenses of preachers in the South.[42]

Many of the missionaries assigned to rural areas could rely only on the funds and food they could raise in the field, literally. In 1868, Bishop John Mifflin Brown rescheduled the regular annual meetings of his southern conferences from spring to winter in order not to interfere with planting time. Bishop Brown explained: "Most of our ministers, save those stationed in the cities, are compelled to depend upon the cultivation of their *little gardens.*" On the other hand, in a city like Charleston, Reverend Cain seemed to be able to raise the money needed to meet the construction costs of Emanuel Church without great difficulty. Citing the pressing need for more workers, Cain, and others like him, urged potential missionaries not to be deterred by the prospect of meager remuneration. "While there are hardships to be encountered," he observed, "yet no man will starve among a people like those in the Southern States, because they are generous to a fault. If they have no money, they will share the last article of food with their pastors."[43]

The ministry of the A.M.E. Church in the South was not made up only of missionaries from the North. In 1869, Reverend Augustus T. Carr, a native of Georgetown, South Carolina, took exception to the way in which the editor of the *Christian Recorder* had described the stalwarts of the missionary corps. "What was meant by your saying . . . that the A.M.E. Church had fifty odd missionaries in the South?" Reverend Carr asked pointedly. "Do you mean to say that those are only regarded as missionaries who were born on the other side of the Potomac?" Reverend Carr's point was well taken; southerners swelled the ranks of the A.M.E. clergy. The growth and development of the denomination ultimately depended on the recruitment of preachers in the South. Reverend T. G. Steward commended the alacrity with which his denomination brought former slaves into its ministry. He observed: " 'Leaders' from the plantations come forth and are clothed with authority and filled with fervor, and go back among their fellows armed with that new power, which sympathy and encouragement and ideas of responsibility give." [44]

While it is clear that some southern black preachers resented the intrusion of northern competitors, it is also true that many of them eagerly seized the ideas and authority that northern denominations offered and used them in their own efforts to secure and increase the fruits of freedom. The battle for the minds and souls of the freedpeople was waged largely by newly ordained, southern stalwarts of the various branches of Methodism. For example, some of the stiffest opposition faced by African Methodism in Louisiana came not from northern white missionaries, or from indigenous preachers protecting their "turf," but from clergymen like the Reverend Emperor Williams, a former slave who became a distinguished and energetic champion of the Northern Methodist Church. [45]

But being from the North was definitely an advantage during the formative years of African Methodist presence in the South. For the most part, northerners directed the mission and defined the content of the A.M.E. social gospel. Being an effective apostle of the Gospel of Freedom required some qualifications that few plantation preachers could offer. "We need those who can teach school as well as preach the Gospel," Cain wrote in 1866, "those who can point out the duties of social life, and of family responsibilities. The people in the country want to be taught how to live like freemen." In time, however, a distinctively southern perspective on denominational policies came into being, and conflicts ensued between those African Methodists who were in the southern field and those who remained in the North. Sectional battlelines were drawn on issues such as the election of bishops, the location of denominational offices, the regional allocation of funds, and the advisability of founding new colleges in the South. In addition, southern supporters of emigration sometimes encountered strong opposition from their northern coreligionists. [46]

The A.M.E. Church was not the only African Methodist denomination sending missionaries to the freedpeople. The African Methodist Episcopal Zion denomination also dispatched its representatives into the cities and rural districts of the South to "seek their brethren." The origins and history of the A.M.E. Zion Church were very similar to those of its slightly older and considerably larger sister denomination; the objectives, dynamics, and structures of the southern missions of the two churches were also similar. As initiator of the A.M.E. Zion mission to the South, Bishop Joseph J. Clinton was the counterpart of Daniel Payne. In January 1864, Bishop Clinton sent Reverend James Walker Hood from a church in Bridgeport, Connecticut, to New Bern, North Carolina. A native of Pennsylvania, Reverend Hood was the Zion counterpart of Richard H. Cain and Henry M. Turner. In fact, Turner regarded Hood as a friend and compatriot. Largely due to his success in the South, Reverend Hood was elected a bishop of the A.M.E. Zion Church in 1872.[47]

Both Hood and Turner were denominational partisans, but they were also exasperated by the fact that the two African Methodist Churches became such unyielding competitors for the allegiance of southern blacks. As a result, Hood and Turner became strong proponents of uniting the two African Methodist denominations. After visiting Hood at his home in New Bern in June 1865, Turner wrote: "I find Brother Hood a strong advocate for union between our connections. He informed me that the name proposed for our connection after its union is, the United African Methodist Episcopal Church. I would suggest that its name be simply, United Methodist Episcopal Church." A few months later, Turner encountered a congregation in Raleigh that was understandably confused by the difference between the denominations. He assured them that there was no cause for concern because the A.M.E.s and the A.M.E.Z.s were going to unite "if *timber heads* in both connections did not raise the devil and prevent it." Despite the best efforts of Reverends Turner and Hood, however, the "timber heads" won out. Once established, institutions tend to take on lives of their own and they steadfastly adhere to the law of self-preservation. The two African Methodist denominations remained institutional rivals, but they also continued to pursue the same vision of the future and to promote the same definition of freedom. Hood's classic history, *One Hundred Years of the African Methodist Episcopal Zion Church* (1895) contains much valuable and interesting information about the Zion mission to the freedpeople and about some of the individuals who planted that denomination in the South. In addition, an impressive, detailed account of Zion Methodism's southern mission is included in Bishop William J. Walls's exhaustive history of his denomination, *The African Methodist Episcopal Zion Church: Reality of the Black Church* (1974).[48]

The most severe challenge confronting African Methodists in the South was not fatigue, economic hardship, interdenominational rivalries, or the demands of trying to be exemplars of black freedom. Missionaries were never entirely free from the threat, or the reality, of violence. The hostilities between the North and South did not end at Appomattox. For many Americans, Lincoln's "new birth of freedom" was followed by a baptism of blood. A pioneer of African Methodism in Texas remembered: "It was no strange sight to feel the horse shy from the road, and see, as the cause, the body of a man dangling from a tree by the roadside."[49] The lives of these missionary preachers were enveloped in crisis. Along with their glowing accounts of new members and new churches came mind-numbing reports of death and brutality. A few of those reports will suffice to convey a sense of the atmosphere in which the missionaries operated, an atmosphere in which boundless optimism was displaced with regularity by utter despair. In June 1866, Bishop J. P. Campbell reported:

> Bishop Campbell, who presides over the Conferences which control the Great Valley of the Mississippi, pleads the cause of the thousands of our brethren in that region. He tells us of the hardships of the noble band of men who suffer almost death, while trying to plant the standard of the Cross of Christ. He tells of our noble brother Rev. Page Tyler, who stood and saw more than twenty of the members of his church shot dead during the recent massacre in Memphis, Tennessee. He saw his churches enveloped in flames, and all his fond hopes laid in the dust.[50]

During the same month, Henry M. Turner reported:

> I have just arrived at this place, from an inspection tour of our work in East Alabama. . . . At Opelika, Ala., I met Rev. Robt Alexander, (Deacon) whom Bishop Payne appointed to the Auburn Mission. He informed me that after church, on Thursday night, (the 14th inst.) he had been severely cut and beaten nearly to death. Four white citizens broke into his room at midnight, and beat and stabbed him till he appeared, when I met him, like a lump of curdled blood. . . . The miscreants told him that no d———d negro schools should be taught there, nor should any negro preacher remain there. . . . I sent Bro. Alexander to Columbus, Ga., for medical aid. Whether he will live or not is to be seen. . . . Brother Alexander is one of the most harmless men I ever saw. . . . He is 26 years of age, and weighs but 101 lbs. . . .
>
> I never saw anything which moved my sympathies more than to see my brother minister's distressed condition on leaving Auburn, the place where he had been assigned to preach the Gospel. This picture is too sad for me [to] draw. O God! Where is our civilization? Is this Christendom, or is it hell? Pray for us.[51]

On 12 November 1870, editor Benjamin T. Tanner reported:

Two of our South Carolina ministers, Revs. Wade Perrin and Griffin Johnson, have just fallen victims to the murderous spirit still rampant in the
South. We simply say, that perfectly outrageous as it is, it is tolerated.[52]

In 1874, Reverend I. S. Grant was assigned to Clinton, South Carolina, the site
of one of the murders referred to above. Reverend Grant reported:

I was sent here by Bishop Campbell to take charge of this work. When
my appointment was read out . . . I was almost persuaded not to go, the
reasons, money was scarce, and I was moved from Bishopville year before
last. . . . But my last reason was the death of Brother Perrin, who had had
charge of this work. He was caught in the road by a band of Ku Klux, and
1st he was made to dance, 2nd to sing, 3rd to pray, 4th and lastly to run,
and in running he was shot dead.[53]

Persecutions notwithstanding, African Methodist missionaries succeeded in
establishing their denominations in the South. Denominational membership
statistics for this period are notoriously unreliable, and their use in studies such
as this implies a degree of precision that can be very misleading. Nevertheless,
it has been estimated that from 1856 to 1880 the membership of the A.M.E.
Church grew from 19,963 to 400,000, and that of the A.M.E. Zion Church grew
from 4,600 to 250,000. Both of the African Methodist denominations surged
past the Colored Methodist Episcopal Church, whose membership stood at
120,000 in 1880. No attempt will be made here to draw hard conclusions from
those highly suggestive statistics, although it appears that the vast majority of
southern blacks could not be held by the old paternalism and were not drawn
to the new paternalism.[54] But even if the accuracy of those figures could be
relied on, by themselves they cannot make clear who was winning the battle
for the souls of black folk, or why.

The fact that Southern Methodism did not begin to organize colored conferences until 1866 put the embryonic Colored Methodist denomination at a competitive disadvantage, and other factors, not under study here, may also have
influenced denominational choices. In her significant and thought-provoking
study, *An African American Exodus*, Katharine Dvorak puts forward the view
that distinctive religious sensibilities and ministerial charisma accounted for
the freedpeople's religious affiliations. She does not stress the significance of external, secular ideas and influences like the ones examined in this study.[55] Final
conclusions must await a direct analysis of the laypeople who were actually
making the choices. At this juncture, prudence and the paucity of local membership lists force me to confine my conjectures to preachers, because there is

sufficient evidence concerning the views of the clergy to make it possible to arrive at some reasonably sound, though limited, conclusions. What is clear is that African Methodism and Colored Methodism offered southern blacks social gospels that were very different, if not entirely incompatible. Fervent apostles of the Gospel of Freedom had contempt for the new paternalism of Colored Methodism. The contrast between the two responses to emancipation will emerge with even greater clarity after the next chapter.

4

EXEGESIS OF THE GOSPEL
OF FREEDOM

"The new era has dawned, the sun has lit up the horizon." Reverend Richard Harvey Cain made that observation after participating in the inaugural session of the South Carolina Conference of the A.M.E. Church. Reverend Cain's vision of the future was shared by most of the African Methodist missionaries who went down to the land of bondage to preach the Gospel of Freedom. They believed that they stood on the threshold of a new era of unlimited possibilities, and they came to the South seeking more than new members.[1] Their mission was really to regenerate a people.

In this chapter, the statements and actions of some of the most prominent, effective, and influential missionaries will be reviewed in order to illustrate the set of attitudes, beliefs, values, and objectives that has been referred to in this book as the Gospel of Freedom. For the most part, the persons whose views are presented here are already familiar to you from the previous chapter. This "exegesis" is not organized chronologically. It will review actions and statements drawn from the entire span of the "new era." The term "African Methodist" will be used generically to refer to either or both the A.M.E. and A.M.E. Zion denominations.

As you make your way through this chapter, it may appear as though African Methodists heaped heavy doses of northern cultural arrogance on the southern freedpeople, and to a large extent that assessment would be correct. On the other hand, the values, methods, and objectives making up the Gospel of Freedom were the very same values, methods, and objectives that northern blacks had been preaching to each other in churches, mutual aid societies, newspapers, and conventions for at least six decades prior to the outbreak of the Civil War.[2] Emancipation and the mission to the South radically heightened its optimism and urgency, but in content, the Gospel of Freedom was essentially the same northern, antebellum "old-time religion" that had always exhorted "middle-class" values, self-help, moral reform, and racial pride.

Northern black evangelicals entered the new era firmly believing that civilization always moves forward and that God is directly involved in the unfolding of human history. Belief in progress as well as in divine providence were integral parts of their creed. In a letter to the *Christian Recorder* in April 1866, Cain referred to "the eternal laws of progress," "the onward march of events," "manifest destiny," and "the decrees of Heaven"—all of which were, in his view, conspiring to bring blacks "certain and full recognition in the mighty march of civilization." One year before his departure for South Carolina, Reverend Cain confidently predicted that "revolutions never go backward."[3]

The missionaries needed vision and faith to sustain them in the South, not only because they faced white opposition, but also because they believed that making it possible for nearly four million people to transcend the cultural legacy of over two centuries of chattel slavery would be a formidable undertaking, no less difficult than the abolition of slavery itself. While still a chaplain in the Union army, Henry McNeal Turner lamented: "Oh, how the foul curse of slavery has blighted the natural greatness of my race!" After two years in South Carolina, Reverend Cain wrote: "The great masses have, by the old systems, been taught that they were inferior to the whites in everything, and they believe it still." As late as 1880, Cain was disturbed to find "the old ideas of negro inferiority" still lingering "in the minds of thousands."[4] According to the Gospel of Freedom, the one unspeakable heresy was for blacks to believe in their own inferiority. The missionaries committed themselves to a relentless campaign to extirpate debilitating notions of inferiority from the minds of former slaves.

African Methodists had a long list of grievances against slavery. The missionaries bemoaned what they perceived to be the moral damage done by the "peculiar institution." Bishop Payne expressed the view that the "greatest curse" of slavery had been the "destruction of the home." Turner once said that "thievish" tendencies and dishonesty were natural by-products of an institution that did not compensate workers for their labor and rewarded unwelcome truth with severe punishment. Cain urged all black Christians to combine their efforts to bring about a "reformation in the moral state of the freedmen."[5]

Those men concluded that slavery had frayed and twisted the moral fiber of its victims. Traditional evangelical moral concerns were closely interwoven with exhortations about racial pride in the Gospel of Freedom.

There were still other problems for which African Methodists held slavery responsible. James Walker Hood noted that two and a half centuries of "the most degrading vassalage" had made it impossible for former slaves to "compare favorably with the Anglo-Saxon in point of intellectual culture." During the summer of 1865, Turner wrote of meeting "hundreds" of newly freed blacks whose mental horizons were limited because of their never having been more than five miles from their cabins. Bishop Payne concluded that slavery was responsible for the freedpeople's "religious errors" and "wild enthusiasm."[6] The missionaries' general assessment of the situation was that emancipation required a great deal more than a proclamation. With more than a little arrogance, African Methodists prescribed a cultural transfusion and a social transformation in order to restore human property to full personhood and in order to make it possible for blacks to occupy their rightful place in the new era.

The missionaries' impressions of the freedpeople were not all so somber. African Methodists saw great potential in the black South. They proudly pointed to examples of intelligence, independence, enterprise, and craftsmanship, and they adamantly refuted whites who implied that the shortcomings of the freedpeople were racial characteristics. In November 1862, a Thanksgiving celebration was held in honor of the contrabands who had found freedom in Washington. During the ceremonies the refugees were subjected to a great deal of learned oratory. Turner, who was then still a Washington pastor, thought the attentiveness of the former slaves showed "a great deal of intelligence." He asserted: "It let gainsayers see, that we could understand something else, besides *dis, dat* and *dem*." James Lynch was also struck by the "mental power" of the contrabands in Washington. After working in the South for a little more than a month, Reverend Lynch wrote that he had discovered in the freedpeople "a desire to hear and learn, that I never imagined."[7]

Turner was also struck by the enterprise of the Washington contrabands, many of whom sought "immediate employment" rather than rations in a government camp. Reflecting on his experiences traveling in the South before the war, he asserted that "the ablest historian, the greatest orator, and the most skillful architect and mechanic I have ever seen, were all slaves in the South." Reverend Cain also observed that the slave states had produced more black craftsmen and skilled workers than had the free economy of the North. Chaplain Turner found that the freedpeople of Columbia, South Carolina, were not afflicted with lingering servility; he reported that they were "brave, independent and fearless." The chaplain observed that blacks in Columbia displayed "none of this foolish crouching before white men."[8]

So, in 1863, African Methodists stood on the threshold of a new era. They saw great problems and great potential in the black South. The missionaries were sobered by the magnitude of their task, and made heady by the power of their vision. They believed that the Gospel of Freedom could regenerate a people whose potential had been smothered under the dead weight of slavery. The missionaries advocated sweeping cultural transformations. They were not the least bit nostalgic, appreciative, or even tolerant of some aspects of the folk culture of southern blacks. The missionaries saw themselves in a battle that pitted the productive, disciplined culture of northern, republican, upward mobility and independence against the static, cavalier culture of slavery and dependency. They might have paraphrased scripture in the following manner: "What shall it profit a man if he gain control from his master, and then lose control over himself?" The missionaries saw no reason to equate blackness with a lack of discipline. African Methodists were cultural Puritans, insisting on discipline and having little patience with what they perceived to be emotional excesses. At times their zeal devolved into arrogance. For example, Turner wrote this derisive characterization of the emotional conversion experiences of some southern black worshipers:

> But let a person get a little animated, fall down and roll over awhile, kick a few shins[,] crawl under a dozen benches, spring upon his feet, knock some innocent person on the nose and set it bleeding, then squeal (or buss) around for awhile, and the work is all done; whereas, if the individual had claimed justification under more quiet circumstances, its legitimacy would have been doubted.[9]

Even after making allowances for Turner's biting satire, the chaplain's words seem unduly harsh and judgmental.

African Methodists preached that in the new era blacks had to become self-reliant, achieve upward mobility, and occupy positions of authority. "To reach the top the black man must go on his own plane, must climb his own ladder," Reverend Hood asserted, expressing one of the main themes of the Gospel of Freedom. Reverend Cain advocated "self-sustenance" and "self-development." Turner urged acceptance of the "help-yourself doctrine, which must ultimately triumph, if we ever triumph." Enterprise and independence could be truly meaningful only in a society that allowed for social and economic advancement. African Methodists argued that blacks held a very limited view of their own potential because they lived in an environment in which positions of distinction were monopolized by whites. Cain explained that problem this way: "We are not so much in want of intelligence among us, as we are in need of position, . . . We know how to serve others, but, have not learned how to serve ourselves. We have always been directed by others in all the affairs of life." Within African Methodism, the freedpeople were offered a model of how society could operate if race were not a controlling factor. Bishop Payne said that African Methodism offered blacks "space to rise," as well as "powerful motives for mental and moral culture; because every office in the gift of this Church was accessible, and the most meritorious obtained it." [10]

The bishop's point was well taken, as is illustrated by an anecdote that had probably already become folklore by the time that it appeared in H. T. Kealing's *History of African Methodism in Texas* in 1885. Kealing relates the story of how a former slave preacher named Haywood closely interrogated an A.M.E. missionary before deciding to abandon his affiliation with the Southern Methodist Church:

"What is your business here?"

"To plant the African Methodist Episcopal Church."

"What kind of a church is that?"

"A church governed by colored Bishops, having colored elders and presiding elders."

"That don't look reasonable. You tell me that your church has negro presiding elders?"

"I do."

"Can they administer the sacrament as white presiding elders can?"

"Just as well."

"Well, I never heard of such a thing, much less saw it."

"I am an elder, sir."

"What! you?"

"Yes."

"Can you baptize like a white elder?"

"Yes, sir."

"And marry?"

"Yes, sir."

"If I wanted license to preach could you give it to me?"

"Yes, sir."

"But would it be legal?"

"Perfectly."

"Just as legal as though a white elder did it?"

"Just as legal."

"And you say you have black Bishops?"

"Yes, sir."

"Can they hold conferences?"

"Why, of course, what would they be good for if they could not?"

"Could they ordain a man?"

"Certainly." [11]

After examining a compilation of the policies governing the A.M.E. Church and hearing an account of the denomination's history, the incredulous Reverend Haywood was won over "and he joined then and there." [12]

African Methodist missionaries saw themselves as the representatives of denominational traditions that stressed racial pride and independence. Both the A.M.E. and A.M.E. Zion denominations were founded in the North during the first quarter of the nineteenth century as protests against segregation and the inflexible, albeit unofficial, limit that white Methodists put on the authority and upward mobility of black preachers. The founding of those denominations symbolized the kind of assertion of independence that the missionaries were urging the freedpeople to make. A biographer of Bishop Hood observed that he was "born into independent manly Church government." In 1866, Lynch proudly asserted that "the formation of the A.M.E. Church was the first attempt of the colored people in this country to vindicate the manhood of the race." Cain attributed his success in organizing African Methodist churches in the South to the fact that the freedpeople "recognize in our organization the idea of Nationality of Manhood. They feel that the time has come for the black man to take his place as a free man." [13] Kealing relates how an African Methodist missionary named Goins won a congregation of tenant farmers away from their Colored Methodist preacher:

> When Goins cried out, "Now all of you that are free, come and join your own church," some started to rise, but the C.M.E. minister seized them, saying, "Don't you go, Mars Young will turn you off'n his plantation." "Come on," cried Goins, "I don't want Mars Young's niggers, I want all who are free." They broke away from the minister, and began to flock forward. [14]

It was not only to the history and traditions of their own denominations that African Methodists referred in order to illustrate the Gospel of Freedom. The missionaries also made use of what historian Bernard Lewis has called the "myth of the glorious past" to further refute the charge that throughout history blacks had been afflicted with congenital insignificance. African Methodists used history to create a powerful, transforming vision of what the future could hold. Hood pointed out that blacks were pioneers in science and art and contended that "instead of being inferior, they stood at the head of the races of the earth." In January 1866, Turner informed an audience of freedpeople in Georgia that blacks were "the first great men of the world. They founded the first cities and formed the first empires; they were the greatest generals." [15] An ex-slave named William Henry Heard remembered hearing Turner give a speech called "The Negro in All Ages." The speech lasted two hours. Heard eventually became an A.M.E. bishop, and in his brief memoir, Bishop Heard recalled the impact of hearing Turner's sermon from the Gospel of Freedom: "I was so impressed with the pictures and historic facts he presented of the Race in past ages, and of the men of the present, that my life is largely what it is because of the impression made at this meeting." [16]

In 1874, after hearing a U.S. Congressman from North Carolina charge that blacks had never produced anything of historical significance, Cain, who was then a member of Congress himself, let loose with a litany of black accomplishment:

I wonder if the gentleman ever read history. Did he ever hear tell of any persons of the name of Hannibal, of Hanno, of Hamilcar, of Euclid—all great men of ancient times—of Aesop and others? No, sir; no; for that kind of literature does not come to North Carolina. [17]

It was not only in ancient history that the missionaries found evidence of historical significance and of the potential for future greatness. The hallowed aura of heritage was already beginning to emanate from the battlefields of the Civil War. Former Chaplain Turner reminded a gathering of freedpeople that black soldiers had bled "gallons of the richest blood that ever coursed its way through the veins of man" fighting for freedom and staking a claim for the inclusion of members of their race as full-fledged citizens of the Republic. Cain was quick to point out to doubters and to the uninformed that at Fort Wagner, Petersburg, Port Hudson, and "on every occasion on the battlefield where the black man met the white man of the South, there was no flinching, no turning back." [18]

Even though the missionaries wrapped themselves in the mantles of tradition and heritage, the Gospel of Freedom was dynamic and forward-looking. Bishop Payne insisted that the new era demanded a "different spirit and different conduct." By temperament, Cain was well suited for the role of cultural ramrod. He once asserted that the goal of the mission to the South was to "mould, fashion and transform the masses." He characterized African Methodism as "aggressive in its character and purposes" and lauded the fact that the denomination "naturally conflicts with the past customs and habits of the people—changes their modes of action and proclaims an advance along the lines of negro nationality."[19]

Reflecting on the impact that African Methodism had on the freedpeople of Texas, Reverend Kealing asserted:

> It [the A.M.E. Church] has established schools, founded a college, erected brick churches, encouraged the building of beautiful cottage residences, instead of the cabin, laughed the open-your-mouth-and-the-Lord-will-fill-it preacher out of countenance, and put him to studying, increased the vocabulary of the masses, by the use of good language—in fine, made the negro ashamed of his foibles and anxious to emulate the better things of life.[20]

The missionaries believed that it was very important for the freedpeople to be ushered into the new era by persons who could themselves exemplify what it meant to be free and black. African Methodists insisted that blacks, like themselves, made the best missionaries. They claimed a special connection with the freedpeople because they were "brethren by virtue of race" as well as "brethren in affliction." But the missionaries were not merely manipulating racial solidarity—the Gospel of Freedom had more substance than that. African Methodists argued that even the most self-sacrificing and committed white missionaries could not serve as exemplars of black leadership ability. Some of the missionaries questioned how wholeheartedly whites would work to wean former slaves from the habit of regarding whites as authority figures. In addition, Cain warned that dependence on the "benevolence of others" would render blacks "subject to their insults." While serving in Beaufort, South Carolina, Lynch urged northern blacks to recognize the "influence and power that can be wielded by colored men and women." In August 1865, Turner contended that "twenty-five colored men of good common sense and education" would be able to "effect a revolution for the better, faster and more surely than any other agency or instrumentality."[21]

But of course, the task of the missionaries was not just to counter the racial ideology on which the enslavement of blacks had been based; African Methodist missionaries also had to pass muster as evangelicals. In his efforts to recruit preachers for service in the South, Reverend Cain called for "young men of learning, integrity, force of character, and indomitable will," but he also warned that "none need hope to be sent there who are not qualified to elevate the standard of Christianity among our beloved brethren." Bishop Payne sent many missionaries to the South. It was a responsibility that he took very seriously. He believed that a missionary became a "*model* man or woman, whose *vices,* as well as whose virtues, the Freedmen will almost always imitate and make their own." Accordingly, the bishop vowed to "never appoint any man to the Freedmen, of whose intellectual, moral or religious character, I have any doubt."[22]

One of the most salient characteristics of the Gospel of Freedom was that it was firmly grounded in northern values. Henry M. Turner was a native of Abbeville, South Carolina, and one of his biographers described him as a "purely southern product." Nevertheless in 1865, Turner wrote of the "lethargical inertness" of the southern lifestyle, and he lauded "that lively interest so characteristic of northern energy." Turner went so far as to suggest that the infusion of northern energy had caused the dogs and cats of Smithville, North Carolina, to bark and meow with increased vigor. Bishop Payne was a native of Charleston, but he maintained that his "noblest ideas of God and man" were the products of his study of "Northern institutions, on Northern soil, under Northern influences." The bishop expressed the hope that the South would be "converted into communities as pure, as powerful, and as noble as Massachusetts."[23] Northern values and attitudes were as much a part of the African Methodist vision of the new era as were racial pride and moral strength.

In part, the northern model was attractive to the missionaries because the North celebrated political inclusion and upward mobility, unlike the aristocratic and tradition-bound South. Cain wrote: "The North has sent forth those leading ideas, which have spread like lightning over the land; and the negro was not so dumb and not so obtuse that he could not catch the light, and embrace its blessings and enjoy them." It should be pointed out, however, that although African Methodists were enthralled with northern ideals, they were less than enamored with northern racial realities. Before they became missionaries, Cain, Hood, and Turner were very critical of the racial attitudes of northern whites and of the lack of economic opportunity for blacks in the North. Northern blacks could not vote except in New England and New York. Even in the state of New York, black citizens had to meet a property qualification for voting that did not apply to whites.[24] It was in the South of the new era that the promise of the North could be made real for blacks for the first time.

The Gospel of Freedom also incorporated the "free soil" philosophy of social and economic mobility espoused by the Republican party. If the Republican party advocated "free soil, free labor and free men," Cain outdid it by advocating "free thought, free speech, free men, free schools, and a free country." Although African Methodists insisted on the removal of all barriers to advancement based on race, they did not advocate the creation of a society without social and economic distinctions. T. G. Steward explained his views on that subject in this way: "In society there will ever remain the high and the low, the small and the great—to which arrangement we have no objection. All we require is, that it not be based upon accidents, such as color, race, previous condition, but that manhood—moral and intellectual worth—be the basis of classification."[25]

In sum, the Gospel of Freedom was confident, aggressive, and dynamic. It called for emancipation from the cultural and moral legacy of slavery and for the development of new, independent, black citizens, who identified with the interests of their race and adhered to northern values. The Gospel of Freedom determined the way in which African Methodist missionaries approached educational, economic, and political issues.

EDUCATION

Education was one of the master symbols of the new era. Its possession was a hallmark of people who were no longer slaves. The year before he left Brooklyn to work in the South, Reverend Cain had called attention to the urgency of the educational mission: "If the human mind is capable of comprehending a period in time when a necessity exists for the general diffusion of knowledge and the proper instruction of youth, it is now." Never one to mince words, Reverend Turner had little patience with those who doubted the supreme importance of education. In 1863, he wrote: "Palsied be the tongue that would utter a word against thee, O Education." Bishop Payne, whose name was synonymous with African Methodist education, remained a teacher at heart throughout his life. As he saw it, an educator "excites the admiration of eternity, the praise of angels, and the approval of God."[26] The missionaries had absolutely no doubts about the utility and intrinsic worth of education.

African Methodists gave short shrift to theories that posited the inherent intellectual superiority of whites or which questioned the freedpeople's aptitude for educational advancement. Writing as editor of the *Christian Recorder,* Benjamin T. Tanner contended: "Gold may be piled up and inherited. Houses and lands may be willed. But brains never." Tanner asserted: "We hazard nothing in saying that the children of the Freedmen will be the full equals of any class at the South." The missionaries' approach to education reflected their belief that they stood on the threshold of an era of unlimited possibilities. Cain wrote: "We must, by a thorough education, prepare the colored youth for the high duties of a citizen, a merchant, a lawyer, or millionaire." Turner told an audience of southern blacks: "Now the channels of learning are free to all; we have only to launch our vessel and sail in its current to the port of distinction."[27]

In accord with the African Methodist vision of the future, an appropriate curriculum for the new era would have to be capable of equipping blacks to fill any station in life. An educational philosophy that promoted vocational or industrial training as the most appropriate kind of schooling for blacks was offensive to apostles of the Gospel of Freedom. Prior to the founding of Tuskegee Institute in 1881, that approach to black education was most often associated with General Samuel Chapman Armstrong and the school he founded in 1869, Hampton Institute.[28] While looking for a school for his daughter in 1878, Turner visited Hampton and wrote this scathing account of his encounter with a member of its faculty:

> Said I, "You have a splendid institution here; have you a class in the higher branches?
> Said she, "What do you mean by the higher branches?"
> "Well," said I, "I mean algebra, geometry, or the higher mathematics in general, Greek, Latin, and the sciences, etc."
> "Oh," said she, "the colored people are not prepared for those studies yet. They are too ignorant. It will be time enough to talk about that, years from this time."
> Her reply was enough. I wanted to hear no more. It set me a fire [sic].[29]

Turner came away with the impression that the teachers of Hampton showed "a great want of respect" for blacks. He concluded his assessment of the school with the following observation: "I am sure that negro inferiority is taught by act, if not by word, as I am that the alphabet is taught." The Hampton philosophy was incompatible with the Gospel of Freedom. Even before Turner made his comments, editor Tanner had dismissed Samuel Armstrong as a man who "doubts our full capacity." It should be made clear that African Methodists were not opposed to industrial training; the denomination itself had attempted to establish a school for industrial education in Ohio in 1853.[30] It was the imposition of racial limits on educational advancement that ran counter to the Gospel of Freedom.

The upshot of this story was that the year after Turner's comments appeared in the *Christian Recorder,* the Virginia Annual Conference met in the city of Hampton, and Armstrong himself visited a session in order to counter "the abuse in different newspapers directed at him." Reverend Turner happened also to be present. It was reported that the general explained "the object of the school was to build up colored young men and women and to teach them to take care of themselves." The "pastor" of Hampton Institute accompanied Armstrong, and he unapologetically informed the delegates that "the classics were not taught in the school and that there was no necessity for them." Turner took issue with that point, reaffirming his belief that the study of the classics was "expedient." He also acknowledged that he had "made some remarks about the school in the papers, however, he did not blame the General but the teachers." Turner diplomatically conceded that Armstrong's comments had caused him to modify his opinion of the Institute.[31]

Of course, religion was also a necessary component of an acceptable curriculum. As Turner put it, education was the "hand maid of religion." The task of the missionary teacher, according to Payne, was to mold the "unlettered mind" into the "intellectual and moral image of the Deity."[32] The inculcation of strong moral values, to undo the damage done by slavery, was a fundamental aspect of the missionaries' educational philosophy.

The African Methodist approach to education was based on a northern model. Cain praised northern efforts to educate "the masses" and blasted the antebellum South for neglecting public education and producing thereby "a vast hoard of illiterates, of both races." Payne acknowledged that most of the southern population would have to be educated in the South, but he urged that the "master minds" of both races be educated in the North, so that they could become "propagandists" of "northern sentiments, northern principles, northern habits."[33]

African Methodists believed that the best teachers for the freedpeople were persons who could offer themselves as instructive examples of black potential. Hood paid homage to the "noble, self-sacrificing devotion" of white teachers from the North, but maintained nevertheless that he would always do what he could to have "colored teachers for colored schools."[34] Writing from Charleston in 1867, Cain put forward the African Methodist position on the desirability of black teachers:

Honest, dignified whites, may teach ever so well, it has not the effect to exalt the black man's opinion of his own race, because they have always been in the habit of seeing white men in honored positions, and respected; but when the colored man, his fellow, comes upon the stage, and does the honorable work, exhibits the same great comprehension of facts, this ocular proof to the mind of that class, is tenfold more convincing, and gives an exalted opinion of the race.[35]

Women and ministers were important agents of cultural change, and so their educational status was of great concern to the missionaries. Bishop Payne had an ongoing interest in education for women. As mothers, wives, and teachers, women played critical roles in shaping and transmitting the culture of the race. Those roles took on even greater significance as African Methodists considered the task of regenerating the freedpeople. Payne contended that "the future demands educated women, . . . who will give unto the race a training entirely and essentially different from the past." Payne also argued that the demands of the new era required that women "descend into the south as educators." Cain echoed the bishop's sentiments and asserted: "We need, and must have schools for *girls*."[36]

Throughout his career in African Methodism, Payne fought to upgrade the educational qualifications for the ministry. In 1844, the denomination adopted his proposal to establish a regimen of required reading and study for preachers working their way through the ranks of the clerical hierarchy. With the dawning of the new era, the need for educated ministers took on increased urgency. Preachers of the "old school" who contended that divine inspiration was the only preparation necessary for the ministry were dismissed by Turner with the following rejoinder: "If God fills our mouths with such senseless gas as we sometimes blow off, God deliver me from such as that." In 1863, Cain wrote that "the necessity of an educated ministry is more apparent now than ever before"; he insisted that "every preacher must be a teacher, if he would be a success in the South." Lynch maintained that it would be "utter folly" to send any but educated ministers to the South. Of course, the need to bring a large number of former slaves into the ministry required flexibility, and some standards had to be relaxed, but the denomination never completely abandoned its educational goals.[37]

Wilberforce University in Tawawa Springs, Ohio, was the most powerful symbol of the A.M.E. educational philosophy, as can be seen in the hopes the denomination had for the school. The A.M.E. Church bought Wilberforce in 1863, the same year in which the Emancipation Proclamation took effect. The link between the acquisition of Wilberforce and the mission to the south was clear to the university's president, Daniel Payne. Bishop Payne hoped that Wilberforce would provide for "the superior education of those who are to be the educators of the freedmen." Of course Payne was pleased by the prospect of training teachers for the freedpeople in a northern environment.[38]

It must have seemed providential to the missionaries that the A.M.E. Church was given the opportunity to buy the school just as blacks were entering an era that held the promise of unlimited possibilities. According to Cain, the new era required an institution of higher learning which could produce "teachers, mechanics, physicians, geologists and botanists and every class of scholar which a civilized and Christian community must have." Wilberforce was not the only college that blacks could attend to receive a liberal arts education, nor was it the first institution established for the purpose of educating black students. The significance of Wilberforce can best be understood within the context of the Gospel of Freedom. Turner explained: "For the first time in the history of these United States, can the colored man boast of having a university in his possession, and under his direct control." In an article entitled, "The Necessity of Wilberforce University for our Youth," Cain urged his denomination to support the university because within its walls, blacks would be permitted to study "every branch of useful knowledge." He also pointed out that under the tutelage of a "faculty of distinguished colored gentlemen" students would be shielded from the "Negrophobia" that was "rampant" at other institutions. Cain argued that blacks who contributed to the cause of Wilberforce were in fact helping to "regenerate and redeem" their race.[39]

By the mid-1880s the A.M.E. Church had founded several colleges in the South, including Johnson Divinity School in Raleigh, North Carolina; Allen University in Columbia, South Carolina; Morris Brown College in Atlanta; Edward Waters College in Jacksonville, Florida; and Paul Quinn College in Waco, Texas. In addition, the A.M.E. Zion Church had founded Zion Wesley Institute and Livingstone College in Salisbury, North Carolina.[40]

ECONOMICS

According to African Methodists, the economy of the antebellum South was inequitable and stagnant. They believed that the new era should bring reforms that make upward mobility possible and throw economic development into high gear. For the black South, dependence and subservience would be left behind as the freedpeople moved forward in "all the different branches of mechanism and labor; in agriculture and in commerce." Cain reasoned that since the South depended on the skills and labor of black workers, former slaves could occupy an "impregnable position" in the economy if they would "enter boldly on the platform and maintain a firm and manly position."[41]

During the antebellum period there were some service positions from which free blacks could earn an adequate income and to which they attached a certain amount of prestige. Included among them were barbering and catering for a white clientele. Although African Methodists encouraged any honest labor, they contended that employment which did not give even the appearance of subservience was more appropriate for the new era. Lynch advised: "It is better that a boy should grow up a competent blacksmith or carpenter, or skilled in any other branch of mechanical art than that he should be a waiter, barber, bootblack, dock-laborer or the keeper of a one-horse restaurant." Turner made much the same point in his own way: "If we saw John out driving 'Massa and Missus' O! how we coveted his big position. But now our big men can be Lawyers, Doctors, Editors, Astronomers, Chemists &c."[42]

Payne stated that his denomination brought "Freedmen into the bosom of the Church of God, there to teach them the habits of industry, thrift and virtue; and to convince them of the necessity of acquiring property for themselves." Those lessons were not new for Payne. When he was a young minister and church historian working on his *History of the A.M.E. Church,* Payne had supported himself, in part, by giving lectures on "Industry and Thrift" and "The Springs of Wealth." In the context of the new era, it might seem that Bishop Payne's preachments on money management were remarkably unimaginative and patronizing approaches to economic advancement, but the bishop and his missionaries believed that they were issuing a radical challenge to the cultural legacy of slavery. Lynch told the freedpeople that Americans believed in "individual accumulation," and he urged southern blacks to "dress less expensively and take less pleasure." Apparently, Turner also felt that the freedpeople needed to be encouraged "to desire the acquisition of money."[43]

The missionaries associated enterprise and industry with the North. Cain was enthused by the arrival of northern black businessmen in South Carolina, and he encouraged northern investors to "take an interest in the economic development of the South." He was pleased to learn that "prudent, thrifty and far-seeing Germans" were making efforts to increase immigration to South Carolina. At times, Cain functioned as a one-man Chamber of Commerce for black entrepreneurs in South Carolina. In April 1866, he proudly reported that there were two steamboats in the state which were owned and operated by blacks. One of the boats was under the command of "Captain Dart, a colored gentleman of enterprise." In 1866, Cain lauded the facts that black veterans had deposited $40,000 in the Freedmen's Bank and that "hundreds" of them were "entering into businesses of different kinds." After pointing out that an "enterprising gentleman" had bought and sold more cotton than anyone else in the state, Reverend Cain asked: "If one colored man can do this, what may not be done by a hundred such in the South?" Cain did more than economic cheerleading. He made a point to employ black workers for the construction of Emanuel Church. He also became president of the appropriately named Enterprise Railroad, which moved freight in and out of Charleston harbor. Finally, in July 1874, Cain was in Philadelphia promoting a new printing press, "the invention of a young negro South Carolinian, James E. Haines." [44]

Most southern blacks were agriculturalists. For them, the path to freedom would have to be cleared with a plow and a mule. For farmers, freedom and independence meant owning your own land. Even before he came to South Carolina, Cain took a strong position on the importance of owning land. In summer 1864 he wrote: "We must possess the soil, be the owner of lands and become independent, or self-dependent." In May 1866, Lynch wrote an editorial for the *Christian Recorder* under the heading "Get Land." Lynch exhorted his readers: "If we want to have influence in the nation, and be respected, we must be landholders." [45]

The missionaries had few illusions about sharecropping or tenant farming. As early as February 1865, Chaplain Turner angrily denounced sharecropping as a stratagem for circumventing the Emancipation Proclamation. He fumed: "The ingenious trickery is designed to keep the old master fat doing nothing, making the Yankee believe 'dis old nigga no wants to leave Massa!'" Turner also charged that landowners were "fizzling" the freedpeople "out of all their claims upon the real estate." As the missionaries had perceived very early on, landless farmers found themselves having to work very hard in order to slow down the rate at which they fell into debt. In August 1866, Cain wrote: "The people see now, that if they remain and work here, they will never accumulate anything, but will always be poor and their children after them." [46]

As a delegate to the South Carolina Constitutional Convention in 1868, Cain charged that crop failure and the dishonesty of landowners had left blacks in the state "in a worse condition pecuniarily than two years ago." Cain demanded that the "utterly destitute" be provided with immediate relief. He also had some long-term concerns about the kind of relief that impoverished farmers received. Any form of dependency was antithetical to the goals of the Gospel of Freedom. Cain stated flatly that he was opposed to people "constantly" receiving rations from the government. Rather than give food to the poor, he argued that the government should provide them with the means to produce their own food. He reasoned: "A man may have rations today and not tomorrow, but when he gets land and a homestead, and is once fixed on that land, he will never go to the commissary again." In arguing on behalf of land reform, Cain linked the immediate needs of landless blacks to the long-term economic interests of the state of South Carolina. He maintained that the development of commerce, banking, and railroads had all been impeded because large tracts of land were concentrated in a few nonproductive hands. The economy needed invigoration. "What we need," Cain argued, "is a system of small farms." [47]

Cain began thinking about ways of making it possible for poor blacks to secure land while he was still a pastor in Brooklyn. In July 1864, he proposed that the National Negro Convention, which was scheduled to meet later that year in Syracuse, establish a "great land company or agricultural association" to purchase government land in the South and the Southwest, which it would then sell to poor and urban blacks at "moderate prices." The proposal was not taken up when the Convention met in October. Cain criticized his fellow delegates because "the interest of the freedmen had not been sufficiently considered." Once in the South, he promoted land reform in the pages of his own newspaper, the *South Carolina Leader.* Cain urged that large landholdings should be broken up and "sold out, to honest laboring men, white or black."[48]

In 1868, at Cain's urging, the South Carolina Constitutional Convention petitioned an unresponsive U.S. Congress to allocate one million dollars for the purchase of lands to be sold to landless blacks and whites. Cain stressed that his proposal was not "simply a scheme for colored men." Specifically, he intended to provide land for "the poor whites of the upper districts." In 1869, he proposed that the state legislature issue bonds for the purchase of land to be re-sold as homesteads. South Carolina did establish a land commission for that purpose, but its effectiveness was severely damaged by the corruption of some of the commissioners. Cain was outraged that his plans for land reform had been rendered ineffective by men with "no sympathy, nor interest, save that of peculation." In an attempt to salvage the situation, he launched an unsuccessful effort to have himself appointed as head of the commission. Having been unable to effect meaningful land reform through the government, Cain attempted to take matters into his own hands, at least on a small scale. In 1871, he bought two thousand acres near Charleston, with the intention of reselling the land in small plots. He called his development Lincolnville. Cain simply refused to be deterred from enacting some strategy for bringing about land reform, but with the Lincolnville project, the ever resourceful missionary overextended himself. Lincolnville turned out to be a financial fiasco. Cain failed to make payments to the original owners of the land and was eventually indicted for fraud.[49]

It is significant that Cain never proposed outright confiscation, nor did he suggest that blacks should be given land free of charge. He was aware of the political realities with which he had to deal, and he probably subscribed to the prevailing beliefs about the sanctity of private property, but there was an additional reason for his conservatism. Cain had a philosophical abhorrence for anything that appeared to undermine the self-sufficiency and "manhood" of his race. He explained: "I do not desire to have a foot of land in this state confiscated. I want these lands purchased by the government, and the people afforded an opportunity to buy from the government." [50]

POLITICS

For African Methodists, politics was an indispensable weapon in the struggle to preserve emancipation and secure the rights, privileges, and protection of citizenship. Five months after Lee's surrender, Elisha Weaver, then editor of the *Christian Recorder,* wrote: "The war is transferred from the field to the forum, and most fiercely will it rage for a long time to come." [51]

The missionaries saw little conflict between their roles as ministers and their involvement in political affairs. In fact, in 1868, Bishop Payne proudly acknowledged the "political influence which the A.M.E. Church exerts over the Freedmen," an influence the bishop contended had a scriptural justification. Payne explained that "in His hands is placed all power in heaven and earth—that by His permission 'kings rule and princes decree justice, even all the judges of the earth.' " But the politics of Reconstruction were disappointing and sometimes sordid. In later years, the bishop had a far less positive view of political religion; in fact, he urged his preachers "to never neglect their calling to mingle in politics." Hood also initially took the position that the involvement of ministers in political affairs violated no scriptural injunction, but years after the end of Reconstruction, he, like Payne, felt constrained to explain that preachers had been "compelled" to enter politics because they were organizers, communicators, and "the only well-informed leaders the people had." Bishop Hood also felt that ministers had been unfairly criticized for radicalizing their followers. As he saw it, the freedpeople were "often more radical, because less thoughtful, than their leaders." [52]

With characteristic modesty, Turner declared that he had done more political work in Georgia than "any five men in the state"; he was, in fact, a tireless organizer for the Republican party. Nevertheless, Turner's career in politics was rocky and unrewarding. He was a delegate to Georgia's Constitutional Convention in 1867 and subsequently was elected to the state legislature in the spring of 1868, only to be expelled from that body with all the other black representatives in September of that year, on the grounds that the state constitution did not sanction office holding by black citizens. In 1870, the U.S. Congress ordered Georgia to readmit the black legislators. Turner served out his term that year and ran for another but was defeated in a hotly contested, fraud-ridden election. The year before, he had served very briefly as postmaster

of Macon, Georgia, but political attacks and allegations of moral and fiscal ir-
regularities forced him to resign from that office after only two weeks. "I have
been the constant target of Democratic abuse and venom and white Republican jealousy," Turner contended. "The newspapers have teemed with all kinds
of slander, accusing me of every crime in the catalogue of villainy." In 1872,
Turner moved to Savannah and was allowed to serve a relatively uneventful
term as inspector of the Federal Customs House in that city.[53]

Richard Cain's political career was at least as significant and as dramatic
as Turner's. Historian Joel Williamson described Cain as the "most spectacular personality politically, as well as religiously, among the African divines"
in South Carolina. In addition to serving as a delegate to the South Carolina
Constitutional Convention in 1868, Cain also served in the state Senate, and
was elected to the United States House of Representatives in 1872 and again in
1876. Far from being ambivalent or apologetic about his political involvement,
Reverend Cain made it clear that he considered it "an honor to my conscience
to vindicate the rights of the whole people of the country." James W. Hood
was also directly involved in politics. He was a delegate to North Carolina's
Constitutional Convention, served as that state's Assistant Superintendent of
Public Instruction, and was a delegate to the Republican National Convention
in 1872.[54]

While he was a delegate to the South Carolina Constitutional Convention,
Cain offered a Jacksonian critique of southern politics. The "curse" of the
political structure of the South was that power had been concentrated in the
hands of a "ruling class" which "dictated the laws that guided the multitude."
The political institutions of the "new era" should be established on a "broad
basis" so that liberty and rights could be enjoyed by "every class of men."[55]
The missionaries saw voting as the sine qua non of citizenship. To them, the
franchise was much more than a symbol of political inclusion. They knew that
the consequences of political impotence could be deadly. Addressing the Constitutional Convention of North Carolina, Hood said: "The idea of those who
were formerly slaves, living in the country without the means to protect themselves from the diabolical prejudices of a portion of the late so-called masters,
is simply ridiculous, and on the whole absurd."[56] Cain made the same point
in the South Carolina Constitutional Convention. He told his fellow delegates
that it was only through the unfettered exercise of the franchise that a man
could "protect himself as a citizen." Cain argued that the right to vote was so
basic and so necessary that it "ought not to be abridged under any circumstances." He was consistent, clear, and outspoken on this issue. In June 1865,

the *New York Times* reported that he had issued an impassioned warning while speaking in the North. "Unless the government give the slave the right of franchise," Cain predicted, "there will be trouble." Even though for the most part these missionaries had a nineteenth-century, male-centered view of the universe, Cain did present a petition to the U.S. Congress on behalf of women's suffrage, and Turner did attempt to secure the vote for women in Georgia.[57]

African Methodists insisted that emancipation could not be complete or secure until blacks were empowered with the vote. Less than three months after Appomattox, the *Christian Recorder* urged the nation to act on the issue of black suffrage "while this great revolution in public opinion, which has riven the chains from the bondsmen of the south, is still in motion." In April 1866, Turner was in Washington lobbying for the vote. Several Congressmen assured him that "the negro must vote," but they thought it unwise to push the issue during an election year. Turner explained their hesitancy in a letter to his white political ally in Georgia, John Emory Bryant: "They are fearful if they hang negro suffrage on the contest they would not get it through sufficiently to keep up a two third power in congress. They are thinking about leting [*sic*] it lie over this congress."[58]

The Fifteenth Amendment was ratified in 1870. The amendment made it unconstitutional to deny anyone the right to vote because of "race, color, or previous condition of servitude." African Methodists hailed the amendment as a triumph in the struggle for black suffrage. "The work is done at last," wrote the editor of the *Recorder;* "the glorious structure of our government is complete." Turner referred to the amendment as "an ensign of our citizenship, the prompter of our patriotism, the bandage that is to blindfold justice."[59]

Of course, African Methodists supported federal civil rights legislation. Congressman Cain was subjected to the indignity of being denied service in restaurants in North Carolina while he was traveling to Washington to take his seat in the 43rd Congress. From the floor of the House of Representatives, Cain made a simple and straightforward argument: "If he [a black person] can pay for his seat in a first-class car or his room in a hotel, I can see no objection to his enjoying it." According to the Gospel of Freedom, the purpose of civil rights legislation was to ensure equal access to public services and accommodations and to guarantee equal protection under the law. The missionaries did not advocate civil rights primarily for the purpose of achieving racial integration or "social equality."[60]

African Methodists saw the politics of Reconstruction in Manichean terms. No disappointment or disillusionment could alter their fundamental political dichotomy. In 1867, Turner put it quite simply: "The contest is between the retrogressive and progressive parties."[61] Eleven years later, editor Tanner wrote:

The Republican party represents progress, prosperity, protection of life and person, national sovereignty, education, manhood equality, and the obliteration of sectional lines and distinctions. The Democratic party on the contrary, is the symbol of retrogression, malignant race-hate, fossil ideas, ante-bellum bloodshed, and midnight assassinations.[62]

The missionaries' support for the Republican party was not merely a sentimental attachment to the party of Lincoln, nor was their support uncritical. Some African Methodists were troubled by the charges of impropriety which came to plague Republican state governments in the South, but on balance, they still found the Republican party enormously preferable to the Democratic alternative. Tanner urged his readers to "contend for honesty, but stick to the Republican party." Corruption was troublesome enough, but the erosion of the party's apparent commitment to ensuring full citizenship for blacks was much more ominous. In 1875, Tanner observed that blacks were confronted with "some new Republican party, with some new shibboleth on its tongue."[63] The editor strained to find some justification for advocating continued loyalty to a party which abandoned the very citizens who most desperately needed its support:

They indeed have lost their ancient fervor for us and for the right; but a negative friend, is to be preferred to a positive enemy. Such friends may not pull us up, but they will not push us down. Possibly, it will be better for us in the long run not to ask for more than this.[64]

The "Compromise of 1877" enabled Rutherford B. Hayes to assume the presidency of the United States and ended what remained of the Republican commitment to use force to protect black voters from violence and intimidation. The ending of federal protection for Republican state governments in the South, on the orders of a Republican president, convinced Turner that the party with which he had so fully identified himself, existed no longer. He recalled how hard and long he had worked for the party and concluded: "It is therefore hard to admit that the Republican party is dead. Any man, however, who has as much brain as a monkey is obliged to see it, and every true Republican must feel it."[65]

Interestingly enough, not long after Turner wrote his obituary for the party of emancipation, it was reported in the *Christian Recorder* that he had met with

President Hayes at the Executive Mansion. Hayes reportedly assured Turner that he did "not entertain the least idea of deserting the colored people" and that he intended to see that ex-slaves were "fairly dealt with." According to the article, Turner left the meeting feeling that blacks should "wait a while longer before despairing."[66]

HEGIRA

Of course, despair was not the only alternative, even for those who had come to realize that the new era had come and gone. Despite bitter political and economic disappointments, it was still possible to see a future of unlimited possibilities on the horizon, by merely shifting one's line of vision. In spring 1878, some prominent African Methodists did just that when they gave their support to the spectacular, but largely unsuccessful, venture of the Liberian Exodus Joint Steamship Company of Charleston. On 21 March, the company "consecrated" its ship, the *Azor,* in preparation for its voyage to Liberia. The *Azor*'s mission was to carry 206 disillusioned black southerners to what they hoped would be a refuge and a land of opportunity.[67]

Some onlookers thought that it was peculiar to "consecrate" a ship, but in this instance a quasi-religious ceremony was appropriate. The president of the Steamship Company was Reverend B. F. Porter, pastor of Morris Brown A.M.E. Church in Charleston. The project had the blessing of Bishop John Mifflin Brown, who had succeeded Daniel Payne as the bishop of South Carolina in 1868. Bishop Brown made the observation that the *Azor* had been "purchased by Christian men, led forward by Christian ministers." He also pointed out that the *Azor*'s passengers could play a role in the redemption of Africa. Indeed, one of the emigrants was an A.M.E. missionary named Samuel Flegler. The project had the strong support of Cain, Turner, and Martin R. Delany, although they did not make the voyage themselves. A newspaper reported that perhaps as many as five thousand people made their way to the Charleston harbor to witness the consecration and to hear Reverend Turner deliver the principal address. Once again, the veteran missionary sounded the familiar themes of the Gospel of Freedom, but this time he urged his anxious listeners to invest their hopes in Africa.[68] The *Charleston News and Courier* reported that at the end of Turner's speech:

> Maj. Delany was heard on the after deck: "Hoist the Liberian flag! Fling our banner to the breeze!": and the flag presented in the morning, went to the masthead amid the shouts of the crowd and the music of the band.[69]

According to Turner, shortly after the consecration of the *Azor,* he and Cain were denounced in a resolution that was brought forward at a meeting of the A.M.E. Preachers Association of Philadelphia. The resolution, which was not officially adopted by the association, charged the two missionaries with being "traitors and enemies of their race, for trying to persuade the colored people to leave this country, and emigrate to the fatal shores of Africa." Turner had seen the freedpeople become victims of economic destitution, political betrayal, and violence. In exasperation he observed: "If men can do worse in Liberia or Siberia than that, they had better ask God to kill them at once." Clearly, there were deep divisions within the denomination on the subject of emigration. The most outspoken African Methodist supporters of emigration tended to be southerners or missionaries working in the South. The strongest opponents tended to be northern clergymen, prominent among whom was Benjamin Tucker Tanner of Philadelphia, the editor of the *Christian Recorder.*[70]

Controversial views on emigration notwithstanding, both Cain and Turner were elected bishops of the A.M.E. Church in 1880. Until his death in 1915, Bishop Turner spoke out against the subordination, segregation and disfranchisement of black Americans, and he became the most prominent advocate of emigration during the late nineteenth and early twentieth centuries. After 1880, Bishop Cain remained as energetic as ever, but he withdrew from political involvements and devoted himself to religion and education. He died in 1887. A comment that one of Cain's colleagues made about him was also an accurate description of many of the African Methodists who rushed to the South at the dawn of freedom: "He was a zealous man even to over-enthusiasm. His dreams of the coming greatness of the race caused him to be perhaps too visionary."[71]

There was yet another Methodist denomination that moved into the South with enthusiasm and a vision of its own. The Methodist Episcopal Church offered southern blacks a radical new model of race relations.

PART 3

NORTHERN METHODISM
AND SOUTHERN BLACKS
"IN CHRIST THERE IS NO
EAST OR WEST"

In Christ there is no East or West,
In Him no South or North;
But one great fellowship of love
Throughout the whole wide earth.

Join hands, then, brothers of the faith,
What-e'er your race may be
Who serves my Father as a son
Is surely kin to me.

—*Methodist Hymnal*

5

THE METHODIST EPISCOPAL CHURCH:
A MISSION TAKES SHAPE

"The famous 'negro question,' instead of having found its final solution in the strange events of the recent past, becomes more and more complicated as the new order of things are more fully developed."[1] So began an editorial entitled "The M.E. Church and the Negro" that appeared in the *Christian Advocate and Journal* (New York) on 20 July 1865. But the relationship between blacks and the Methodist Episcopal Church had never been uncomplicated. Throughout its history in America, the Methodist Episcopal Church had tried to embrace its black membership while holding it at arms length. Custom had confined northern black M.E. clergy to a subordinate sphere in the denomination and black laity to segregated pews, although official policy made no distinctions at all between blacks and whites.[2]

Black frustration with the disparity between policy and practice led to the founding of three independent black denominations: the Union Church of Africans in 1813, the African Methodist Episcopal Church in 1816, and the African Methodist Episcopal Zion Church in 1822. The black clergymen who remained in the M.E. Church petitioned every General Conference from 1844 to 1860 for the right to exercise the full authority of the ministry—without success. When they tried again in 1864, they found that the attitudes and priorities of their white coreligionists had gone through a remarkable transformation.[3]

In that year, the Committee on the State of the Country observed: "No previous General Conference of the Methodist Episcopal Church has met in a period so important as the present. It is crowded with thrilling events that must affect the highest interests of the Church, of our country, and of the world." The denomination stood on the threshold of an unprecedented opportunity for expanding its mission work. In their address to the conference, the bishops of the denomination reported: "The progress of the Federal arms has thrown open to the loyal Churches of the Union large and inviting fields of Christian enterprise and labor. In the cultivation of these fields it is natural and reasonable to expect that the Methodist Episcopal Church should occupy a prominent position."[4]

For committed evangelicals, the cultivation of any new field of missionary endeavor is an imperious obligation, but it was not that alone that focused Northern Methodist attention on the South. In 1844, irreconcilable differences over slaveholding had split Methodism into separate southern and northern denominations and excluded the M.E. Church from almost all of the South. A generation later, divine providence seemed to be vindicating the antislavery position of Northern Methodists, and M.E. bishops envisioned the recovery of lost territory with the fervor of irredentists:

> She [the M.E. Church] occupied these fields once. Her network of conferences, districts and pastoral charges spread over them all: all indeed, both within and beyond the Federal lines. For nineteen years they have been in the occupancy of the Methodist Episcopal Church, South, to the wrongful exclusion of the Methodist Episcopal Church. But her days of exclusive occupancy are ended.

To gear up for the southern crusade, the General Conference created the Church Extension Society to support the purchase or construction of churches in the South and elsewhere. The Conference also expanded the scope of the Board of Missions to include "third-class" missions, which were defined as "missions in the United States and territories, not included in any of the Annual Conferences."[5]

Because of the rapidly changing situation, it finally had become possible to link the long-standing interests of black preachers to an immediate and pressing concern of their white brethren. In its report, the Committee on the State of the Work among the People of Color reasoned: "If it be a principle patent to Christian enterprise that the missionary field itself must produce the most efficient missionaries, our colored local preachers are peculiarly important to us at this time. With these properly marshaled, what hindereth that we go down and possess the land?"[6]

The bishops questioned whether the denomination's policies concerning blacks were adequate, and they informed the delegates that "the time has now come, in our judgement, when the General Conference should carefully consider what measures can be adopted to give increased efficiency to our Church among them." As a result, the petitions from black preachers and churches were treated with an urgency that would have been incomprehensible just four years earlier. The ability to exercise the full authority of the ministry was the exclusive prerogative of ordained itinerant elders who were members in good standing of one of the denomination's annual conferences. No black clergyman had ever been granted the privilege of such membership, and even in the heady atmosphere of 1864, the Committee on Colored People concluded that admitting black ministers to white conferences would be "attended with difficulties too formidable in every way to be readily disposed of." [7]

The General Conference resorted to the pragmatic alternative of authorizing the formation of two new mission conferences to which all black M.E. preachers in the North and border states would belong. The two new bodies were called the Washington Conference and the Delaware Conference, even though their constituencies were determined primarily by race and only secondarily by geography. Because they had only mission status, the Washington and Delaware Conferences did not have the full standing of regular annual conferences, but it was understood that they would be granted full powers after a period of transition and adjustment. In an effort to avoid the stigma of segregation, the General Conference stipulated that white ministers could be assigned to the new conferences. In addition, the delegates resolved that the creation of racially defined conferences would not "impair the existing constitutional rights of our colored members." But those stipulations were weak efforts to uphold principles that really had never been adhered to in the first place. The whole episode was a strange prelude for a crusade with the objective of ushering in a new era of brotherhood and racial egalitarianism in the South. The *Christian Advocate and Journal* observed that no action taken by the General Conference had been more "significant of the strange times in which we live." [8]

The times were strange and stirring, especially for those Northern Methodists who were already in the southern field. Accounts written from the South reveal how profoundly some white Methodists were affected by their encounters with blacks whose lives had only recently been transformed by freedom. Experiences in the South put flesh on ideas, ideals, and abstractions.

While stationed in North Carolina in January 1863, Chaplain J. E. Round wrote to *Zion's Herald and Wesleyan Journal* in Boston about his "stout contraband" servant named Frank, who left camp to rescue members of his family held in slavery a few miles away. Chaplain Round recalled that the next day Frank "appeared with his wife and child by his side, his black eyes shining with a lustre that you at the North will scarcely understand." The chaplain concluded that "a few scenes such as that" would make every "philanthropist" want to pursue emancipation "with such energy and success as to give deliverance to all the oppressed in our land." In March 1864, another Methodist chaplain wrote to the *Christian Advocate and Journal* from Huntsville, Alabama: "The colored people are congregating here by scores. They are the most joyful and grateful creatures I ever saw. . . . If I hated slavery before I entered the service, now I loathe, abhor, and execrate it."[9]

John Emory Bryant was a Methodist layman from Maine who served in the Union army and later became prominent in Reconstruction politics in Georgia. In May 1865 he wrote his wife about an experience he shared with a Methodist missionary named Mansfield French at a meeting of blacks in Augusta:

> It does my soul good to witness their joy. They almost consider Mr. French and myself their deliverers and wherever we go they all want to shake hands with us. . . . I wish you could see this people as they step from slavery into freedom. Men are taking their wives and children. Families which had been for a long time broken up are united and Oh! such happiness. I am glad I am here.[10]

There was much speculation about the ability, character, and potential of the newly freed race. The General Conference of 1864 established a "Committee on Freedmen" and its report reflected an interesting kind of northern, antislavery paternalism. In expressing its concern for the freedpeople, the committee stated: "Wherever properly cared for they may soon become qualified for the blessings and responsibilities of freedom. But dwarfed by slavery, they, as a race, are children, subject to become victims of the heartless and avaricious." From his post as a chaplain in Jacksonville, Florida, Reverend H. H. Moore came to a similar conclusion: "I think they give evidence that they are hardly qualified to go out into the world, surrounded by sharpers, haters of their race, and scoundrels, and fight successfully the battles of life."[11]

The situation appeared to be even more bleak because blacks emerged from slavery without the wherewithal to sustain themselves or to protect their interests. For the most part, they were vulnerable, dependent, and destitute. As the title of Eric Foner's book on the subject suggests, emancipation vested the southern black population with *Nothing but Freedom*. Most Methodists who published opinions about the freedpeople expressed the view that slavery had severely damaged their character and values. The denomination's Missionary Society summarized such observations in this way: "As a whole, their condition excites our pity. Poor, ignorant, superstitious and debased, they are a sad commentary on the institution of domestic slavery."[12]

But northern evangelicals also firmly believed that minds and bodies could be redeemed, as well as souls. Whatever was wrong with the freedpeople could be remedied. Their shortcomings were the consequence of having been slaves, not characteristics of being black. Furthermore, there were some very positive indications that the freedpeople would overcome their disabilities if given the opportunity and the tools to do so. Their intense desire to secure education and to have the ability to work for themselves on land of their own, were indications of the enormous potential waiting to be developed. Part of the mandate of the missionaries would be to make free black communities strong, sound, and infused with northern values.[13]

Even before the denomination had organized an official mission to the freedpeople, Methodists in the military found it difficult to separate their commitment to the Union from their commitment to plant the flag of Northern Methodism in the South. Dramatic reports of denominational victories began to appear in the Methodist press even while the military phase of the Civil War still wore on.

On 28 February 1863, a Northern Methodist minister reported from Beaufort, South Carolina, that he had been preaching in that city since December: "I have endeavored to proclaim the same truths I did in New England during sixteen years in the ministry; and it has not diminished my zeal or made my feelings less intense, to realize that my pulpit was so near the slave market." The Reverend T. W. Lewis also worked in Beaufort during the winter of 1863. In March, he wrote an account of his activities for the *Christian Advocate and Journal,* employing the crisp, no-nonsense language of a military commander: "Immediately, on my arrival," Reverend Lewis reported, "I took possession of the Church and parsonage and commenced meetings." In the winter and spring of 1863, J. E. Round functioned in North Carolina both as a chaplain of the Union army and as a missionary of the M.E. Church. During that time, he successfully brought at least three black Methodist congregations into the Northern Methodist fold. Reverend Round proudly proclaimed that one of the congregations "unanimously by a rising vote disavowed all connexion with the Methodist Episcopal Church, South."[14]

Some officials of the military also found it difficult to make a distinction between the cause of Northern Methodism and the cause of the Union. On November 30, 1863, the War Department issued a directive which put at the disposal of the M.E. Church "all houses of worship belonging to the Methodist Episcopal Church South in which a loyal minister, appointed by a loyal bishop of said church, does not now officiate." In effect, the Secretary of War enlisted the whole Union army in the effort to establish the M.E. Church in the South. Before the war's conclusion, Northern Methodist outposts were scattered through the territory once claimed by the Confederacy and by the Southern Methodist Church.[15]

Throughout the initial, uncoordinated phase of the Northern Methodist re-entry into the South, missionaries and their supporters urged the denomination to pursue its work with greater vigor and in a more organized fashion. They argued that the work suffered because it lacked men and method. In March 1863, Chaplain C. Nasson of the 8th Maine Volunteers wrote to *Zion's Herald* from his post in South Carolina: "A principal object of my writing at present, is to urge upon you, and through you the proper authorities of our own church, the importance of sending a Methodist minister, . . . to immediately occupy this interesting and important field."[16] Many such appeals were sent up from the South by Methodist missionaries attempting to stake out new territory.

During the winter of 1864, Reverend R. Wheatley toured the South and wrote an account of his travels for the *Christian Advocate and Journal*. Reverend Wheatley was not encouraged by what he saw. He reported that in New Bern, North Carolina, he found Unionist whites and loyal blacks "in great need of a pastor," and in New Orleans he found "not a single Methodist preacher habitually officiating." In April of the following year, Reverend William T. Gilbert expressed a similar concern over the denomination's lack of initiative in New Orleans. Reverend Gilbert insisted that success required only "that a plan be adopted which shall be worthy of the Church and worthy of the work." An editorial appearing in the *Christian Advocate and Journal* in May 1865 lamented that the Church had "occupied only a few of many chief points," even though the gates to the South had been open for nearly three years. In August, Chaplain H. H. Moore wrote from his post in Jacksonville, Florida, to express his impatience with the denomination's inaction. "The question seems to be about settled," he wrote; "*organized* Methodism is afraid to grapple with the problem of the moral reconstruction of the South."[17]

In time, the denomination responded to pleas like those and mounted a large-scale, multifaceted mission to the South, but there were some Methodists, infused with missionary zeal and caught up in the urgency of the moment, who could not wait for the church's plan of operation to emerge. Instead, they poured their energy and resources into the efforts of nominally nonsectarian agencies that were already working in the South.

Reverend Mansfield French launched his work with the freedpeople in spring 1862 by sailing from New York to Port Royal Island, South Carolina, with a group of sixty-four "Gideonites." The group undertook what historian Willie Lee Rose called a "Rehearsal for Reconstruction." Their project had the sponsorship of the National Freedmen's Relief Association of New York, the Educational Commission of Boston, and the Port Royal Relief Committee of Philadelphia. One Baptist missionary connected with the project took note of the disproportionately large number of Methodist participants: "Our Freedmen's Relief Association have [sic] sent down about 30 persons today to take charge of the plantations—The greater part were Methodists—scarcely a Baptist among them." With wounded denominational pride he concluded, "the Methodists are ahead of us." [18]

The M.E. Church gave strong support to all the projects sponsored by the National Freedmen's Relief Association (N.F.R.A.). A resolution adopted by the General Conference of 1864 deemed the Relief Association worthy of Methodist "sympathy and support." The Association also received enthusiastic endorsements from several of the denomination's newspapers and annual conferences. Perhaps it was in recognition of those facts that in March 1864, the N.F.R.A. invited M.E. bishop, Matthew Simpson, to speak at its second annual meeting in New York, an honor he shared with luminaries such as William Cullen Bryant and Henry Ward Beecher. Other relief agencies also had strong support from the Methodists. A cleric of the M.E. Church served as president of the Western Freedmen's Aid Commission, and the denomination's clergy occupied prominent positions in the Northwestern Freedmen's Aid Commission. In addition, Bishop Simpson was the first president of the American Freedmen's Union Commission, which was established in 1866 to coordinate the efforts of all the major nonsectarian relief agencies.[19] But coalitions require compromise, and some uncompromising Methodists were anxious to march under their own banner.

On 30 July 1866, nine Methodists from Ohio and Illinois issued a call for "a meeting of a few leading ministers and laymen of the Methodist Episcopal Church in the West, to confer in regard to the relation of our Church to the work of relief and education in behalf of the Freedmen." Several fissures in the edifice of cooperative benevolence had led to the issuing of the call. Methodists chaffed at constraints imposed by nonsectarians against the admixture of religion and education. They were also aware that their church bore an increasingly large share of the financial burden for cooperative efforts, as other denominations withdrew in order to form relief agencies of their own. Energy and money put into efforts that would not produce new Methodists was energy and money denied to ones that could. Although they endorsed the concept and objectives of broadly based relief organizations, Methodists could never invest themselves fully in associations that neglected the evangelical imperative.[20]

So, in response to the "call," twelve prominent Methodists met at Trinity Church in Cincinnati on the 7th and 8th of August and founded the Freedmen's Aid Society (F.A.S.) of the Methodist Episcopal Church. It is significant that all the persons present were from the states of Ohio and Illinois. In his important work, *Northern Methodism and Reconstruction,* Ralph E. Morrow suggests that the formation of the new society was in part an internal denominational revolt by western radicals against the sluggishness and conservatism of the eastern-based Missionary and Church Extension Societies. The founders of the F.A.S. pledged to work in tandem with the two older Methodist societies, but they did not invite an official representative of either organization to the meeting in Cincinnati. Perhaps in order to avoid conflicts over turf as much as to prevent duplication of effort, the Freedmen's Aid Society made its primary mission the promotion of education, leaving the support of ministers and the establishment of churches to the Missionary and Extension Societies, respectively. The new Methodist organization received the endorsement of the Board of Bishops when that body met on 8 November in New York City, and the General Conference gave its official sanction to the F.A.S. in 1868.[21]

Creating and mobilizing the institutional apparatus for the mission was only one aspect of the denomination's preparation for its work in the South. Far more problematic was the debate over what the objectives of the mission should be and what principles should guide it. "How Shall the Church Go South?" was the title of an article that appeared in the *Christian Advocate and Journal* on 1 June 1865. It was a succinct expression of the issue with which the Church had been grappling since Methodist chaplains first moved into the South with Union troops. The subject of "Church reconstruction" had occupied so much space in the *Advocate and Journal* that the paper's editor felt it necessary to explain: "the importance of the subject, and the interest felt respecting it, must be our apology (if any is deemed necessary)." The editor was unduly apologetic, because interest in the subject was intense, particularly on the part of the persons who had to execute nonexistent denominational policies. Reverend T. W. Lewis wrote from Charleston: "I have long waited for definite instructions from the proper authorities. . . . We ought to act in concert with each other as missionaries to be efficient, and how can we do this until some 'plan' is adopted at 'headquarters?' "[22]

The church had failed to provide clear answers to several key questions. What would be the relation of Northern Methodism to the Methodist Episcopal Church, South, and to southern whites in general? Would the church support and assist the work of African Methodists among the freedpeople, or would it compete with the black denominations? Would mission churches and conferences be organized on an integrated basis? Would blacks be granted full equality in church membership and decision making? Eventually, time and experience provided answers, but until they did, policy remained ad hoc and inconsistent.

Some Northern Methodists believed that the end of the division between the states of the North and South would naturally lead to the end of the division between Northern and Southern Methodism. Even an abolitionist as resolute and uncompromising as Mansfield French became an advocate of reconciliation with the Southern Methodist Church. Writing from Beaufort, South Carolina, in June 1865, Reverend French asserted: "Now is the time, the golden moment, to forgive, restore, and extend the open hand of fellowship to them." French reported having favorable conversations with several of the leading figures in the Southern denomination. He also observed that the laity of Southern Methodism "stand ready, yea, are anxious to return." He predicted that the times and the prevailing attitudes were so propitious that reunion could be effected in "less than six months." A few other missionaries shared French's optimistic assessment of the potential for, and desirability of, reconciliation. That was also the view of the editorial boards of two M.E. publications based in New York, *The Methodist* and the *Methodist Quarterly Review.*[23]

Other northerners were not so sure. They doubted whether Southern Methodism had really undergone conversion experiences at the deathbeds of slavery and the Confederacy. "Who believes in southern professions?" asked the Reverend Daniel Wise. "Their leading minds, and it is to be feared, most of their members, are steeped to the chin in disloyalty and proslaveryism. They led the rebellion, gloried in it, adhered to it as long as it lived, and now that it is dying, they do homage to its departing spirit." Reconciliation would entail ingesting the very attitudes with which the mission intended to do battle. From the point of view of some northern radicals, reunion would require an unwise, unnecessary, and unholy compromise.[24]

White southern Unionists surpassed even northern radicals in the intensity of their disdain for Methodist reunion. They had no desire to join ranks with the denomination that had treated them like outcasts and reprobates during the war. They were drawn to Northern Methodism precisely because it had no official ties with the Southern Methodist Church. One of the most prominent of the southern Unionists was the outspoken preacher and politician from Tennessee, William G. Brownlow. "Parson" Brownlow, as he was known, stated that he would "feel more honored to be associated with a pack of Professional Gamblers than with a Conference of Methodist Rebel preachers." Another southern Unionist asserted: "I would rather live and die out of the church . . . than to be in connection with the Church South."[25]

There were still other Methodists who took the position that reunion was not really an issue because Southern Methodism was on the verge of becoming nonexistent. The denomination had been disrupted and thrown into disarray by the war. Its finances were shaky, and many of its preachers were fugitives. A vigorous, expansive Northern Methodism could simply sweep down and absorb what remained of the once proud Church of the Confederacy, without the unpleasant necessity for compromise or concessions. Of course, the obituary for the Methodist Episcopal Church, South, was more than a little premature, as became evident when the Southern denomination held its first postwar General Conference in May 1866, and gave no indication that it was considering going out of existence by death or by merger. That put to rest any lingering hope that reunion would be the route by which the Northern Church would reenter the South. By default, then, the field of missionary endeavor would also be a field of competition.[26]

Although at this point it did not seem possible to reunite a denomination that had been torn asunder by slavery, that did not mean that Northern Methodists abandoned hope for gaining large numbers of white members. In fact, it was by no means a foregone conclusion that primary emphasis would be put on evangelizing the freedpeople; after all, southern whites outnumbered blacks by two to one. Some of the first missionaries functioned under the assumption that blacks were a secondary concern. In July 1865, an exasperated Reverend William T. Gilbert reported from his post in New Orleans:

> The labors of our Church have hitherto been almost exclusively devoted to the whites. That we should have spent more than a whole year in comparatively fruitless labors among them, while we have virtually repelled multitudes of blacks who were only waiting for the opportunity to join us, is a responsibility for which I am thankful I have not to answer.

Reverend Lucius Hawkins made a similar observation from Tennessee in August: "When I came to this place some three months ago, I came with the expectation of building up a white Church. I had no instructions to do anything among the colored people."[27]

The problem was that most southern whites had no use for Northern Methodists. Of course, there were some significant exceptions: Southern Unionists and other disaffected whites were not automatically repelled by northern evangelical overtures, and many of them found a home in the M.E. Church; there was also a growing number of transplanted northerners who gravitated to the denomination. For the most part, however, the missionaries encountered indifference or hostility. Reverend T. Willard Lewis tried to defend himself and his fellow missionaries from the burden of unreasonable expectations: "If we do not succeed in organizing a single Church in the gulf states with *white* men, . . . be not harsh in your judgement; it may be the fault is in the *material* we have to work." The church continued its pursuit of whites, but it became clear very quickly that its primary mission would have to be to the freedpeople.[28]

The church did not focus on blacks only because it was spurned by whites. Guilt and a sincere sense of moral obligation had always been among the missionaries' motivations. Neither Methodists nor northerners in general were free from complicity in the national sin of slavery. Its victims were now left broken and plundered, like the man left by the side of the road in the biblical parable about the Good Samaritan. More than one Methodist writer made use of that parable to explain why the church had a moral obligation to minister to the freedpeople. "Can any Christian evade the responsibility?" asked Reverend Lewis. "He that passeth by, . . . and only *looks* at this matter, is the priest and the Levite. But he that hath 'mercy on him,' and helps him up, or gives 'two pence' to start him on his journey of Christian civilization, is the good *Samaritan*." A missionary in Memphis pointed out that the primary mission of Methodism had always been to serve the "poor and outcast," and no element of the southern population fit that description better than former slaves.[29]

Northern Methodists also had some strong secular reasons for giving priority to the freedpeople. Some argued that blacks had played a key role in tipping the scale on the side of the Union during the war. As a consequence, freedpeople were deserving of special consideration from a Unionist denomination and would most probably seek a home in a loyal church. Further, there was the pragmatic rationale that if former slaves were given the opportunity to develop their strengths, they would contribute them to society. On the other hand, black southerners would just as surely infect the commonweal with their weaknesses if they were left within the grip of the debilitating culture of slavery. Anyone who wanted to build a strong, reconstructed nation had an interest in the uplift of the black South.[30]

Pragmatism, principle, and Providence directed Northern Methodism to the freedpeople, but the same forces seem to have given the same directions to the African Methodist denominations. On what basis could the M.E. Church compete with African Methodist missionaries who went south to redeem and uplift the flesh of their flesh and the bone of their bone? The very existence of separate African Methodist denominations was evidence that the Northern Methodist mission did not rest on a foundation of good race relations and that the church's commitment to blacks was of a very recent vintage. Even the editor of the *Christian Advocate and Journal* conceded that in the North "nearly all the colored people abandoned us a generation ago."[31]

The Northern Methodists' response to the African Methodist challenge was to point out the shortcomings of the black denominations, directing most of their fire at the A.M.E. Church. "So far as the 'African M.E. Church' is concerned," wrote Reverend Lucius Hawkins, "they can never do the work required. . . . They have neither the wealth nor the intelligence." Inadequate resources and manpower were cited by several Northern Methodists as the chief liabilities of their A.M.E. competitors. Some also argued that the very existence of African Methodist denominations had become outmoded and that "race" churches had no place in the reconstructed nation. In August 1865, the editor of the *Christian Advocate and Journal* pushed that point to its logical conclusion: "It is quite time that our colored people ceased to call themselves Africans. . . . And equally so it is time that these special organizations of colored people, as such, were merged into the great body of our cosmopolitan Americanism and catholic Methodism." But, African Methodists were no more inclined to rejoin the M.E. Church than Southern Methodists were.[32] As a consequence, there would be at least three Methodist bodies contending for the souls of black folk.

A blemished record on race relations and two formidable challengers notwithstanding, Northern Methodists were confident that the future of the black South should be shaped by the values and the vision of the Methodist Episcopal Church. The most distinctive part of that vision was the denomination's opposition to "caste," a term which Methodists used to describe a social hierarchy that made one race separate from, and subordinate to, another. Reverend Gilbert Haven of the New England Conference was probably the most unequivocal and outspoken advocate of the radical anticaste position. In November 1864, Reverend Haven wrote: "The first, greatest, all absorbing duty of the Church is to secure the absolute oneness of all its members in Christ."[33] Egalitarians like Haven did not push merely for the symbolic interspersing of black and white bodies within Methodist structures. The radical anticaste position envisioned the full integration of blacks into the powers and privileges of the denomination.

The temperament of the radical, activist minority within what was a relatively conservative denomination, requires a few words of explanation. Anticaste radicalism could be referred to as the "new abolitionism," or more correctly as the continuation of the perfectionist, immediatist approach to social change that had characterized radical antebellum abolitionism. Historian John Thomas reflected on the meaning of perfectionism in the following manner: "Perfectibility—the essentially religious notion of the individual as a 'reservoir' of possibilities—fosters a revolutionary assurance 'that if you can so rearrange society by the destruction of an oppressive order then these possibilities will have a chance and you will get progress.' " Anticaste radicals believed that individuals could be redeemed from the sin of racism and that Methodism could be purged of the moral evil of racial caste. Redeemed individuals and the purified denomination could then become powerful examples and agents who could in turn reform society as a whole. As immediatists, the radicals believed that gradualist approaches to ending moral evils and societal sins were inappropriate and unacceptable. To a large degree, the concepts of perfectionism and immediatism were both legacies of the intense evangelical revivals that swept through the "burned-over district" of western New York state in the 1820s. Perfectionism gave the radicals their idealism and optimism. Immediatism gave them their passion. The emergence of anticaste radicalism during the period of emancipation bears out historian James M. McPherson's thesis that the ethos and the principles of radical abolitionism were not casualties of the Civil War.[34]

In light of the competition from African Methodists, Reverend George Lansing Taylor asked: "What is more preposterous than to talk of inviting the colored people to unite with us in a membership where they have no voice or influence in the councils of the Church?" Reverend Taylor was not merely a pragmatist. He contended that humanity, Christianity and the "spirit of the age," made "ecclesiastical equality" an imperative of the southern mission. Using the vocabulary of political reconstruction, Reverend Mansfield French urged the church to enter the mission field with " 'Negro Ecclesiastical Suffrage' blazoned on her banners." If Methodism met French's anticaste standards, blacks would participate in decision making at all levels and would not "stop short of a seat on the bench of bishops." Anticaste radicals set out to make their denomination a model of egalitarian possibilities.[35]

In order to move the church toward their position, anticaste radicals had to confront what appeared to be a procaste precedent that had been set by the General Conference of 1864 when it created two mission conferences for black M.E. ministers. Would the Delaware and Washington Mission Conferences serve as prototypes for new conferences in the South? When the New England Annual Conference met in April 1865, its delegates passed a resolution that condemned the racially separate conferences, urged their abolition, and warned that such conferences would "result in evil, and only evil, and that continually." Other egalitarians argued that the Washington and Delaware precedents could not be extended to the South because southern blacks would not be receptive to membership in mission conferences that were not equal in status to regular annual conferences. Defenders of the action of the General Conference responded to the radicals by pointing out that the separate conferences were created at the behest of ecclesiastically disfranchised black ministers. Furthermore, they were established "only to meet a temporary emergency, and without any intention that they were to be perpetual." [36]

The debate over objectives, policies, and precedents aired critical issues and helped clarify the denomination's positions, but officially it settled nothing. No new legislation could be enacted until the General Conference convened again in 1868. Nevertheless, some working assumptions had emerged. Northern Methodism would carry out its mission work primarily under its own banner, although it would continue to support nonsectarian benevolent agencies. The church would not seek reunion with Southern Methodism. The freedpeople would be the primary focus of the mission, although the denomination would not neglect efforts to build its southern white membership. Finally, Northern Methodism would attempt to enter the South as an opponent of caste. Even those positions would have to be refined by time and experience, but the rush of history could not wait for greater clarity. Nor could it wait for the organizational structure of the mission to take shape and get up to speed. The missions advanced and grew largely due to the initiatives of individual preachers in the field, and not in response to the orchestrations of the Missionary Society, the Church Extension Society, or the Freedmen's Aid Society, although those agencies each provided critical support in order to keep things moving forward. Furthermore, as it turned out, the Delaware and Washington Conferences did not actually send many missionaries to the South, although they did become very important entities for black ministers in the North. So, guided largely by idealism, ambition, hopes, impressions, and a good many untested assumptions, the Methodist Episcopal Church launched its mission to the South.

6

THE APPEAL OF NORTHERN
METHODISM

Northern Methodist missionaries went to the South as evangelical Reconstructionists with a special mission to the black population. They attempted to supplant Southern Methodism, to compete with African Methodism, and to organize new congregations. The missionaries tried to convey to the freedpeople an understanding of what was distinctive about the Methodist Episcopal Church and its vision of the future. The content of the appeals made to southern blacks varied from missionary to missionary, but generally they addressed the following themes: the denomination's anticaste position; the return of the M.E. Church to a region from which it had been wrongfully excluded; the antislavery tradition of Northern Methodism; and the denomination's claim to be the appropriate church home for Methodists who were loyal to the Union. Through its Freedmen's Aid Society, Northern Methodism also provided southern blacks with access to education.

In 1865, Reverend T. W. Lewis successfully persuaded the black members of Trinity Church in Charleston to transfer their allegiance from Southern to Northern Methodism. A history written twenty years after the event gives the following account of the most dramatic moment in Reverend Lewis's appeal:

Brother Lewis arose and said: "Brethren and sisters, there will be no galleries in heaven. Those who are willing to go with a Church that makes no distinction as to race or color, follow me to the Normal School on the corner of Baufain and St. Phillips Streets." The congregation rose to a man, and marched with enthusiasm to the Normal School.[1]

If the story is accurate, the congregation that followed Reverend Lewis seized Northern Methodism's anticaste radicalism as a means of transcending the strictures of southern racial traditions. At that moment, it really didn't seem to matter that the "church" to which they were going was a school building in which virtually all of the worshipers would be black. Through their collective act of self-assertion, the black members of Trinity Church crossed a symbolic dividing line separating chattel slaves from free human beings, and by doing so took unto themselves the power to define who they were and how they should be regarded by others.

In his appeal, Reverend Lewis identified himself as a representative of the "John Wesley Church," the mother denomination. Northern Methodists presented themselves as both the insistent apostles of change and as the legitimate heirs of the traditions of early Methodism. In a sense, they were offering southern black Methodists an opportunity to *renew* their affiliation with the church of their fathers, which had not been a presence in the region since the founding of the Methodist Episcopal Church, South, in 1844. The missionaries argued that slaves had had no option other than to go with their masters into the church of the slavocracy and leave the denomination that had opposed black bondage. A missionary in Louisiana apprised a group of new black members of how the situation had changed since emancipation: "And, now the war having made you free," he informed them, "the M.E. Church comes again to throw around you her fostering care." Missionaries made sure that blacks understood that Northern Methodism had been an antislavery church and that it had given steadfast support to the Union. They presented an image of their denomination that made it appear as though no black person who valued freedom, loved the church of John Wesley, or was loyal to the Union could refuse to join the Methodist Episcopal denomination.[2] The M.E. Church projected an image that claimed to represent the best of the past and the hope of the future.

The Northern Methodist message to the freedpeople was at times a mixture of idealism and pragmatism. For example, a missionary in Grenada, Mississippi, gave this account of the appeal he made to blacks there:

I did not preach a formal sermon, but explained "Our work—its principles, purpose and spirit," and spoke of the conference, Biblical Institute, Book Depository, N.O. [New Orleans] Advocate and Missionary appropriations. . . . When all was explained I asked for an expression from the colored people as to whether they would remain in the Church South, or come to us? and they voted unanimously to join the "Mother Church."

Education, books, newspapers, and the promise of financial support for the work of the mission all contributed to making the Northern Methodist Church an attractive option for free people in search of a new religious identity.[3]

The acquisition of church buildings was very important to the success of the mission. In addition to providing a place for worship and organization, church buildings served as powerful symbols of the reality and permanence of the Methodist Episcopal presence in the South. Initially, some missionaries had to resort to holding services in mechanics' halls, schools, or other public buildings, which they secured through the cooperation of friendly federal government officials. Some made use of a directive issued by Secretary of War Edwin M. Stanton in November 1863 giving Northern Methodists permission to occupy the sanctuaries of "disloyal" Southern Methodists. But Lincoln later limited the scope of that directive, and then Andrew Johnson reversed it altogether. The control of church property became a particularly complicated and contentious issue when black Southern Methodist congregations chose to affiliate with the Northern Methodist Church. Even in cases when churches had been built by and for blacks, the buildings remained the legal property of the M.E. Church, South, and few white Southern Methodists could countenance the prospect of their property falling into the hands of the Yankee church.[4]

The missionaries found that there was far greater certainty in buying or building churches of their own. The General Conference of 1864 created the Church Extension Society to serve as a conduit for contributions earmarked for securing places for worship. In a letter soliciting support for the society, Bishop Davis W. Clark observed: "No other want is now so pressing for the colored people as places of worship. Aid them in getting places of worship, and they will come to the church by thousands." In addition to assistance from the North, the missionaries relied on the sacrificial offerings of poor but dedicated black members to raise the walls of new houses of worship throughout the South. Particularly striking was the case of the purchase of Centenary Church in Charleston in 1866, toward which black Methodists contributed $5,000 in gold.[5]

At its annual meeting in November 1864, the Missionary Society had divided its southern work into four departments, each of which was under the supervision of one of the bishops. The society had official responsibility for providing direction and support for missionary personnel.[6] Within that general administrative framework, northern missionaries brought into being what was really a new denomination in the South, even though it was an organic part of a church that celebrated its centennial in 1866. The new denomination had the potential to issue a bold and exciting challenge to many of the fundamental assumptions upon which southern society had been based. Surely, the experiment was deeply flawed from the outset, but, for a time, the new church attempted to live up to its potential.

Northern Methodism took root naturally in the Unionist strongholds of eastern Tennessee, and it was there that Bishop Clark organized the first mission conference in the South on 1 June 1865. In some important respects, the Holston Mission Conference, as it was called, was atypical. It was organized at the request of local white Methodist preachers who wrote to Bishop Clark informing him that they were urgently seeking an alternative to Southern Methodism. The Holston Conference was also atypical in that of the 5,284 persons who were members of its congregations in 1865, only 128 were black.[7]

Bishop Edward Thompson organized the next new conference on Christmas Day, 1865, in New Orleans. It was called the Mississippi Mission Conference even though it encompassed a preposterously expansive territory that included Mississippi, Louisiana, and Texas, within which Northern Methodism could claim only nine congregations, five church buildings, and 2,216 members, all but 88 of whom were black. Reverend John P. Newman served as secretary for the inaugural session of the conference. Newman was a white missionary who had come to New Orleans from the New York Conference in early 1864. The tone and language of his minutes reveal the emotion he felt as the significance of the events he recorded became manifest. The conference approved four men for ordination as elders, and Newman wrote: "The ordination service was noticeable from the fact that the candidates were three colored brethren and one white brother. There they stood side by side before the same altar, and the same hands which were laid upon the latter were placed upon the heads of the former. Was not this the commencement of a new era in the South?" Twelve black preachers were ordained as deacons, and again Reverend Newman captured the moment: "The number suggested the twelve apostles. In his quiet manner, Bishop Thompson proceeded with the ordination service, while the whole audience, composed of whites and blacks, were affected, some with tears, some to shouts."[8]

The first session of the Mississippi Mission Conference founded the Thompson Biblical Institute, primarily for the education of black preachers, and it endorsed a newspaper called the *New Orleans Advocate*, which began publication less than two weeks after the conference adjourned, with Newman serving as editor and publisher. During the months after the dramatic beginning of the Mississippi Conference, the following Mission Conferences had their inaugural convocations: South Carolina, 23 April 1866; Tennessee, 11 October 1866; Texas, 3 January 1867; Virginia and North Carolina, 3 January 1867; Georgia, 10 October 1867; Alabama, 17 October 1867. By the end of 1867, the denomination could claim 66,040 southern members.[9]

Black preachers were key figures in the success of the mission. They interpreted the message of the denomination and conveyed it in a manner that resonated with the freedpeople's values, aspirations, and modes of expression. It was the mediation of black preachers that made it possible for many black southerners to take possession of the Northern Methodist vision of the future. In a more immediate way than their white colleagues, black ministers became the embodiment of the Methodist Episcopal Church for the freedpeople, and from the very start the denomination recognized the need for cultivating a cadre of effective black emissaries.[10]

The Reverend Pierre Landry provides a very interesting illustration of how that racially pragmatic approach to proselytizing actually worked. Landry was born a slave in Louisiana and grew up as a Catholic. In 1862, he was converted to Methodism by a group of slaves, among whom was a preacher named David Ingram. That group of Methodist slaves had been brought to Louisiana from Baltimore, where they had been members of the Sharp Street Methodist Episcopal Church. In his unpublished autobiographical sketch, Landry wrote that it was from those slaves that he learned "what the old Methodist Church stood for." In December 1865, Landry read in the *Daily Picayune* about the impending inaugural session of the Mississippi Mission Conference. He and the other members of his little group of Methodists received additional reports about the organization of the conference from the "mighty voices" of three respected preachers, who had been slaves in the area and were going to the conference themselves in order to be ordained. Landry's fellow Methodists then decided to send him to the conference with instructions to secure a minister for them, and they scraped together eighteen dollars to cover his traveling expenses. The conference did respond to the request by sending a black M.E. minister, who organized several churches, with the assistance of an eager Pierre Landry. Landry later received ordination himself and subsequently had a very distinguished career as a Northern Methodist clergyman. Reverend Landry's story shows how the advances of the Northern Methodist mission were sometimes promoted, prodded, and made possible by southern blacks, acting on their own initiative.[11] It is likely that a disproportionately large number of the documents about mission work were generated by and about urban missionaries, although at least as much work was being done in the hinterlands by little-known preachers, like Landry and his compeers. As a result, our understanding of these events and the people who took part in them has been limited and distorted by the "iron law of available sources."

In 1864 and 1865, Reverend John P. Newman directed the work of missionaries in the area that was to become the aforementioned Mississippi Conference. After establishing the denomination in the city of New Orleans, Reverend Newman organized the work in the outlying areas in the following manner:

> Knowing that the freedmen awaited the coming of the "old church," I sent two colored brethren to travel through all that section of Louisiana lying on the east bank of the Mississippi, between New Orleans and Baton Rouge; another was sent to Thibodeaux and Houma; a fourth to Donaldsonville, on the opposite bank of the river; and two were employed in Texas, one in Galveston and the other in Houston.[12]

When Reverend J. E. Round organized congregations in New Bern, North Carolina, in March 1864, he found "quite a number of men who have regularly officiated as local preachers and exhorters without the formality of a license." Some of them were seasoned veterans in the Methodist ministry who had been unable to secure licenses since the hostile overreaction against all black preachers that swept the South following the Nat Turner revolt of 1831. The old regime had denied them formal education, but Round observed that the unlettered black preachers "have a great deal of practical shrewdness, and certainly understand better how to manage their own class than any one else." Round's experience convinced him that the best policy was to make "freedmen the pastors of freedmen." The organization of mission churches and conferences generally included the licensing and ordination of local black clergymen, accompanied by urgent appeals for more black clergymen. In 1865, Reverend T. W. Lewis directed mission work in the area that later became the South Carolina Conference, and he also relied heavily on black preachers. In his report for that year, Lewis indicated that twelve mission posts had been established and that seven of them were being supervised by black clergymen. Reverend Lewis reported the names of two of those seven men, the others he identified simply as "colored preachers."[13]

Who were the "colored preachers" who decided to embrace a new denomination and become exemplars of Northern Methodism for southern blacks? Many of them were former slaves like Reverends Scott Chinn, Henry Green, and Anthony Ross, who were ordained at the first session of the Mississippi Mission Conference, after many years of unordained service in the Southern Methodist Church. In addition, however, some black M.E. clergymen were drawn from the relatively wealthy and well-educated free black elite, like Reverend James A. Sasportas, a charter member of the South Carolina Conference, who had amassed valuable real estate holdings before the war, and Reverend Henry Cardoza, a member of the exclusive Bonneau Society of Charleston, who was admitted to the South Carolina Conference in 1868. A few missionaries came from the two conferences that had been established in 1864 for black M.E. preachers in the North and border states. Among them were Reverends George Dardis and Charles Fisher, both of whom belonged to the Washington Conference before they went to the deep South to build churches for the freedpeople. In addition, there were some ministers, such as Reverends Hiram Revels and James Lynch, who came to the South as African Methodist missionaries and then decided to switch their allegiance to the M.E. Church. On occasion, the church gained ministers from non-Methodist denominations. For example, Benjamin F. Randolph was an ordained Presbyterian clergyman and a graduate of Oberlin College who came to the South as a chaplain with a colored regiment. After the war, he decided to stay in the South to participate in shaping the new era. He also decided to become a member of the Methodist Episcopal Church.[14] Reverend Randolph probably believed that those two decisions were connected in some important way.

Why would such a disparate group of black religious leaders choose to invest themselves in furthering the mission of the Methodist Episcopal Church? Why did they believe that Northern Methodism was the best alternative for them and for the thousands of southern blacks whom they brought into the denomination?

Anticaste was a powerful and precious principle that could engage the fondest hopes of a people grown accustomed to seeing their loved ones treated as things. To stake one's career on the belief that a denomination could be built on such a principle was to risk being characterized as willfully mushy-headed, but the gravity of the idea was so strong that it pulled many blacks into the orbit of the M.E. Church. Reverend C. S. Smith was an A.M.E. minister who switched over to the Methodist Episcopal Church and gushed the following account of the first time he attended the Tennessee Conference: "Instead of discovering any thing like 'snubbing' or 'contempt,' I beheld an interchange of Christian greeting, which at once dispelled my fears, sent a thrill of joy to my soul, and caused me to feel that I was in the midst of an assembly of saints."[15] Overstatement by new converts is to be expected, but for a moment, Reverend Smith really may have felt that he had entered the new era.

Anticaste also had its practical aspects. Some black southerners chose Northern Methodism in part because they sought an arena within which they could associate with people who had some of the skills, knowledge, and values that might prove beneficial to a race trying to move out of the culture of slavery. Reverend Smith made reference to "the power of association to reform." Another black M.E. minister explained: "We want to associate with those who have what we have not, and what we so much need, and who are willing to contribute to our necessities, till we can stand alone."[16] It should be clear that those preachers were not seeking paternalistic relationships with white Northern Methodists. The Methodist Episcopal Church appeared to be willing to provide access to a world few black people knew firsthand—the world on the other side of the deprivations of slavery and caste. Preachers like Smith may well have been paying homage to the culture and resources of northern whites, but their objective was to empower southern blacks so that equality could be achieved.

Had the term been in usage at the time, many of the freedpeople would have regarded "empowerment" as just another word for education. The ambitious educational mission undertaken by individual conferences and by the Freedmen's Aid Society of the Methodist Episcopal Church distinguished Northern Methodism from its competitors and won it the allegiance of many black ministers and members. At its inaugural session, the Mississippi Conference established the Thompson Biblical Institute in New Orleans "for the education of colored ministers of the Methodist Episcopal Church." The Institute began operation on 16 January 1866 with very few students, but at the end of the month the *New Orleans Advocate* expressed the hope that the school would "send forth educated black men to be the pastors of their own people." Similarly, the South Carolina Conference established the tuition-free Baker Theological Institute at its first session in April 1866. The school became the alma mater of many of the premier ministers of the South Carolina Conference. Other mission conferences also made efforts to provide black preachers with some kind of training or to encourage them to acquire training on their own.[17]

The M.E. Church benefited from its association with education and educational resources. Reverend C. S. Smith wrote that his primary reason for leaving the A.M.E. Church was that he "had become convinced of the importance of securing an educated ministry," and he did not believe that African Methodism had the resources to meet that need. Northern Methodism also addressed the need for secular education through the impressive efforts of the denomination's Freedmen's Aid Society to provide schools and teachers for the freedpeople. A good shepherd might have found it difficult to turn away from a denomination that attempted to offer the schooling which his people needed and wanted so desperately. In the mid-1870s, a black M.E. minister named J. C. Tate challenged a bishop of the A.M.E. Zion Church to tell him of "one colored school in the South supported by the Zion Church." The implacable critic of African Methodism continued: "I told him if he would call on me, I would cite to him various schools in the South that are supported by the white people, and many of them entirely by the Methodist Episcopal Church." [18]

The Methodist Episcopal Church seemed to be able to usher blacks into the new era and provide them with some of the resources they would need to succeed in a free environment. An A.M.E. minister until 1868, Hiram Revels gave a straightforward explanation for his switch to Northern Methodism: "The grand old Church . . . could do more than any other Church in the world for the colored people of America." One of the things the denomination's Missionary Society did was provide missionaries with half their annual salary of $400; the missionaries were expected to raise the other half from their congregations. Missionary work was far from a sinecure, and the salary supplement could not always be counted on, but any offer of support was attractive and made a difficult life a little less uncertain. [19]

The Methodist Episcopal Church may have had an additional attraction for ministers who were also politicians like Revels, a U.S. Senator from Mississippi, and Benjamin Randolph, who served as member of the South Carolina legislature and as chair of that state's Republican Central Committee. The denomination provided a religious link with some influential white Republicans during a time when finding common ground between black and white leaders was of crucial importance. Political networking was probably a key factor in securing the nomination of the Republican party. For ministers seeking entrée into the political arena, it must have been a great advantage to have the kind of religious credential that could give them connections with both black congregations and influential white politicians. Of the black ministers who were elected to serve in the radical South Carolina legislature, more belonged to the M.E. Church than to any other denomination. [20]

The advantages that could be derived from affiliating with the Methodist Episcopal Church had to be weighed against the disadvantages, and the disadvantages could be severe. It was not uncommon for opposition to the denomination to degenerate into violence. In January 1866 an article in one of the first issues of the *New Orleans Advocate* warned missionaries to expect the kind of violent opposition that "some colored preachers . . . have already experienced." It was good advice. "Another Preacher Murdered," was the headline for a story that appeared in the same newspaper on 14 November 1868. This time a preacher in Natchitoches, Louisiana, had been shot to death. His assassins were unknown, and the local authorities showed no interest in apprehending them. The report ended with anxious uncertainty: "How many more of our ministers have been killed, we can not tell. . . . We know that some were absent from their charges previous to the election, but whether dead or simply run off, we have not learned." Just the previous month, Reverend Benjamin Randolph had been shot down in broad daylight while holding a conversation on the platform of a railroad car in South Carolina. His murderers also escaped without being apprehended or even pursued.[21] Race, religion, and politics could be a dangerous mixture in the South.

All the same, black preachers continued to be drawn to Northern Methodism because of their own assessment of what was best for them and for the members of their race. In sum, black preachers joined the M.E. Church because the denomination made it possible for them to strike a blow against caste, and because it provided a milieu in which to develop beneficial associations with progressive white colleagues from the North. The denomination provided schools, and it had the financial resources to give some assistance to black congregations trying to acquire church buildings. Northern Methodism also supplemented the modest salaries that fledgling black churches could offer missionary preachers. In addition, there were probably some preacher/politicians who found the denomination attractive because it provided an opportunity to engage in political networking with influential white Republicans. The mix and priority of the motivations varied with the individual, but despite all of those incentives, the choice between Methodisms was not always an easy one to make. Other denominations had other attractions that could be just as compelling. The case of Reverend James Lynch shows just how difficult and significant deciding between denominations could be.

The A.M.E. Church issued its initial call for missionaries to serve in the South in April 1863 at its Baltimore Annual Conference. The very first volunteer was a twenty-four-year-old preacher named James Lynch. Less than a month after volunteering to serve in the South, Reverend Lynch was in Union-occupied, coastal South Carolina, sharing and shaping the wonder of new freedom.[22]

For the next two years, Lynch threw himself into the work of organizing African Methodist congregations in South Carolina and Georgia. He urged the A.M.E. Church not to leave the salvation of the freedpeople to whites who brought prejudices, as well as missionary zeal, to their work. Lynch derided critics who did not see the need for the "formation of colored churches by colored ministers under colored organizations." He explained that in a segregated society "colored people have no other way to maintain untrammelled their religious privileges, than by having churches under their own control." But the young missionary was no cynic. "This, it is hoped, will not always be a necessity," he wrote in August 1864. "I think it only a question of time."[23]

In May 1865, Lynch served as the secretary for the first session of the South Carolina Conference of the A.M.E. Church. The conference was presided over by Bishop Daniel A. Payne, who many years earlier had been Lynch's teacher when the future missionary was a boy in Baltimore. A few months after the conference adjourned, Lynch returned to the North to become Bishop Payne's assistant. In February 1866, the twenty-seven-year-old minister was selected to be editor of the *Christian Recorder,* the official organ of the A.M.E. Church and one of the most important black newspapers in the nation. In May of the following year, yet another honor was bestowed on Lynch when he was appointed to serve as pastor of historic Bethel Church in Philadelphia, the "mother" church of the A.M.E. denomination—but after some anguished indecision, he declined the appointment. At the time, only a few of Lynch's confidants understood that he was not merely declining a distinguished assignment. He was leaving the denomination he had served so well in order to join ranks with its arch rival in the South, the Methodist Episcopal Church.[24]

On a Saturday night about two months earlier, Lynch had stood outside the door of the Philadelphia home of the highly influential M.E. bishop, Matthew Simpson, and wondered whether he should knock. He decided that 9:15 was too late to disturb the bishop, so instead he wrote him a letter "in the strictest confidence" expressing his desire to affiliate with the Methodist Episcopal Church and explaining his reasons for wanting to do so. Obviously, his decision to leave the A.M.E. Church had been far from easy. "I must be true to my church while in her pales," he wrote. "I indeed, owe her much. She has done more than most know of. I rejoice in her glory. Would to God my brethren could appreciate the inexorable logic of events, and meet the demand of this hour. *They will not;* a hundred considerations will hinder."[25]

After much reflection, Lynch had come to the conclusion that "the Mission of the A.M.E. Church, as a seperate [sic] organization is drawing to a close." A denomination defined by race was symbolically and philosophically an inappropriate instrument for the task of constructing a casteless society. African Methodism was based on the assumptions and historical circumstances of the old order; the M.E. Church attempted to embody the hopes of the new. Lynch believed that Northern Methodism represented the "radicalism of the nation," and he believed himself to be a radical. Lynch wrote his letter to Bishop Simpson in March 1867, the same month in which Congress passed the Reconstruction Acts that gave the first indication that blacks would be permitted to participate in the political process, but the prescient young minister observed that "political enfranchisement is not ample protection against political oppression." Rather, Lynch put forward the view that the future could be made secure only through "the development of our intellect and a fellow feeling with our white neighbors." He told the bishop that "the relations being established in your denomination with colored men is [sic] indispensable to this development and contributes more than anything else to beget this *fellow feeling.*"[26]

Lynch also questioned whether the A.M.E. Church had sacrificed racial uplift on the altars of independence and pride. The resources needed for the reconstruction of the race could not be found in black communities. "We can help ourselves amazingly, and our salvation depends on such action," Lynch explained, "but we must be *helped* out of the turbid waters of our degradation— we can *grasp* the rope and *hold* it, but it must be thrown to us and drawn upward."[27] The Methodist Episcopal Church was the rope that Lynch intended to use to lift his people from the morass of slavery's legacy.

The day after he wrote to Bishop Simpson, Lynch left for Massachusetts where he visited the sessions of the New England Annual Conference of the M.E. Church as the guest of Reverend Gilbert Haven, the outspoken proponent of anticaste principles. In July, Lynch was in Mississippi to begin work as a presiding elder of the Methodist Episcopal Church. The *New Orleans Advocate* welcomed the young dynamo to Northern Methodism and predicted that "*it will not be long till other leading men in his denomination will follow his example.*" A few months later, Lynch wrote a letter to the *Advocate* in which he affirmed that his decision to change denominations had been the correct one. "The M.E. Church is dotting the South with temples, where white and black can meet as equals around God's altar," he wrote. "Every day increases my attachment to the 'old mother church.'"[28]

So, for many and varied reasons they came and committed themselves to the work. In effect, by the spring of 1868, James Lynch and his compeers had created a visionary, biracial, anticaste denomination in the South. The nation had seen nothing like it before. The missionaries, black and white, established a new church and a new racial covenant, conceived in the exhilaration of emancipation and born in hostile territory, through several years' labor, in hardship and hope. Delegates from eight remarkable new conferences presented their credentials to the General Conference of 1868. It was a bold beginning.

REPUBLICANISM AND THE RISE AND FALL
OF ANTICASTE RADICALISM

Beneath the dazzling beacon of anticaste, the Southern Mission preached a social gospel that was often conventional and conservative. At its inaugural session in December 1865, the Mississippi Conference advised its missionaries that they would "doubtless have opportunities of benefiting the bodies as well as the souls of men" and that in the course of meeting that responsibility they should inculcate "industry, economy and frugality." In addition, the ministers were instructed to "promote peace and order, by urging upon the emancipated a cheerful obedience to law, and a patient waiting for those civil rights to which they aspire." The Gospel of evangelical morality was preached by the denomination's missionaries and promoted in its press. The *New Orleans Advocate* carried an occasional exhortatory column under the heading "The Freedmen," which was written in "large, plain print, so easy to read." The column admonished blacks to value honesty, sobriety, hard work, and family life. A similar column, although written in regular type, appeared occasionally in the *Methodist Advocate* of Atlanta.[1]

Northern Methodists believed that the classical liberal assumptions of "republicanism" would be sufficient to regenerate the freedpeople and transform the South. Freedom required discipline, morality, education, opportunity, and the franchise—not radical measures like land reform or disruptive collective actions like strikes or sit-ins. Slavery had spawned its own social values and had created economic, legal, and political cultures in its own image. Methodist Episcopal missionaries believed that freedom would in a similar manner call its own infrastructure into being, with some assistance from Northern Methodism.

At the outset and on the margins there were some interesting unconventional proposals for economic uplift, but they were quickly swallowed up by the mainstream and disappeared without a trace. One such proposal was put forward in spring 1864 by Reverend Mansfield French. Reverend French advocated that the government "place an army of one hundred thousand colored soldiers in the South," and give them, as well as all heads of families "a home with from twenty to eighty acres of land, at a very low price." His proposal grew from his frustration with the policies that were being pursued in the Union-occupied sections of the coast of South Carolina. Those policies required ex-slaves to compete for land with northern investors and had the effect of undermining the blacks' plans to become independent farmers. Reverend French asked: "Does the government need most to make money out of these lands, or to raise upon them an enlightened and industrious people?" Similar concerns led Reverend H. H. Moore to advocate that black soldiers be authorized to establish colonies of from three to four thousand people "for mutual assistance and protection." According to Moore's plan, the government would "grant to such colony without charge from five thousand to one hundred thousand acres of public or confiscated lands in the South." [2]

Moore's plan went nowhere, and in time French's proposals became much more conventional. In June 1865 the *Augusta Constitutionalist* reported that French told an audience of recently emancipated blacks that their "primary and chief duty . . . was to remain on the plantations and at the homes where they had been engaged." French also told them that they "must be industrious, must cultivate the social virtues, and, above all, be true to their masters and mistresses." Reverend French did not disavow the *Constitutionalist*'s account of his speech; in fact, he had parts of it reprinted in the *Christian Advocate and Journal*.[3] Perhaps chastened by criticism, the once impatient missionary had found his way to the mainstream of Methodist Episcopal discourse on economic reform.

The parameters of that mainstream were defined by "republicanism." At its very center was the belief in the efficacy of individual effort and the reality of upward mobility. A few of the positions taken by Northern Methodists will help illustrate the axioms on which the denomination based its approach to economic reform. The editor of the *Christian Advocate and Journal* contended that former slaves should seek no special consideration from the government. Those who wanted to buy land should compete with white investors on the open market. Maintaining philosophical consistency, the *New Orleans Advo-*

cate opposed the restrictive provisions of the Black Codes that prevented black workers and craftsmen from marketing their labor and skills on an equal basis with white workers and craftsmen. In July 1866, a Methodist minister in Jackson, Mississippi, successfully persuaded the members of his congregation not to participate in a strike planned by black workers in that city and proudly announced that his intervention represented "another victory to the church." Finally, even after a season of disastrous crop failures, the Mississippi Conference urged blacks not to look to the government for help or to "depend upon the bounty of others."[4]

There was a striking disjuncture between the missionaries' reports of destitution, violence, and exploitation and the homilies they offered to rectify the situation. Even the most devout farmers must have been a little perplexed to learn from a black M.E. preacher that "America, with her broad lands offers wealth to any man who will 'put his hand to the plow.' "[5] Long after it seemed apparent to some observers that most sharecroppers could no more work their way into landownership than serfs could work their way into the nobility, the church continued to sound the old nostrums, exhorting impoverished, hardworking farmers to exercise economy, to labor with diligence, and to pull themselves up through their own exertions. Having reached the limits of its social gospel, Northern Methodism simply had no other solutions to offer.

The M.E. Church strongly supported the position that race or previous condition of servitude should not impair the ability of any person to be a citizen, exercise the franchise, serve on juries, or run for elective office. In November 1866 the Tennessee Conference passed a resolution stating that the war had rid the nation of "the destructive dogma of inequality in human rights" and given Americans the opportunity to lay "the foundations of our political institutions upon the broad and enduring principle of equal and exact justice to all men." Those sentiments were affirmed by other conferences and proclaimed in the denomination's newspapers. The Church also supported federal, state, and local legislation designed to ensure impartial access to public accommodations and services, but not without some dissent over the tactics of some civil rights advocates.[6]

In May 1867, the *New Orleans Advocate* denounced the efforts of some blacks in that city to integrate segregated streetcars. The paper counseled blacks to "allow society time to adjust itself to the new order of things" and contended that they should press their case in the courts, not in the streets. The next issue of the paper repeated the criticism and also deplored the involvement of "some white men in this community who call themselves Republicans, who instigate the black men, to such violations of the peace." In June 1874, the *Methodist Advocate* questioned the wisdom of the provision of the then pending federal Civil Rights Bill requiring integration of public schools. The *Advocate* feared that white taxpayers would withdraw their support for public education, leaving blacks in a worse situation than before.[7] But, allowing for some differences of opinion over tactics and the provisions of some pieces of legislation, Methodists were generally solid in their support of civil rights.

Social equality was quite another matter, or at least so it seemed to a great many otherwise clearheaded people. Few terms have caused so much fear, loathing, consternation, and confusion. Its definition was elusive, but it had the impact of an open invitation to interracial intercourse on a grand scale. Northern Methodism took pride in its support of civil rights, but the church was thrown on the defensive by the charge that it was a reckless purveyor of social equality. For the most part, M.E. ministers took the position that their denomination had no policy on social intermingling. Social relationships were purely personal matters. Neither the church nor the government could mandate personal affinities. As one preacher put it: "This question of social negro equality is a scarecrow concocted by our enemies to injure us as a church."[8] Northern Methodists insisted that social equality was a non-issue, but they had a problem.

The problem was Gilbert Haven. As the editor of *Zion's Herald and Wesleyan Journal* in Boston, Haven earned a reputation for being his denomination's most outspoken and uncompromising opponent of caste. The editor of Southern Methodism's *Raleigh Christian Advocate* charged Haven with having "great admiration for the negro, social equality and for mixed blood." Other white southerners referred to him as "a redmouth, miscegenating, ranting, howling hypocrite" and an "old negro-affiliating political preacher and shameless propagandist of every radicalism." In 1873, the "shameless propagandist" moved to Atlanta to become the newly elected resident bishop of the Methodist Episcopal Church in the South. After assuming his new duties, Bishop Haven continued his crusade against caste and did nothing to allay the fears of his detractors. A white M.E. preacher who had great respect for Haven observed that "the Bishop was generally misunderstood and cordially hated."[9]

As the most prominent Northern Methodist in the South from 1873 to 1876, Bishop Haven cast a long shadow and made it difficult for his denomination to escape being tainted with the charge of social equality, with all its lascivious implications. In April 1874, Reverend James Mitchell wrote an article for the *Methodist Advocate* entitled "Amalgamation." Mitchell complained that "the word that stands at the head of this article is hurled with the force of a bombshell into our young and struggling conferences." It was his assessment that the "pretended foundation for all this agitation was 'the appointment' of Bishop Haven to the South." The controversy was primarily a concern for the white Northern Methodists who had hopes of becoming less objectionable to the white South. For them, the issue of race was becoming a burden that limited the denomination's growth. For most blacks, however, Bishop Haven's appointment was a welcome affirmation of the denomination's commitment to anticaste principles.[10]

White Southern Methodists objected strenuously to Northern Methodism's violation of their sense of racial propriety. From the southern perspective, the M.E. Church gave every indication that it was "hell-bent" on destroying the principle of black deference to whites and all of the boundaries of a well-ordered society. Not only did northerners fail to understand that blacks had a proper place, they also seemed to be tragically unaware that the church also had an appropriate sphere to which it should confine itself. "There is a difference between the two Methodisms and the distinction is easily made," the *Raleigh Christian Advocate* informed its readers. "Southern Methodists do not interfere with politics and Northern Methodists preach and write and talk more about politics than about the Gospel of the Lord Jesus Christ."[11]

The relationship between Northern Methodists and politics was not always comfortable, but for the most part the churchmen stayed in it, for better or worse. Some M.E. ministers embraced politics with great enthusiasm; others were drawn into it with grave misgivings. James Lynch was a good example of both types. As soon as he arrived in Mississippi, Reverend Lynch became involved in political organizing. Few politicians in the state could match his effectiveness or zeal. In October 1869, Lynch informed Bishop Simpson that the Republican party of Mississippi had nominated him for the position of secretary of state by an "overwhelming majority." Lynch felt a great responsibility to the people who looked to him for political leadership, but he was torn. "I feel that Christ's Church is starving and suffering for the bread which I would give were I devoted with singleness to the ministry," Lynch confessed. He then offered to resign from the ticket if Simpson thought that he should. Apparently Simpson did not, because Lynch went on to victory in the election. Not all Northern Methodists agreed with the bishop's position. The previous year, the Georgia Conference had passed a resolution prohibiting its ministers from accepting any "nomination to civil office."[12]

But, as architects of a new society, missionaries found it difficult to refuse to handle a tool as powerful as politics or to resist the "whirlwind of political excitement" as Lynch put it. Nor could they let politics become the exclusive instrument of persons who did not share their vision of the future. Besides, northern preachers found something disingenuous about their southern counterparts' protestations against political involvement. "As if the Methodist Episcopal Church South had not plunged 'neck and heels' into the politics of slavery and rebellion," the *Christian Advocate and Journal* of New York sputtered in indignation.[13]

Methodist Episcopal missionaries saw themselves as the rear guard of the Union Army and the vanguard of Republican Reconstruction.[14] The denomination and the Republican party entered the South together, protecting each other's flanks as they attempted to establish themselves in hostile territory. Northern missionaries helped prepare the soil in which the Republican party could take root. The party mobilized the government and the military in ways that helped the racially iconoclastic denomination survive in the South. But the match between the denomination and the party was more than a marriage of convenience. The social gospel of the M.E. Church meshed with the civil religion of the Republican party. The religious institution and the secular organization entered the task of Reconstruction from different points of departure, but they had similar goals for reforming the South.

In 1870, the South Carolina Conference pledged "to hold no entangling alliances with any party or organization." The minutes of the conference were printed by the Republican Book and Job Office in Charleston, and the back cover carried an advertisement for the *South Carolina Republican* newspaper, which promoted the principles of the Republican party because they were the "only sound and safe principles."[15] If there was a contradiction in that arrangement, neither the Methodists nor the Republicans seemed to be troubled by it.

On the national level, Methodists were not greatly disturbed by the implications of their associations with politics and with prominent politicians. Bishop Edward R. Ames was a close friend of Secretary of War Stanton. It was at the request of Bishop Ames that Stanton issued the directive giving the M.E. Church control of the church buildings of disloyal Southern Methodists during the war. Bishop Simpson gave the sermon at Lincoln's funeral service, and was well known for his influence in Washington. In January 1868, the bishops of the M.E. Church published an "Address" to General Grant urging him to run for the presidency. Five months later, the General Conference of 1868 passed a strongly worded resolution urging the Senate to remove Andrew Johnson from office so that "tyrannical usurpation may be rebuked." After Reverend John P. Newman left his mission work in New Orleans, he became chaplain of the United States Senate. While serving in that position he also became an outspoken supporter of the policies of President Grant. Reverend Newman, who was reputed to be a member of the president's inner circle, also served as pastor of the church attended by the Grant family. In addition, the first black person to become a U.S. Senator was the Reverend Hiram Revels of Mississippi.[16]

Ultimately, though, Methodist Episcopal politics were larger than partisan politics. The denomination's churches, schools, sermons, social gospel, and partisan activities were all components of a larger political mission to plant "American ideas" in the South. According to the Northern Methodist analysis, the revolution of 1776 had failed to free all of the new American republic from vassalage to "feudal" European ideas. European notions of politics and social organization remained in the "aristocratic" South, because there they were protected by slavery, the epitome of undemocratic institutions. Slavery had effectively repelled the ideas that could challenge its legitimacy. The destruction of slavery gave Americans the opportunity to complete their aborted revolution by transforming the South. Completion of the revolution required the destruction of caste and all of the other social, economic, and political vestiges of slavery's reign. Completion of the revolution also required churches that would replace the theology of slavery and social hierarchy with the gospel of liberty and republicanism. The Northern Methodist mission was to bring the South into harmony with the ideas and institutions of the rest of the nation.[17] In that sense, every missionary was a "political missionary."

"Political missionary" was the term used by a prominent Northern Methodist layman named John Emory Bryant to describe himself and his colleagues in the Southern Advance Association. Bryant was a native of Maine who came South as a Union soldier. After the war, he settled in Georgia where he became passionately involved in Republican politics. Bishop Haven called Bryant one of the "leading members" of the denomination in that state. Bryant expressed the Northern Methodist interpretation of the American dichotomy succinctly: "The civilization of the North is modern, Christian, American: that of the South is European, feudal, un-American." As part of the effort to put an end to southern exceptionalism, Bryant founded the Southern Advance Association in 1877. He intended the organization to be a "political missionary association" which would promote American ideas. Bryant also wanted the Association to counter the influence of the Southern Historical Society, which had been founded by "un-Reconstructed" southerners in 1869 as part of an effort to enshrine southern exceptionalism. The first volume of the *Southern Historical Society Papers* was published in 1876. The president of the Southern Advance Association was Erasmus Q. Fuller, who was also the editor of the *Methodist Advocate*, the Northern Methodist newspaper published in Atlanta. Officially, Bryant was only the association's business manager.[18]

Bryant felt a kinship with Albion Tourgée, another prominent Northern Methodist layman. Tourgée was a native of Ohio and a veteran of the Union army who became embroiled in Reconstruction politics in North Carolina. He achieved fame in 1879 for a novel he wrote based on his experiences in the South, entitled *A Fool's Errand*. The book's main character gives this assessment of the American dichotomy: "The constitutions of the North had fostered individual independence, equal rights and power, and general intelligence among the masses. . . . In the South the reverse was true. The ballot and the jury-box were jealously guarded from the intrusion of the poor. . . . It was a republic in name, but an oligarchy in fact." John Bryant was "very much pleased" with Tourgée's novel and agreed with its portrayal of the situation in the South. Bryant also agreed with Tourgée's conclusion: "The remedy he proposes is substantially the same as I propose—The conversion of southern whites to American ideas." [19] Political missionaries could not bring about the kind of victory that they wanted to achieve relying only on the mission to blacks. If the situation in the South was going to be changed, organizations like the Southern Advance Association and the M.E. Church would have to "convert" a significant part of the white population.

For several years before Erasmus Fuller became president of the Southern Advance Association, he had strongly advocated that the M.E. Church put greater emphasis on efforts to secure the allegiance of southern whites. In order to accomplish that goal, Fuller and those who shared his views argued that Northern Methodism should put less emphasis on its anticaste positions and end race-mixing within the denomination. Nevertheless, Reverend Fuller pronounced himself to be "as free from the influence of caste as the apostle Paul or the angel Gabriel." Before the decade of the 1870s was over, the plans of pragmatic separatists like Fuller defined the contours of Northern Methodism in the South, not the moral imperatives of anticaste radicals like Bishop Haven or the vision of missionaries like James Lynch. [20] On the surface, that appeared to be quite a turnabout.

Actually, the Methodist Episcopal Church had never officially adopted an anticaste policy. The mission to the South was launched by the General Conference of 1864. The same General Conference also created two "colored" mission conferences for all of its black members outside the South. The church left open the possibility that similar "colored" conferences could be organized in the South, but it issued no clear directives. Additional guidance could be gleaned from the many articles and editorials on southern policy that appeared in the denomination's press, but newspapers do not produce church law. The missionaries had to enact policies in the field based on their own understanding of what was appropriate and effective. They had a considerable amount of leeway because most of their organizing took place during the four-year interim before the next General Conference convened. Furthermore, there was little fear that experiments in the South would have any impact on practices in the North. The situation gave an unusual amount of influence to the kinds of idealists who became missionaries, many of whom were imbued with the ethos of radical abolition.[21]

As the missionaries penetrated the southern frontier, they found no welcome except among the freedpeople and in a few white Unionist strongholds. Blacks became the mission's primary focus, and as such, their aspirations played a role in shaping denominational policy. For a time, anticaste principles made as much sense to conservatives, who were primarily interested in church expansion, as they did to the radicals, who were committed to building a new social order. So, because of a complex set of circumstances, the missionaries and their supporters were able to bring into being a Southern Mission Church, whose racial policies bore little resemblance to those of the M.E. Church in the North. Anticaste policies were instituted without a clear mandate, but those policies also had a far more serious weakness—they didn't work, at least not on the level of individual congregations.

"It is a beautiful theory, and eminently Christian, that white and colored, former masters and slaves, be seated indiscriminately in the same church, and side by side kneel at the same communion altar," observed a wistful Reverend T. W. Lewis in 1865. Reverend Lewis had tried to organize a church in Beaufort, South Carolina, "on the basis of 'no distinction on account of color, and no separate sittings for the whites.'" The result was that after two years, no white person had joined. Elsewhere in South Carolina and in Florida, Lewis tried to organize congregations on the same basis, with the same result.[22]

Reverend J. E. Round became skeptical of "ecclesiastical amalgamation" after he began working with freedpeople in North Carolina. He warned that "it is a great mistake to suppose that these people are generally desirous of connecting themselves with the same congregations and conferences with the whites." Reverend John Newman sometimes became rhapsodic when he wrote about the anticaste practices of the Mississippi Mission Conference. Nevertheless, when he built Ames Chapel in New Orleans, he intended it to be expressly for the use of white worshipers. Even Bishop Haven himself failed when he tried to reorganize churches in Atlanta on a nonracial basis.[23]

Anticaste congregations were a lost cause from the start. It was on the conference level that the "beautiful theory" could be put into application. Conferences, after all, were primarily ministerial organizations and surely M.E. pastors would be able to conduct business and have fellowship on a nonracial basis. Conferences in parts of the deep South did maintain a fierce fidelity to anticaste principles. The Louisiana, Mississippi, and South Carolina Conferences never wavered from the moral commitment they made to banish caste from their proceedings, but the number of white ministers associated with those conferences was very small. Too small, some critics said, for caste to become an issue. After a preaching engagement in South Carolina, Reverend W. G. Matton returned to his work in North Carolina "much impressed with the idea that the non color-line, of which the South Carolina Confce [*sic*] boasted so much, was a myth."[24]

In other conferences there was significant representation of both races. In those conferences, racial idealism and racial disaffection were conjoined in contentious coexistence. Like the tragic mulattoes of literature, the "mixed" conferences were ill at ease about their identity. They were unsure whether they belonged to the black or the white South. Were they products of the new South or aliens from the North? They hoped they might be accepted as progressive hybrids but assumed they would always be scorned as pathetic mongrels. Some mixed conferences tried to achieve peace and respectability by drawing the color line and requiring the races to fall back to their respective sides, quieting taunts and uncertainties by abandoning the common ground.

Mixed conferences were the frameworks on which radical missionaries hoped to build an anticaste denomination that would itself become one of the main supports of a new social order in the South, but as early as 1868 the frameworks began to give way. The General Conference which met in that year gave the Kentucky Conference permission to divide along racial lines. The church appeared to be following the precedent it had established four years earlier by authorizing the organization of two colored conferences to cover the eastern border states and the North. The General Conference did not find that precedent to be applicable to the lower South and so denied a similar request for racial division from the Alabama Conference.[25] The division of the Kentucky Conference and the petition of the Alabama Conference to follow suit marked the beginning of an effort to dislodge anticaste principles from the Northern Methodist creed. That effort increased in intensity during the 1870s, as the vision of a promising New Era of black freedom receded and the image of a New (white) South came into view.

By the early 1870s, most of the black South had already sifted itself out into denominational affiliations, and the potential for explosive new growth in black membership was over. By then, it was also becoming evident that blacks would be force-marched into a future of political and economic marginalization. As editor of Atlanta's *Methodist Advocate,* Erasmus Fuller helped mobilize an effort to prevent Northern Methodism from becoming trapped in an exclusive relationship with a race with such dismal prospects. The future of the South belonged to its white population, and Reverend Fuller knew it. Fuller was a northerner, a Methodist, and a Republican, but clearly he was no radical. He came to Georgia from Illinois in 1869, after the first wave of missionary idealism had subsided.[26]

In an article entitled "The White Work," Fuller reminded his readers that whites comprised two-thirds of the population of the South. Whites controlled the schools and the governments. They owned "the mines and mining interests, the railroads, the commerce, the manufactories, the stock, the implements of industry." The editor asserted that one of the "great embarrassments" of Northern Methodism was its reliance on the membership of landless laborers who "may go from place to place." Fuller did not suggest that the work among blacks should be diminished, but he argued that the denomination should also "form societies among the owners of the soil, white societies, even where the colored people are in the majority."[27]

Fuller was only one of an increasing number of advocates of the "white work." Whites who had joined the denomination were keen on reducing their own marginality by bringing other whites into the fold. Proponents of an invigorated mission to whites argued that such an effort was a practical necessity to ensure the future strength of the denomination in the South. They also pointed out that a truly evangelical church could not neglect the salvation of the majority of the region's population. The problem was that the existence of mixed conferences made it nearly impossible for Northern Methodism to reach large numbers of whites. Mixed conferences evoked fears of church-sponsored social equality. They made Northern Methodism appear to be radical, alien, and hostile to the sensibilities of southern whites. As a rule, even Unionists and reconstructed whites had no desire to affiliate with racial radicals or to be associated with mixed conferences.[28] So, the Methodist Episcopal Church was faced with a dilemma: it could adhere to anticaste principles, or it could work effectively with whites. It had to make a choice.

On one side of the issue were the pragmatic divisionists who argued that mixed conferences had nothing to do with moral or religious principles. Anticaste was merely the pet abstraction of radical theorists; as such it should not take priority over saving souls or strengthening the denomination. The pragmatists also contended that cultural dissonance made it difficult for the races to work together efficiently in the same conferences, and as a result the work of the church suffered. Generally, white pragmatists were careful not to give the impression that they were motivated by any ill will toward blacks. Although, on occasion, one would concede that "perhaps some who advocate a division do not care particularly where the colored members go." For the most part, however, opponents of mixed conferences took the position that division would serve the interests of both races. In separate conferences, blacks would have more opportunities to develop leadership, but they would still remain in the Methodist Episcopal Church and have access to its resources. Finally, one of the white divisionists' strongest arguments was their assertion that they represented the true feelings of black preachers in the denomination.[29]

It is difficult to assess the magnitude and character of black support for separate conferences. Some black divisionists were motivated by a desire to govern their own affairs and be free from even the appearance of white oversight. Others were realists who bent to the will of their white coreligionists for the sake of denominational harmony. In 1872, the Georgia Conference adopted a resolution proposing the creation of a separate conference for blacks. Subsequently, the black members of the conference held a convention to discuss the issue among themselves. The delegates to the black convention endorsed the proposal to separate, but contended that in doing so they were not capitulating to caste. In fact, they argued that division was the true anticaste position because a separate conference would enable blacks to "feel as men, and the peers of our white brethren." The convention took the position that caste was an issue of status, not proximity. The delegates also supported the view that division would make it possible for their "white brethren to more vigorously prosecute the work among their own race." It is not clear how large a majority of those who attended the convention voted to support division or how widely their views were shared by black Northern Methodists elsewhere in the South.[30]

It is clear that there were other black clerics who vehemently disagreed with them. "There is one thing certain," wrote a black minister from Tennessee in 1875. "We colored brethren will fight it out on this line if it takes all summer. We can not afford to separate in this country. United we stand—divided we destroy ourselves." Another black preacher was even more blunt about his refusal to draw down the anticaste standard. "I have concluded to stay with you a while," he declared. "You put us in here and we will stay till you turn us out."[31]

Hiram Revels was one of the black M.E. ministers who vowed to "work and pray" against separation. Reverend Revels urged his adopted denomination not to abandon the principles upon which it entered the South. Like Revels, James Lynch had once been an African Methodist. Less than a year after Reverend Lynch left the A.M.E. Church in order to escape racial exclusivity, he found himself in a struggle to prevent Northern Methodism from dividing its ministry into black and white compartments. Lynch argued that the denomination ought not give in to the pressures of prejudice. He and those who shared his views insisted that the church was not called to conform to the world. A black presiding elder from Tennessee put it this way: "I do not believe that the Gospel is hindered or that a single soul will be lost by our having mixed conferences. But I do believe that scores, yea thousands will be lost by professors of religion and ministers seeking to please men rather than God." Black opponents of separate conferences argued that drawing the color line was un-scriptural, un-Christian and a betrayal of trust. They also pointed out that southern legislatures and the United States Congress managed to function on a "mixed" basis, and questioned whether the Methodist Episcopal Church could allow itself to do less.[32]

White anticaste radicals also refused to yield to the rising tide of divisionism. As an editor and then as bishop, Gilbert Haven tried to be the conscience of his denomination on this issue, but he was not alone. One of the most prominent of the white opponents of separate conferences was Lucius C. Matlack, author of the "Louisiana Platform" of 1872, which called on the church to repudiate the color line. Matlack exhorted his denomination not to be dissuaded from anticaste by white or black divisionists. He warned that compromise of principle would render the church worthy of contempt. Matlack was no stranger to controversy. In the 1830s his abolitionism had cost him his preacher's license as well as his membership in the Philadelphia Local Preachers' Association. For twenty-five years, he was one of the leaders of a group of abolitionist dissenters called the Wesleyan Methodist Connection of America.[33]

Reverend Isaac J. Lansing of Atlanta also waged war on the divisionists in a series of articles entitled "Church without Color" published in the *Methodist Advocate* in 1876. Reverend Lansing insisted that the continued existence of mixed conferences was itself the "most powerful sermon which God permits the Church to preach from year to year." Lansing pointed out that it was particularly shameful to push for racial division at the very time when the political and economic fortunes of blacks were at their lowest ebb. He reminded his readers that southern whites had been slow to join the M.E. denomination because of their own racial haughtiness, not because they had been neglected or spurned by the church. At least one southern white minister publicly declared himself to be a supporter of mixed conferences: Reverend O. R. Franklin was a native of the South who became a presiding elder in the Alabama Conference. Before the war he had been a slave owner. Reverend Franklin observed that the races were mixed in business, in politics, and on juries and asked: "Shall our annual conferences be made the exception?" When the Alabama Conference voted in favor of division in 1876, Reverend Franklin registered his dissent and asked to be excused from voting. He later wrote a letter of protest to the *Methodist Advocate* which he closed in this way: "I am, respectfully, the white man of the Alabama Conference who declined to vote."[34]

The contours of the debate over anticaste could be seen in the positions taken in and by the southern conferences, but ultimate decision making on the matter remained the exclusive prerogative of the General Conference. It was at the General Conferences of 1872 and 1876 that the struggle for the soul of Northern Methodism was waged in earnest.

The General Conference of 1872 convened in the spring in Brooklyn, New York. E. Q. Fuller was one of the delegates, but so was James Lynch. Petitions asking for authorization to establish separate conferences were submitted by the Alabama and Georgia Conferences. An additional petition in support of racial division was submitted by Fuller on behalf of the "convention of colored people of Georgia." On the other side of the issue, the South Carolina Conference submitted ten separate petitions against the color line, bearing a total of 785 signatures. In addition, a petition from Mississippi was submitted bearing the signatures of 112 opponents of caste. James Lynch and a black delegate from South Carolina named James B. Middleton both made speeches against division. At one point in the proceedings, Fuller proposed that the General Conference adopt a resolution authorizing colored conferences in Alabama and Georgia, but Middleton successfully countered the proposal with a motion to table.[35]

In 1872 the machinery of the General Conference worked in favor of the opponents of caste. The Committee on Boundaries was charged with responsibility for making a recommendation in response to the calls for and against racial division, and that committee was chaired by none other than Lucius Matlack, the inveterate anticaste stalwart. It came as no surprise that Matlack's committee recommended that the petitions for separate conferences be denied. It may be more than coincidental that the same General Conference that sustained Matlack's recommendation also made Gilbert Haven a bishop and removed E. Q. Fuller from his position as editor of the *Methodist Advocate*. Fuller was replaced by Nelson E. Cobleigh, who had been Haven's predecessor as editor of *Zion's Herald and Wesleyan Journal,* the newspaper of the New England Conference.[36] The anticaste position seemed to be secure for at least four more years.

In 1876, the General Conference met in Baltimore. This time, the supporters of mixed conferences had no reason to be sanguine. E. Q. Fuller was a delegate again, but James Lynch had died of a bronchial infection and Bright's disease at the end of 1872. At the time of his death he was not quite thirty-four years old. By 1876, Fuller had been restored to his position as editor of the *Methodist Advocate* as a result of the untimely death of Cobleigh in early 1874. Finally and ironically, opposition to mixed conferences had been galvanized by Bishop Haven's war on the color line. The bishop's anticaste policies generated an adamant divisionist backlash that looked to the General Conference of 1876 for relief.[37]

The Alabama Conference requested division and called for the reelection of Fuller as editor of the *Methodist Advocate*. Fuller presented a request from the Georgia Conference for division on geographic lines that would have the same effect, if not the odium, of dividing on racial lines. He also presented two petitions on the subject from "white ministers and laymen" in Georgia. In addition, the Arkansas and Holston Conferences requested the authority to create colored conferences. The Tennessee Conference was sharply divided on the issue. It presented a petition in favor of division, but also reported that a majority of the conference had voted to maintain its mixed status. Finally, the anticaste position was also put forward in official communications from the Louisiana, North Carolina, South Carolina, and Texas Conferences.[38]

In 1876 the issue of conference division was referred to the Committee on the State of the Church instead of to the Committee on Boundaries as had been done in 1872. The Committee on the State of the Church was chaired by Otis Haven, a cousin of Bishop Haven, but Otis and Gilbert had very different perspectives on anticaste. In fact, Otis Haven was interested in reunion with the Southern Methodist Church and was keenly aware that mixed conferences made that virtually impossible. The majority of his committee recommended that Southern Conferences be allowed to draw the color line as long as a majority of both their white and black ministers voted to do so, a proposal sometimes referred to as the "local option" plan. There was opposition to the majority's proposal. Lucius Matlack championed a minority report that took the position that the General Conference should not compromise the anticaste policy it had adopted four years earlier. Matlack asked: "Shall the pledge of our church made in 1872 be broken in 1876?" He said that he was making that case on behalf of the black delegates from the South who did not ask for, and did not support, "local option." Matlack said that "the question would be quickly settled if submitted to them alone." In the end, the General Conference approved the majority's recommendation by a vote of 226 to 66. The vote revealed that anticaste radicals had become a small and ineffective minority. Their principles were relegated to the status of historical artifacts. Lucius Matlack's lengthy argument against the color line was printed in full on the front page of the *Christian Recorder* of the A.M.E. Church. After reporting that Northern Methodism had rejected Matlack's position, the editor of that newspaper reminded his readers that "the millennium has not yet come."[39]

The marginality of radicalism was underscored when Bishop Haven was assigned to spend a year touring the Liberian Conference.[40] In effect, the foremost crusader against caste was banished to an African Elba. For a time, the churning waters of the Atlantic would muffle the sound of Haven's strident protests against the color line. At least he was spared the ignominy of being put in the impossible position of having to preside over the dissolution of the policies he had fought so hard to establish. Divisionists like Fuller must have regarded Haven's exile as a positive response to their complaints.

Yet another blow was delivered to the proponents of anticaste principles when the General Conference responded to an overture from the M.E. Church, South, by establishing a five-member commission to meet with the southerners "in order to remove all obstacles to formal fraternity between the two Churches." E. Q. Fuller was appointed to serve on the Commission, as was John P. Newman, one of the pioneer missionaries of the Mississippi Conference. Actual union between Northern and Southern Methodism was still just an idea that wouldn't be realized until 1939, but establishment of the commission indicated clearly how much things had changed.[41]

Once the General Conference gave its qualified approval to division, the experiment with anticaste principles collapsed in conference after conference, like divisionist dominoes. The Alabama, Georgia, and West Texas Conferences divided in 1876; the Tennessee Conference followed suit in 1877. In 1878 the races separated in the Arkansas Conference, and in 1879 they did the same in the Holston and North Carolina Conferences. Separation seldom occurred without opposition. For example, the first time the North Carolina Conference voted on a proposal to establish separate conferences, division was blocked by a majority of the black ministers. Seven of the eight white ministers voted for the color line. Two days later, the North Carolinians reconsidered their vote. This time, sixteen blacks voted in favor of division and the remaining twelve black ministers asked to be excused from voting. The white vote remained the same, with one white preacher holding out against division until the end. Following the final vote, the black members adopted a resolution which stated: "While we wish the Church at large to know that we, as colored members of the North Carolina Conference, did not wish a separation from our white brethren, we pray that God's blessing may go with them in their work, and that our common Father may watch over and bless us all."[42]

By the time that the General Conference of 1880 convened, only the Louisiana, Mississippi, and South Carolina Conferences claimed to be integrated, but even they were de facto black conferences with only token white membership. And, by the time that General Conference convened, Gilbert Haven was dead. He had contracted malaria during his tour of duty in West Africa and never fully recovered. Death came to Bishop Haven on 3 January 1880.[43] The *Christian Recorder* of the A.M.E. Church reported his death in this way:

> Alas! Alas! that we should be called upon to chronicle the death of Bishop Gilbert Haven. . . . He was the one man of his church that dared treat the "negro question" other than in a sentimental way. For much of the legislation of 1876, at Baltimore, he blushed. Separate Conferences and separate churches and separate schools were alike hateful to him. . . . Whether in the North or in the South, his was always a certain sound.[44]

As the possibility of real integration became remote, the energy invested in securing symbolic integration increased, and a campaign to elect a black bishop became the last refuge for anticaste idealism in the religious mission to remake the South. The election of a black Methodist Episcopal bishop would demonstrate that the hierarchy of the denomination had no caste barriers and that although blacks were separate they were not second class. Black appeals for the election of a black bishop were particularly numerous and insistent at the General Conferences of 1876 and 1880, although the campaign for such a position began before those years and continued until 1920 when two black ministers were elected bishops for the express purpose of administering black conferences.[45]

The Methodist Episcopal mission to the freedpeople ended as it had begun at the General Conference of 1864, with the creation of separate conferences for blacks. Between the establishment of the Delaware and Washington Conferences in 1864 and the division of the North Carolina Conference in 1879, a great deal had happened. Northern Methodists had gained almost twice as many black members as the C.M.E.'s, but less than either of the African Methodist denominations. And at the same time that the missionaries were organizing congregations, Northern Methodism's Freedmen's Aid Society had been establishing a network of schools and colleges, including institutions like Bennett College in North Carolina, Claflin College in South Carolina, Clark College in Georgia, and Rust College in Mississippi. Although it falls beyond the purview of this study, the story of the missionary educators is every bit as dramatic and as significant as the story of the preachers.[46]

In sum, sustained by little more than their idealism, anticaste radicals had attempted to remake a denomination, transform a region, and abolish segregation. For a time, the best of them, black and white, became the embodiments of immediatist, perfectionist integrationism. That they failed is not nearly as remarkable as is the fact that they had pursued objectives that were so visionary, with such tenacity, in such unlikely places, so soon after slavery.[47] Indeed, the times had been strange and stirring.

CONCLUSION

The scriptures instructed some Methodists to look after the errant, sable children, admonished others to seek their brethren, and advised still others to be Good Samaritans for the travelers who had been waylaid by slavery. Ultimately, the freedpeople themselves would be the final arbiters of which Methodists' interpretation of the Bible was most appropriate. The new paternalism, the Gospel of Freedom, and anticaste radicalism were engaged in a battle for the hearts and minds of the black South until each could claim its own adherents. The major objective of this book has been to demonstrate that each of these views held by Methodist preachers was substantial, clear, distinctive, and significant enough to be usefully analyzed in order to develop a typology of some of the ways in which freedom was understood and pursued.

The new paternalism did not see the coming of freedom as a sudden, transforming event. New paternalists were traditionalists who assumed that the forces that had exerted powerful influences over their lives in slavery would continue to do so in freedom. When freedom came, Lucius Holsey continued to work for the man who had been his master, and, of course, he continued to regard his first master as his father. Even the Union army couldn't change some relationships. New paternalists expected that their ties to the white South would remain strong, but not as direct as they had been before the war. Traditionalists believed that it was unwise to directly challenge the ideology of white supremacy. They developed ways of allowing black freedom to be mediated through white paternalism. Traditionalists did expect that freedom would bring change and advancement, but they believed that southern whites would set the limits and determine the pace of progress. The new paternalists believed that freedom meant they had won a little more breathing room in which to pursue the strategies for advancement they had developed before the war. The preachers of the new paternalism represented an important and influential group of emancipationist leaders who were not involved in electoral politics. Therefore, the meaning and significance of the new paternalism can barely be detected in studies of this period that focus primarily on the political arena.

According to the Gospel of Freedom, emancipation struck like a bolt of lightning. It destroyed an old world and brought a new one into being. Becoming free was like a religious conversion experience. Emancipation from the burden of slavery was the secular equivalent of redemption from the burden of sin. Conversion made one a wholly new person. Nevertheless, ministers of the Gospel of Freedom always had to guard against backsliders and Democrats. According to that Gospel, the essence of slavery had been the control and subordination of blacks by whites. Freedom was to be made real through the assertion of independence and racial pride. The promised land of freedom would be reached, whether in this country or in another, in this world or the next, but the ultimate goal would not be compromised. The Gospel of Freedom defined freedom as the abolition of all of the social, economic, and political limits that were imposed because of race. The Gospel of Freedom incorporated republican values and celebrated individual achievement, but it also stipulated that the victims of slavery would have to be restored and regenerated as a race in order for them to flourish as individuals. African Methodist missionaries did not see anything intrinsically white or unalterably alien about the values variously associated with republicanism, the "middle class" and the work ethic— and if their response is any indication, most Methodist freedpeople didn't either.

Anticaste radicals did not make up the majority of their denomination, but they did put forward Northern Methodism's most distinctive and arresting interpretation of the meaning of freedom. From the perspective of the radicals, slavery had been a rigid social hierarchy and a racial caste system that was antithetical to American/republican values because it completely deprived individuals of opportunity and personal sovereignty. The radicals made their boldest symbolic statement of freedom when they attempted to aggressively transgress caste barriers.

The differences between anticaste radicalism and the Gospel of Freedom were not categorical, but they were clear. On the one hand, the Gospel of Freedom was a kind of black nationalism based on the premise that a corrective racial philosophy was absolutely necessary in order to move the dead weight of ongoing racial oppression, so that individual achievement, in the mainstream, would be possible. Advocates of the Gospel of Freedom sought to empower their race and to build up its institutional bulwarks so that the freedpeople could confront the ideology of white supremacy. On the other hand, anticaste radicals believed that white supremacy could be transcended altogether. Anticaste radicalism was a kind of uncompromising, immediatist, integrationist individualism based on the premise that it was possible to create a new social order in which individuals would be treated equally and color would have little significance. Anticaste radicals sought a color-blind society. For them, freedom meant republican integration, pure and simple.

It could be argued that Northern Methodism provides a model illustrating the dynamics and the trajectory of the history of radicalism within the national Republican party. In some important ways, the fortunes of the anticaste radicals did parallel those of the radical Republicans. Both groups believed deeply in achieving the goal of racial equality. Both groups were radical minorities operating within conservative/moderate organizations, and for a time both groups enjoyed unusual influence and prominence because of an unusual set of external circumstances. When the principles of the radicals no longer seemed to further the interests of their national organizations, those principles were abandoned and the radicals themselves returned to the margins of the power structures of the Methodist denomination and the Republican party. It should be underscored that the chief spokesperson for the fight against anticaste radicalism was not an "un-Reconstructed" southern slave owner, but a white northerner from Illinois, who also served as head of the politically progressive Southern Advance Association. Erasmus Q. Fuller was a solid Northern Methodist and a loyal Republican, through and through.

As it turned out, only the new paternalists were free of illusions. They expected the least from freedom, and they were the least disappointed by subsequent events. The new paternalists did not seek protection or advancement from politics or from the North. It could be argued that collapse of Reconstruction and the rise of Booker T. Washington validated the Colored Methodist's position. But, according to a perceptive essay by Glenn Eskew, at the end of the century Lucius Holsey discovered, to his disgust, that paternalism provided no defense from the humiliation of segregation or from the terror of lynching. The bishop became a separatist and wrote that it was "impossible for the two separate and distinct races to live together in the same territory in harmonious relationship."[1] Nevertheless, the institutionalization of the Gospel of Freedom and of anticaste radicalism in southern churches and denominational schools may have helped the descendants of the freedpeople keep faith in themselves and in the ideals that eventually fueled the Freedom Movement of the 1960s.

This study has focused on a particular moment in history when denominational choices had a significance they had not had before, and have not had since. In time, the distinctions between Methodist denominations became less clear and less important. In 1939, the M.E. Church, South, united with the M.E. Church to form the Methodist Church. At the same time that the reunion between Northern and Southern Methodism took place, the black congregations and conferences of the M.E. denomination were set apart in a separate administrative unit called the Central Jurisdiction. From 1964 to 1968, with the civil rights movement as a backdrop, the Central Jurisdiction was gradually abolished. As a result, black conferences were dismantled and black churches were administratively integrated into what became the United Methodist Church. In 1954, the Colored Methodist Episcopal Church changed its name to the Christian Methodist Episcopal Church. The change of name was an important symbolic statement, but it did not signify a significant change in the makeup of the denomination's membership. Finally, African Methodists are still African Methodists, and they are still preaching the gospel in two separate denominations. Since the mid-1960s, all Methodist denominations have been participants in the Consultation on Church Union, which has as its ultimate goal the union of all the major Protestant denominations in the United States.[2]

This case study of Methodism and the meaning of freedom suggests that similar questions can be asked of other denominations to gain additional perspectives on the battle of ideas that engaged the black South during emancipation. Studies comparing Baptists and Episcopalians, as one example, could help illuminate important issues of class, status, culture, and community. If elusive membership lists from black Methodist churches can be found from this period in sufficient number for meaningful comparative studies, they will open up a whole new range of investigations concerning the demographics and attitudes of the laity. Of particular importance would be the information such studies could provide about the key roles played by black women in the church and in society during the upheavals of this period. It is obvious that the freedwomen must have played crucial roles in determining denominational choices and in shaping denominational values as their race went through the process of emancipation. Using a time frame larger than the period of emancipation, Jualynne Dodson has chronicled the unsuccessful struggles of women preachers to secure ordination from the A.M.E. Church during the nineteenth century. In addition, Evelyn Brooks Higginbotham and Kathleen C. Berkeley have shown some of the ways in which black women have shaped and carried out the social reform agenda of the black church. Finally, Sara J. Duncan's *Progressive Missions in the South* (1906) would be a useful starting point for a study focused specifically on African Methodist women and reform. In 1898 Ms. Duncan was appointed general superintendent of the Women's Home and Foreign Missionary Society of the A.M.E. Church, an organization that had been organized five years earlier by Bishop Henry M. Turner. Toward the end of her book she wrote: "In presenting this little volume to the public, my wish is that there be some inspiration left in the hearts of the dear women and girls of my race into whose hands it may chance to fall."[3]

Here I have explored and clarified some of the ways in which freedom was perceived and pursued. This book suggests that far from having their independence circumscribed by the complex reciprocal relationships of a paternalistic "hegemony," most Methodists who had been slaves seem to have eagerly embraced black leadership and northern ideas. On the eve of the Civil War, all of the slaves who were Methodists were already members of the Southern Methodist Church and the objects of its paternal care. Remaining in the Southern Methodist paternalistic tradition was the only denominational choice that did not require the freedpeople to take action of any sort. All things being equal, Southern Methodism should have had a distinct advantage in the competition for black membership, but most black Methodists just walked away from paternalism as soon as it was possible for them to do so. This study has also tried to explain why a much smaller, yet still significant, number of freedpeople, who were just as intent on securing the fruits of freedom, rejected northern ideas and attitudes and cleaved to the old familiar strategies and traditions that they associated with paternalism.[4]

In addition, this volume has provided a different perspective on the complexity of the relationships that existed between segments of the black population. It offers a way of delving into the battle of ideas that raged among emancipationists, without simplistically reducing that complex internal debate to a straightforward contest between "radicals" and "conservatives," or even more problematically to a struggle between representatives of progressive and nonprogressive "classes." The story told here has also shown some of the factors that complicated efforts to forge an alliance between blacks and northern whites. Perhaps most important, an effort has been made here to demonstrate why churches and preachers ought not be relegated to the sidelines in the current scholarly investigations of emancipation. Of course, electoral politics and economics can tell us a great deal, but they cannot explain some of the things that lay near the core of how the freedpeople made sense of existence after emancipation.

I have attempted no theological analyses of the spiritual component of the missionaries' work, but it is difficult not to be moved by the faith that motivated and sustained them. Theirs is a story of struggle and sacrifice and commitment and courage of heroic dimensions. The mission to the freedpeople was an American epic. With all of that, it still seems appropriate to end this book with an observation that was made by H. Richard Niebuhr in the concluding chapter of *The Social Sources of Denominationalism:*

> Denominational Christianity, that is a Christianity which surrenders its leadership to the social forces of national and economic life, offers no hope to the divided world. Lacking an integrating ethic, lacking a universal appeal, it continues to follow the fortunes of the world, gaining petty victories in a war it has long lost. From it the world can expect none of the prophetic guidance it requires in its search for synthesis.[5]

CHRONOLOGY

(AME = African Methodist Episcopal; AMEZ = African Methodist Episcopal Zion; CME = Colored Methodist Episcopal; GOVT = U.S. government; ME = Methodist Episcopal; MES = Methodist Episcopal Church, South)

1861

May 24: (GOVT) Gen. Benjamin Butler at Fortress Monroe, Virginia, proclaims refugees from slavery to be "contraband of war."

August 6: (GOVT) First Confiscation Act decrees that slaves used in Confederate war effort will be claimed as U.S. government property.

August 30: (GOVT) Gen. John C. Freemont proclaims freedom for the slaves of disloyal Missourians.

September 11: (GOVT) President Lincoln countermands Freemont's freedom proclamation.

1862

January: (ME) Rev. Mansfield French begins work with the freedpeople in Port Royal, South Carolina.

April 16: (GOVT) Congress emancipates slaves in the District of Columbia and appropriates funds to colonize them outside the United States.

May 9: (GOVT) Gen. David Hunter proclaims freedom for all slaves in South Carolina, Georgia, and Florida.

May 19: (GOVT) Lincoln countermands Gen. Hunter's freedom proclamation.

(GOVT) Lincoln proposes gradual emancipation for the border states.

June 19: (GOVT) Congress bans slavery from the territories.

July 12: (GOVT) Lincoln again proposes gradual emancipation.

July 17: (GOVT) Second Confiscation Act proclaims freedom for slaves of all active supporters of the Confederacy.

September 22: (GOVT) Lincoln issues Preliminary Provisional Emancipation Proclamation and supports proposal to colonize blacks outside the United States.

1863

January 1: (GOVT) Emancipation Proclamation goes into effect, declaring all slaves in the Confederacy free and authorizing enlistment of black troops.

March 10: (AME) AME denomination purchases Wilberforce University (Xenia, Ohio) from ME denomination.

May 20: (AME) Revs. James D. S. Hall and James Lynch depart from New York harbor to undertake mission work in South Carolina.

December 8: (GOVT) Lincoln announces "ten percent plan" for Reconstruction.

1864

January: (AMEZ) Rev. James Walker Hood begins missionary work in New Bern, North Carolina.

May: (ME) General Conference of Northern Methodism reverses racially exclusionary tradition and adopts plan to ordain black ministers in two newly created black conferences.

July 2: (GOVT) Wade-Davis Bill passed.

July 8: (GOVT) Lincoln announces pocket veto of Wade-Davis Bill.

July 29: (ME) Organization of the Delaware Conference for black Northern Methodist ministers.

October 27: (ME) Organization of the Washington Conference for black Northern Methodist ministers.

December 17: (AMEZ) Organization of the North Carolina Conference.

1865

March 3: (GOVT) Freedmen's Bureau established.

(SECULAR) Freedmen's Saving and Trust Company chartered.

March 13: (AMEZ) Organization of Louisiana Conference.

April 14: (GOVT) Assassination of Lincoln.

May 15: (AME) Organization of South Carolina Conference.

May 29: (GOVT) President Johnson announces his plan for "restoration" of southern states.

November 1: (AME) Organization of the Louisiana Conference.

December 4: (GOVT) Congress refuses to recognize representatives from Johnson governments.

December 13: (GOVT) Congress establishes the Joint Committee on Reconstruction.

December 18: (GOVT) Ratification of the Thirteenth Amendment making slavery unconstitutional.

December 25: (ME) Organization of the Mississippi Mission Conference.

1866

April 9: (GOVT) Passage of the Civil Rights Bill, conferring basic rights of citizenship, excluding the franchise.

April 20: (CME) General Conference of the Southern Methodist Church adopts plan for the ordination of black ministers and the formation of the Colored Methodist denomination.

April 23: (ME) Organization of the South Carolina Mission Conference.

May 1: (SECULAR) Antiblack riot takes place in Memphis.
June 6: (AMEZ) Organization of the Kentucky Conference.
July 30: (SECULAR) Antiblack riot takes place in New Orleans.
October: (AMEZ) Organization of the Virginia Conference.
October 11: (ME) Organization of the Tennessee Mission Conference.

1867

January 3: (ME) Organization of the Texas Mission Conference.
(ME) Organization of the Virginia and North Carolina Mission Conference.
March 2: (GOVT) Passage of the first Congressional Reconstruction Act.
March 22: (GOVT) Passage of the second Congressional Reconstruction Act.
March 24: (AMEZ) Organization of the South Carolina Conference.
March 29: (ME) Rev. James Lynch leaves AME denomination and affiliates with the ME denomination.
April 3: (AMEZ) Organization of the Alabama Conference.
May 10: (AME) Organization of the Virginia Conference.
May 30: (AME) Organization of the Georgia Conference.
June 8: (AME) Organization of the Florida Conference.
June 15: (AMEZ) Organization of the Georgia Conference.
July 19: (GOVT) Passage of the third Congressional Reconstruction Act.
October 10: (ME) Organization of the Georgia Mission Conference.
October 17: (ME) Organization of the Alabama Mission Conference.
November 20–24: (CME) Organization of the Memphis Colored Conference.

1868

February 24: (GOVT) Johnson impeached.
March 11: (GOVT) Passage of the fourth Congressional Reconstruction Act.
May: (ME) General Conference gives permission for the Kentucky Conference to divide along racial lines.
June 25: (GOVT) Alabama, Florida, Louisiana, North Carolina, and South Carolina readmitted to the Union.
July 25: (AME) Organization of the Alabama Conference.
July 28: (GOVT) Ratification of the Fourteenth Amendment, conferring state and federal citizenship on "all persons born or naturalized in the United States."
August 11: (GOVT) Death of Rep. Thaddeus Stevens of Pennsylvania, prominent "radical" emancipationist.
October 1: (AME) Organization of the Mississippi Conference.
October 6: (AMEZ) Organization of the Tennessee Conference.
October 17: (ME) Assassination of black minister and politician Benjamin Franklin Randolph in South Carolina.
November 19: (AME) Organization of the Arkansas Conference.
November 20: (CME) Organization of the Kentucky Colored Conference.

1869

January 6: (CME) Organization of the Georgia Colored Conference.
January 7–9: (CME) Organization of the Mississippi Colored Conference.

April 22: (AMEZ) Organization of the Florida Conference.

October: (AMEZ) Organization of the West Tennessee and Mississippi Conference.

October 4: (GOVT) Biracial Republican government defeated in Tennessee.

November 25–29: (CME) Organization of the Alabama Colored Conference.

1870

January 26: (GOVT) Virginia readmitted to the Union.

February 23: (GOVT) Mississippi readmitted to the Union.

February 25: (ME) Rev. Hiram Revels of Mississippi becomes the first black U.S. Senator.

March 30: (GOVT) Texas readmitted to the Union.

March 30: (GOVT) Ratification of the Fifteenth Amendment, establishing the right to vote regardless of "race, color or previous condition of servitude."

July 15: (GOVT) Georgia readmitted to the Union.

November 2: (CME) Organization of the Texas Colored Conference.

November 3: (GOVT) Biracial Republican government defeated in North Carolina.

December 12: (GOVT) Joseph H. Rainey of South Carolina becomes the first black to serve in the U.S. House of Representatives.

December 16: (CME) Inaugural session of the General Conference of the CME denomination takes place in Jackson, Tennessee.

December 21: (CME) William Henry Miles and Richard H. Vanderhorst become the first bishops of the CME denomination.

1871

November 1: (GOVT) Biracial Republican government defeated in Georgia.

1872

May: (ME) The General Conference refuses to grant requests from the South for permission to form racially segregated Conferences.

(ME) Rev. Gilbert Haven, prominent anticaste radical from Massachusetts, elected bishop and assigned to preside over Southern Conferences.

July 18: (CME) Death of Bishop Vanderhorst after illness.

December 18: (ME) Death of Rev. James Lynch at age thirty-three after illness.

1873

January 14: (GOVT) Biracial Republican government defeated in Texas.

March 4: (AME) Rev. Richard H. Cain of South Carolina becomes member of the 43rd U.S. Congress.

March 22: (CME) Joseph H. Beebe, Lucius H. Holsey, and Isaac Lane elected bishops at special session of the General Conference.

1874

March 11: (GOVT) Death of Sen. Charles Sumner of Massachusetts, prominent "radical" emancipationist.

November 10: (GOVT) Biracial Republican government defeated in Arkansas.

November 14: (GOVT) Biracial Republican government defeated in Alabama.

1875

March 1: (GOVT) Passage of the Civil Rights Act establishing the legal right of equal access to public accommodations.

November 3: (GOVT) Biracial Republican government defeated in Mississippi.

1876

May: (ME) The General Conference permits racial division in Southern conferences, except when separation is opposed by a majority of black ministers. Alabama, Georgia, and West Texas Conferences divide before the end of the year, and other conferences follow suit. By 1880 only Louisiana, Mississippi, and South Carolina remain "integrated" through the presence of a few white ministers.

1877

February 26: (GOVT) "Compromise of 1877" negotiations begin, ultimately resulting in a presidential pledge of nonintervention in southern politics.

March 4: (AME) Rev. R. H. Cain of South Carolina becomes a member of the 45th U.S. Congress.

March 5: (GOVT) Inauguration of President Rutherford B. Hayes.

April 10: (GOVT) Withdrawal of federal troops from South Carolina.

April 24: (GOVT) Withdrawal of federal troops from Louisiana.

1878

April 4: (AME) AME missionaries give their support to 206 disillusioned black emigrants who depart from Charleston harbor for Liberia.

1880

January 3: (ME) Bishop Gilbert Haven dies after illness.

May 14: (AME) Revs. Richard H. Cain and Henry M. Turner elected bishops.

1883

January 19: (CME) Incorporation of Paine Institute (later to become Paine College) in Augusta, Georgia.

October 15: (GOVT) Supreme Court declares the Civil Rights Act of 1875 unconstitutional.

1895

September 18: (SECULAR) Booker T. Washington delivers the "Atlanta Compromise" Address, advocating both black accommodation to white racial attitudes and black uplift through basic economic development.

1896

May 6: (GOVT) In *Plessy v. Ferguson,* the Supreme Court gives approval to racial segregation by pronouncing the doctrine of "separate but equal."

NOTES

INTRODUCTION

1 W. E. B. Du Bois, *The Souls of Black Folk* (New York: Penguin, 1989), 6–7.

2 George P. Rawick, ed., *The American Slave: A Composite Autobiography,* vol. 10, supplement, series 1, part 5: *Mississippi Narratives* (Westport, Conn.: Greenwood Press, 1977).

3 Ira Berlin et al., eds., *Freedom: A Documentary History of Emancipation, 1861–1867,* vol. 2, series 1: *The Destruction of Slavery* (Cambridge, U.K.: Cambridge University Press, 1985); Berlin et al., *Slaves No More: Three Essays on Emancipation and the Civil War* (Cambridge, U.K.: Cambridge University Press, 1992); William Cohen, *At Freedom's Edge: Black Mobility and the Southern White Quest for Racial Control, 1861–1915* (Baton Rouge: Louisiana State University Press, 1991); Seymour Drescher and Frank McGlynn, eds., *The Meaning of Freedom: Economics, Politics, and Culture after Slavery* (Pittsburgh, Pa.: University of Pittsburgh Press, 1992); Russell Duncan, *Freedom's Shore: Tunis Campbell and the Georgia Freedmen* (Athens: University of Georgia Press, 1986); Robert F. Engs, *Freedom's First Generation: Black Hampton, Virginia, 1861–1890* (Philadelphia: University of Pennsylvania Press, 1979); Barbara Jeanne Fields, *Slavery and Freedom on the Middle Ground: Maryland during the Nineteenth Century* (New Haven, Conn.: Yale University Press, 1985); Eric Foner, *Nothing but Freedom: Emancipation and Its Legacy* (Baton Rouge: Louisiana State University Press, 1983); Leon F. Litwack, *Been in the Storm So Long: The Aftermath of Slavery* (New York: Alfred A. Knopf, 1979); Edward Magdol, *A Right to the Land* (Westport, Conn.: Greenwood Press, 1977); Jay R. Mandle, *Not Slave, Not Free: The African American Economic Experience since the Civil War* (Durham, N.C.: Duke University Press, 1992); Clarence L. Mohr, *On the Threshold of Freedom: Masters and Slaves in Civil War Georgia* (Athens: University of Georgia Press, 1986); Roger L. Ransom and Richard Sutch, *One Kind of Freedom: The Economic Consequences of Emancipation* (Cambridge: Cambridge University Press, 1977). Two path-breaking studies of emancipation in the

Caribbean have been written: see Thomas C. Holt, *The Problem of Freedom: Race, Labor, and Politics in Jamaica and Britain, 1832–1938* (Baltimore: Johns Hopkins University Press, 1992), and Rebecca J. Scott, *Slave Emancipation in Cuba: The Transition to Free Labor, 1860–1899* (Princeton, N.J.: Princeton University Press, 1985).

4   William E. Montgomery, *Under Their Own Vine and Fig Tree: The African-American Church in the South, 1865–1900* (Baton Rouge: Louisiana State University Press, 1993), xi–xii; Thomas C. Holt, *Black over White: Negro Political Leadership in South Carolina during Reconstruction* (Urbana: University of Illinois Press, 1977), 80–91; Peter Kolchin, *First Freedom: The Responses of Alabama's Blacks to Emancipation and Reconstruction* (Westport, Conn.: Greenwood Press, 1972), 107–27; Alrutheus A. Taylor, *The Negro in the Reconstruction of Virginia* (Washington, D.C.: Association for the Study of Negro Life and History, 1926), 174–207; Vernon L. Wharton, *The Negro in Mississippi, 1865–1890* (Chapel Hill: University of North Carolina Press, 1947), 256–65; George B. Tindall, *South Carolina Negroes, 1877–1900* (Columbia: University of South Carolina Press, 1952), 186–208; Joel Williamson, *After Slavery: The Negro in South Carolina during Reconstruction, 1861–1877* (New York: W. W. Norton, 1975), 180–208. It should be noted that Williamson's chapter on the church stands out because of the thoughtful and serious way in which he explores the subject. Even more of an exception because of its thorough and thoughtful treatment of the church is James M. McPherson's, *The Abolitionist Legacy: From Reconstruction to the NAACP* (Princeton, N.J.: Princeton University Press, 1975), 148–57, 222–43, 262–74.

5   Eric Foner, *Reconstruction: America's Unfinished Revolution, 1863–1877* (New York: Harper and Row, 1988), 88–95, quotations from pp. xxiv, 93.

6   Litwack, *Been in the Storm So Long*, 450–71.

7   Ralph E. Morrow, *Northern Methodism and Reconstruction* (East Lansing: Michigan State University Press, 1956); Clarence E. Walker, *A Rock in a Weary Land: The African Methodist Episcopal Church during the Civil War and Reconstruction* (Baton Rouge: Louisiana State University Press, 1982).

8   Montgomery, *Their Own Vine and Fig Tree*, esp. 1–141.

9   E. Franklin Frazier, *The Negro Church in America* (New York: Schocken Books, 1963), 1–9; Albert J. Raboteau, *Slave Religion: The "Invisible Institution" in the Antebellum South* (New York: Oxford University Press, 1978).

10   Robert L. Hall, " 'Yonder Come Day': Religious Dimensions of the Transition from Slavery to Freedom in Florida," *Florida Historical Quarterly* 65 (April 1987): 418; Montgomery, *Their Own Vine and Fig Tree*, 254; Wilbert Lee Jenkins, "Chaos, Conflict and Control: The Responses of the Newly-Freed Slaves in Charleston, South Carolina to Emancipation and Reconstruction, 1865–1877" (Ph.D. diss., Michigan State University, 1993), 264–65.

11   Readers seeking general information about emancipation and Reconstruction should consult the following: John Hope Franklin, *The Emancipation Proclamation* (Garden City, N.Y.: Doubleday, 1963); Franklin, *Reconstruction after the Civil War* (Chicago: University of Chicago Press, 1961); Foner, *Reconstruction;* James M. McPherson, *The Struggle for Equality: Abolitionists and the Negro in the Civil War and Reconstruction* (Princeton, N.J.: Princeton University Press, 1964); Michael Perman, *Emancipation and Reconstruction, 1862–1879* (Arlington Heights, Ill.: Harlan Davidson, 1987); Emma

Lou Thornbrough, ed., *Black Reconstructionists* (Englewood Cliffs, N.J.: Prentice-Hall, 1972).

12 Montgomery, *Their Own Vine and Fig Tree*, 33, 307.

13 Traditional accounts tend to suggest that the founding of the C.M.E. denomination should be regarded as the southern equivalent of what happened when the African Methodist denominations declared their independence from the Methodist Episcopal Church in the North. While it is clear that blacks did take much of the initiative in the effort to establish a separate Colored Methodist church, it is also true that white Southern Methodists organized the first Colored Methodist conferences, ordained and licensed the first Colored Methodist ministers, and presided over the first sessions of the inaugural C.M.E. General Conference. Southern whites also edited the C.M.E. newspaper and served as presidents of C.M.E. schools. The best and most important traditional accounts of the history of the C.M.E. Church have been written by a bishop of that denomination. See Othal H. Lakey, *The Rise of "Colored Methodism": A Study of the Background and the Beginnings of the Christian Methodist Episcopal Church* (Dallas: Crescendo Book Publications, 1972), and Lakey, *The History of the C.M.E. Church* (Memphis: C.M.E. Publishing, 1985). My own thinking on the subject was influenced greatly by William B. Gravely, "The Social, Political and Religious Significance of the Formation of the Colored Methodist Episcopal Church (1870)," *Methodist History* 18 (October 1979): 3–25.

14 Donald G. Mathews, *Slavery and Methodism: A Chapter in American Morality, 1780–1845* (Princeton, N.J.: Princeton University Press, 1965), vii–viii; James M. Washington, *Frustrated Fellowship: The Black Baptist Quest for Social Power* (Macon, Ga.: Mercer University Press, 1986), 49–131; David O. Moore, "The Withdrawal of Blacks from Southern Baptist Churches following Emancipation," *Baptist History and Heritage* (July 1981): 12–18; J. Carleton Hayden, "After the War: The Mission and Growth of the Episcopal Church among Blacks in the South, 1865–1877," *Historical Magazine of the Protestant Episcopal Church* 42 (December 1973): 403–27; Joe M. Richardson, "The Failure of the American Missionary Association to Expand Congregationalism among Southern Blacks," *Southern Studies* 18 (Spring 1979): 51–73; and Richardson, *Christian Reconstruction: The American Missionary Association and Southern Blacks, 1861–1890* (Athens: University of Georgia Press, 1986).

METHODIST DENOMINATIONS REFERRED TO IN THIS BOOK

1 1822 was the year in which Zion Methodism became an independently governed denomination with ordained black superintendents. A historic preliminary meeting took place in June of the previous year, and for that reason some sources say that the A.M.E. Zion Church was founded in 1821.

1 SOUTHERN METHODIST PATERNALISM, OLD AND NEW

1 Othal H. Lakey, *The History of the C.M.E. Church* (Memphis: C.M.E. Publishing, 1985), 145–46, 431.

2 Both quotations are by Rev. William Martin and are from Harrison, *Gospel among the Slaves*, 256–61. For a thoughtful analysis of the social status of early Southern Methodists, see Donald G. Mathews, *Religion in the Old South* (Chicago: University of Chicago Press, 1977), 35–38. For a graphic account of the "persecutions and fiery trials" that beset

Methodist pioneers in the Carolinas, including the successful efforts of Henry Evans, a free black, to establish Methodism in Fayetteville, N.C., see William P. Harrison, ed., *The Gospel among the Slaves: A Short Account of Missionary Operations among the African Slaves of the Southern States* (Nashville: Publishing House of the M.E. Church, South, 1893), 142–43; Thomas A. Smoot, "Early Methodism on the Lower Cape Fear," in *Historical Papers of the North Carolina Conference Historical Society. . . . 1925* (Greensboro: North Carolina Christian Advocate, 1925), 13–19; William M. Wightman, *Life of William Capers D.D., One of the Bishops of the Methodist Episcopal Church, South, Including an Autobiography* (Nashville: Southern Methodist Publishing, 1858), 124–27; Carter G. Woodson, *The History of the Negro Church,* 3rd ed. (Washington, D.C.: Associated Publishers, 1972), 47–48. See also Francis Asbury Mood, *Methodism in Charleston: A Narrative of the Chief Events relating to the Rise and Progress of the Methodist Episcopal Church in Charleston, S.C.* (Nashville: E. Stevenson and J. E. Evans, 1856), 181–85; John O. Willson, *Sketch of the Methodist Church in Charleston, S.C., 1787–1887* (Charleston, 1888), 21–22. Membership figures are from Donald G. Mathews, *Slavery and Methodism: A Chapter in American Morality, 1780–1845* (Princeton, N.J.: Princeton University Press, 1965), 68. In addition, see Greensboro *Weekly Message,* 12 March 1860.

3 Antebellum black preachers who were not associated with the mission to plantations played an important role in the spread of Christianity in general and of Methodism in particular. For information concerning their significance, see Albert J. Raboteau, *Slave Religion: The "Invisible Institution" in the Antebellum South* (New York: Oxford University Press, 1978), 135–37, and Woodson, *History of the Negro Church,* 34–49, 58–60. Re the Methodist Episcopal mission to the slaves, see Harrison, *Gospel among the Slaves,* 137, 181, 196, 283, 297, and Milton C. Sernett, *Black Religion and American Evangelism: White Protestants, Plantation Missions, and the Flowering of Negro Christianity, 1787–1865* (Metuchen, N.J.: Scarecrow Press, 1975), 37, 41, 46, 293–94; Wightman, *Life of Capers,* 291–92.

4 Quotation from Harrison, *Gospel among the Slaves,* 310; statistics ibid., 325. See also C. C. Goen, *Broken Churches, Broken Nation: Denominational Schisms and the Coming of the American Civil War* (Macon, Ga.: Mercer University Press, 1985), 81–89; A. H. Redford, *History of the Organization of the Methodist Episcopal Church, South* (Nashville: Published by A. H. Redford, Agent for the M.E. Church, South, 1871). See also *Annual Report of the Board of Missions of the Methodist Episcopal Church, South, June 1, 1876* (Nashville: Southern Methodist Publishing, 1876), 3, 14: Albert M. Shipp, *History of American Methodism in South Carolina* (Nashville: Southern Methodist Publishing, 1884), 449–63.

5 Quotations from Harrison, *Gospel among the Slaves,* 143, 247–48. See also Wightman, *Life of Capers,* 294–95.

6 *Southern Christian Advocate* [hereafter SCA], 26 April 1859; Harrison, *Gospel among the Slaves,* 151–52, 186, 217, 242, 291. See also Greensboro *Weekly Message,* 2 March 1860; John Spencer Basset, "North Carolina Methodism and Slavery," *An Annual Publication of Historical Papers Published by the Historical Society of Trinity College, Durham, N.C.,* Series 4 (1900), 10; Brantley York, *The Autobiography of Brantley York* (Durham, N.C.: Seeman Printery, 1910), 108.

7   Mathews, *Religion*, 144. See also Harrison, *Gospel among the Slaves*, 240; *SCA*, 26 January 1865; *Raleigh Christian Advocate*, 3 June 1863.

8   Capers's quotation from Wightman, *Life of Capers*, 296. See also Harrison, *Gospel among the Slaves*, 220–21, 246–47, 283, 291–92.

9   *Annual Report of the Missionary Society of the S.C. Conference [M.E. Church, South]*, *December 14, 1861*, 34; Harrison, *Gospel among the Slaves*, 233–58; Mathews, *Religion*, 149–50; Wightman, *Life of Capers*, 291–92.

10   The Mission Church referred to here was organized by the South Carolina Annual Conference in December 1863 upon the recommendation of Rev. Mood. He proposed that the black members of the Methodist churches in Charleston be "thrown together as one charge" in an edifice that would be "out of reach of the shells." Mood, "Autobiography" [n.d.], TMs, 126, Manuscripts Department, South Caroliniana Library, University of South Carolina, Columbia, S.C.

11   Ibid., 125–26.

12   Ibid., 121; Mason Crum, "What Became of the Negro Membership?" [n.d.], TMs, 2–6, Manuscripts Department, Perkins Library, Duke University, Durham, N.C.

13   Percentages based on membership figures in Lakey, *History*, 105, 108; quotation in *SCA*, 9 February 1865.

14   Daniel W. Stowell, " 'We Have Sinned, and God Has Smitten Us!' John H. Caldwell and the Religious Meaning of Confederate Defeat," *Georgia Historical Quarterly* 78 (Spring 1994): 4–5.

15   Quotations from *SCA*, 5 January 1865. See also Clarence L. Mohr, *On the Threshold of Freedom: Masters and Slaves in Civil War Georgia* (Athens: University of Georgia Press, 1986), 262–64; George F. Pierce, "Sermon of Bishop Pierce before the State Assembly of Georgia, March 27, 1863," in George B. Smith, *The Life and Times of George Foster Pierce, D.D., LL.D. Bishop of the Methodist Episcopal Church, South* (Sparta, Ga.: Hancock Publishing, 1888), 475.

16   *SCA*, 5 January 1865.

17   S.C. Missionary Society quoted in *SCA*, 30 November 1865; Georgia Conference quoted in *SCA*, 23 November 1865; *New Orleans Christian Advocate*, 5 April 1866. See also a strongly worded letter by Bishop G. F. Pierce in which he instructed Methodist clergymen to stand by their posts "both among whites and blacks," *SCA*, 31 August 1865; Pierce, "Sermon," 471; *Minutes of the South Carolina Annual Conference of the Methodist Episcopal Church, South, 1865*, 14; Hunter D. Farish, *The Circuit Rider Dismounts: A Social History of Southern Methodism, 1865–1900* (Richmond: Dietz Press, 1938; reprinted, New York: Da Capo Press, 1969), 162–68; Harrison, *Gospel among the Slaves*, 303, 313. Some whites were not displeased by the departure of black members, see *SCA*, 28 September 1865; William B. Gravely, "The Social, Political and Religious Significance of the Formation of the Colored Methodist Episcopal Church (1870)," *Methodist History* 18 (October 1979): 6.

18   I am much indebted to the analyses of the significance of "place" and "order" in southern society that appear in Mathews, *Religion*, 177 and passim, and in Joel Williamson, *The Crucible of Race: Black-White Relations in the American South since Emancipation* (New York: Oxford University Press, 1984), 28–35, 70–80, and passim.

19   *SCA*, 13 April 1866.

20   The efforts of some white Southern Methodists to mount an educational mission to the freedpeople probably merit greater attention than they have received thus far in the literature on Reconstruction. Southern evangelicals frequently commented on the need to establish both "Sabbath" and "day" schools, under white supervision. See *SCA* for the following: "Montgomery Conference," 14 December 1865; "Virginia Conference," 21 December 1865; "Committee on Interests of Colored People, Report 1," 27 April 1866; "District Conference, Athens District, Ga.," 21 September 1866; "Morven District Meeting, Florida Conference," 9 November 1866; "Griffin District Meeting," 20 September 1867; "Augusta [Ga.] District Meeting," 25 September 1868. See also "Minutes of the Salisbury, N.C. District Conference, 1868–1877," 1869 (Bound, Hw.), 50–51, Manuscripts Department, Perkins Library, Duke University, Durham, N.C.

21   *SCA*, 27 April 1866. Parentheses added for clarity.

22   *SCA*, 1 June 1866.

23   For a discussion of the black input into the proposal to establish a separate denomination, see Orthal H. Lakey, *The Rise of "Colored Methodism": A Study of the Background and the Beginnings of the Christian Methodist Episcopal Church* (Dallas: Crescendo Book Publications, 1972), 67–70. For an account of the brief debate on the proposal that took place at the General Conference, see *SCA*, 4 May 1866. See also Gravely, "Social . . . Significance," 10–12, and Lakey, *History*, 132–38. Evans quotation from *SCA*, 15 June 1866.

24   *SCA*, 4 May 1866.

25   Ibid.

26   See *SCA* for: "Augusta District Meeting of Colored Members," 27 November 1868; "Augusta Colored District Meeting, M.E. Church, South," 12 November 1869; "Colored Annual Conference," 5 July 1867; "The Colored Conferences," 13 November 1868; "Memphis Colored Conference," 4 December 1863; "Georgia Annual Conference of the M.E. Church, South (Colored)," 15 January 1869; "The Georgia Conference for Colored People," 22 January 1869; "The Colored Conferences," 1 October 1869; "The Tennessee Colored Conference," 15 October 1869; "Colored Georgia Annual Conference, M.E. Church, South," 24 December 1869. See also Lakey, *History*, 151–63.

27   *SCA*, 24 August 1866.

28   Paine quotation from *SCA*, 5 July 1867. North Carolina Annual Conference, "Conference Journal, 1867–1873," 1869 (Bound Hw.), 129–30, Manuscripts Department, Perkins Library, Duke University, Durham, N.C.

29   John W. Cromwell, "'The Aftermath of Nat Turner's Insurrection," *Journal of Negro History* 5 (April 1920): 218–19, 230–33; Reginald F. Hildebrand, "'An Imperious Sense of Duty': Documents Illustrating an Episode in the Methodist Reaction to the Nat Turner Revolt," *Methodist History* 19 (April 1981): 155–74; *SCA*, 23 November 1866, 31 May 1867.

30   *SCA*, 4 May 1866, 25 May 1866, 15 June 1866, 29 June 1866, 20 July 1866; Gravely, "Social . . . Significance," 12–19; Lakey, *History*, 138–43.

31   *SCA*, 9 November 1866, 18 September 1868.

32   *SCA*, 13 November 1868; Paine quotation from *Episcopal Methodist* (Raleigh), 14 October 1868. See also North Carolina Annual Conference, "Conference Journal, 1867–1873," 1869, 39–40 and Gravely, "Social . . . Significance," 20.

33   *SCA*, 15 January 1869; *Episcopal Methodist* (Raleigh), 10 February 1869.

34   Lakey notes that the idea to establish the newspaper was first put forward by the Memphis Colored Conference at its inaugural meeting in 1867. See Lakey, *Rise*, 102–4. The first editorial of the *Christian Index* was reprinted in *SCA*, 17 December 1869. See also *SCA*, 1 February 1871; *Episcopal Methodist* (Raleigh), 6 October 1869, 2 February 1870, 25 January 1871, 1 February 1871; *Raleigh Christian Advocate*, 21 January 1874, 7 April 1875.

35   *SCA*, 17 December 1869.

36   In 1871 there were 7,841 black Southern Methodists. As late as 1880 there were still 1,081 black members. *Minutes of the Annual Conferences of the Methodist Episcopal Church, South: 1871* (Nashville: Southern Methodist Publishing, 1872), 642; ibid., *1880* (Nashville: Southern Methodist Publishing, 1881), 250; Lakey, *Rise*, 78; Lakey, *History*, 191–219; *SCA*, 25 January 1871.

37   *SCA*, 25 January 1871.

2   COLORED METHODISM AND THE NEW PATERNALISM

1   Quotation from Lucius H. Holsey, *Autobiography, Sermons, Addresses and Essays of Bishop L. H. Holsey, D.D.* (Atlanta: Franklin Printing and Publishing, 1898), 25. See also Hunter D. Farish, *The Circuit Rider Dismounts: A Social History of Southern Methodism, 1865–1900* (Richmond: Dietz Press, 1938; reprint, New York: Da Capo Press, 1969), 173–74; Isaac Lane, *The Autobiography of Bishop Isaac Lane, LL.D, with a Short History of the C.M.E. Church in America and of Methodism* (Nashville: Publishing House of the M.E. Church, South, 1916), 21: Othal H. Lakey, *The History of the C.M.E. Church* (Memphis: C.M.E. Publishing, 1985), 239; Charles H. Phillips, *The History of the Colored Methodist Episcopal Church in America* (Jackson, Tenn.: Publishing House of the C.M.E. Church, 1900), 51–53, 60–61; Clarence E. Walker, *A Rock in a Weary Land: The African Methodist Episcopal Church during the Civil War and Reconstruction* (Baton Rouge: Louisiana State University Press, 1982), 103–6. Bishop Vanderhorst died in Charleston on 18 July 1872, at the age of fifty-eight after contracting pneumonia. See *Christian Recorder* (Philadelphia), 3 August 1872; *Nashville Christian Advocate*, 3 August 1872; *Texas Christian Advocate*, 7 August 1872.

2   Quotation from John B. Cade, *Holsey: The Incomparable* (New York: Pagent Press, 1964), 53. It was possible (and quite common) for antebellum white northerners to be antislavery and also be opposed to radical abolitionism and racial equality. Also, by reporting that the pronouncements of Northern Methodist missionaries were egalitarian, I am not suggesting that their denomination's policies actually were egalitarian in practice.

3   Lakey, *History*, 390, 670–71; William B. Gravely, "The Social, Political and Religious Significance of the Formation of the Colored Methodist Episcopal Church (1870)," *Methodist History* 18 (October 1979): 23; William P. Harrison, ed., *The Gospel among the Slaves: A Short Account of Missionary Operations among the African Slaves of the Southern States* (Nashville: Publishing House of the M.E. Church, South, 1893), 109, 380.

4   Holsey, *Autobiography*, 9–10; Cade, *Holsey*, 2–3; Glenn T. Eskew, "Black Elitism and the Failure of Paternalism in Postbellum Georgia: The Case of Bishop Lucius Henry Holsey," *Journal of Southern History* 58 (November 1992): 639. Other scholars, less careful than Eskew, have written that Johnson was a professor at the University of Georgia.

5   Holsey, *Autobiography*, 10–11; Eskew, "Black Elitism," 642, 646; Cade, *Holsey*, 2–3, 11.

6   Lane quotations from Harrison, *Gospel among the Slaves*, 381–82, and Lane, *Autobiography*, 48. See also Paul R. Griffin, "Black Founders of Reconstruction Era Methodist Colleges: Daniel A. Payne, Joseph C. Price and Isaac Lane, 1863–1890" (Ph.D. diss., Emory University, 1983), 17; Horace C. Savage, *Life and Times of Bishop Isaac Lane* (Nashville: National Publication Company, 1958), 33–34, 65.

7   *SCA*, 25 January 1871; *Raleigh Christian Advocate*, 25 January 1871; Lakey, *History*, 213, Harrison, *Gospel among the Slaves*, 380.

8   Lakey, *History*, 211–12; *Raleigh Christian Advocate*, 28 June 1871. The quotation from the *Trenton Gazette* is twice removed from its original source. It was first reprinted in an article that appeared in the *Christian Index*, which was in turn reprinted in the *Raleigh Christian Advocate*, 31 May 1871. Other articles in the *Raleigh Christian Advocate* described Miles as being "of yellow complexion" (25 January 1871) and "not more than one-third removed from white" (28 June 1871). A letter published in *SCA*, 25 January 1871, described him as "one fourth Caucasian." One student of Colored Methodism makes the following observation: "According to oral tradition, light skin was just as necessary for c.m.e. leadership as jet blackness was for an a.m.e. bishop. Certainly, five of the first seven c.m.e. bishops were in fact mulattoes." David M. Tucker, *Black Pastors and Leaders: Memphis, 1819–1972* (Memphis: Memphis State University Press, 1975), 20.

9   Harrison, *Gospel among the Slaves*, 382–83; Lane, *Autobiography*, 47.

10   Quotations from Harrison, *Gospel among the Slaves*, 383, and Lane, *Autobiography*, 52–53.

11   Lane, *Autobiography*, 55; Harrison, *Gospel among the Slaves*, 384.

12   Harrison, *Gospel among the Slaves*, 384.

13   Savage, *Life of Lane*, 42.

14   Lakey, *History*, 212.

15   Ibid.; William E. Montgomery, *Under Their Own Vine and Fig Tree: The African-American Church in the South, 1865–1900* (Baton Rouge: Louisiana State University Press, 1993), 121–22.

16   The introduction was written by George W. Walker, a Southern Methodist minister who became president of Paine College. See Holsey, *Autobiography*, 5. Ironically, the Turner referred to here became an a.m.e. minister and one of the chief antagonists of Colored Methodism. See also Sara J. Duncan, *Progressive Missions in the South and Addresses with Illustrations and Sketches of Missionary Workers and Ministers and Bishops' Wives* (Atlanta: Franklin Printing and Publishing, 1906), 214, and Cade, *Holsey*, 55. Holsey quotation from Harrison, *Gospel among the Slaves*, 387.

17   Harrison, *Gospel among the Slaves*, 381.

18   Othal H. Lakey, *The Rise of "Colored Methodism": A Study of the Background and Beginnings of the Christian Methodist Episcopal Church* (Dallas: Crescendo Book Publications, 1972), 110–11. Some historians have argued that Vanderhorst left the a.m.e. Church because he was moved from place to place so often. Statements made by Vanderhorst show that he also had a philosophical predilection for Colored Methodism. Stephen Ward Angell, *Bishop Henry McNeal Turner and African-American Religion in the South* (Knoxville: University of Tennessee Press, 1992), 72; *SCA*, 25 January 1871; Montgomery, *Their Own Vine and Fig Tree*, 122.

19   Quotation from Lane, *Autobiography,* 48. See also Holsey, *Autobiography,* 17–18; Harrison, *Gospel among the Slaves,* 384–86; Eskew, "Black Elitism," 640; and Savage, *Life of Lane,* 18. Griffin asserts that Cullen Lane "winked at" his son's efforts to acquire an education. See Griffin, "Black Founders." Even after becoming a bishop, Lane professed that he had feelings of inadequacy when speaking before educated audiences. See *Nashville Christian Advocate,* 6 December 1879. In 1880, Rev. C. H. Phillips became the first Colored Methodist minister to have a college education. See Charles H. Phillips, *From the Farm to the Bishopric: An Autobiography* (Nashville: Parthenon Press, 1932), 262–63. In 1910, Bishop Phillips led a reform movement that charged that the denomination suffered because of a bias against college educated ministers. See Lakey, *History,* 365–66.

20   Lakey, *History,* 212–14; Harrison, *Gospel among the Slaves,* 380–81.

21   Quotation from William L. Graham, "Patterns of Intergroup Relations in the Cooperative Establishment, Control, and Administration of Paine College (Georgia) by Southern Negro and White People: A Study of Intergroup Process" (Ph.D. diss., New York University, 1955), 36–39, quotation 37, 95. The Southern Methodist General Conference of 1866 first proposed that Colored Methodism constitute "a separate General Conference jurisdiction" that would have had no more than a "fraternal union" with the M.E. Church, South. That language was rejected specifically because it did not provide for an official link between the two denominations. The amended proposal stipulated that Colored Methodism would have "the same relation to the Southern Methodist General Conference as the Annual Conferences bear to each other." *SCA,* 4 May 1866. See also Kenneth K. Bailey, "The Post Civil War Racial Separations in Southern Protestantism: Another Look," *Church History* 46 (December 1977): 464–65; George Esmond Clary Jr., "The Founding of Paine College: A Unique Venture in Interracial Cooperation in the New South, 1882–1903" (Ed.D. diss., University of Georgia, 1965), 35; *SCA,* 4 January 1871; and Lakey, *History,* 199–202.

22   *SCA,* 25 January 1871. For a similar quotation from another pioneer Colored Methodist, see Tucker, *Black Pastors and Leaders,* 18–19.

23   Holsey, "Speech Delivered before Several Conferences of the M.E. Church, South," in Holsey, *Autobiography,* 246–47.

24   Ibid., 243–44. Studies of postemancipation paternalism, old and new, have an old and distinguished lineage. See C. Vann Woodward, *The Strange Career of Jim Crow,* 3rd ed. (New York: Oxford University Press, 1974), 47–59; George M. Frederickson, *The Black Image in the White Mind: The Debate on Afro-American Character and Destiny, 1817–1914* (New York: Harper and Row, 1971), 198–227; John David Smith, *An Old Creed for the New South: Proslavery Ideology and Historiography, 1865–1918* (Westport, Conn.: Greenwood Press, 1985), 17–67; and Joel Williamson's masterfully written, *The Crucible of Race: Black-White Relations in the American South since Emancipation* (New York: Oxford University Press, 1984), 79–93.

25   Cade, *Holsey,* 60–61, 114; Lakey, *History,* 128–29.

26   Holsey, *Autobiography,* 22. See also Harrison, *Gospel among the Slaves,* 384.

27   Rev. A. R. Spencer was the C.M.E. organizer in Talbutton, Georgia, who was quoted in *SCA,* 3 September 1869. Final quotation from *Raleigh Christian Advocate,* 12 November 1879. See also Lakey, *Rise,* 73–74, 87–88, 91; North Carolina Annual Conference,

"Conference Journal, 1874–1881," 1875 and 1876 (Bound Hw.), 88–89, 156–57, Manuscripts Department, Perkins Library, Duke University, Durham, N.C.; *Nashville Christian Advocate*, 6 December 1879; Savage, *Life of Lane*, 99–100.

28   Holsey quotation from Holsey, "The Colored Methodist Episcopal Church," in Holsey, *Autobiography*, 216; final quotation from *SCA*, 6 September 1871. The delegates to the first General Conference of the C.M.E. Church adopted the Southern Methodist rule that churches should be "plain and decent." They then added the following amendment: "and they shall, on no account be used for political assemblages or purposes." *SCA*, 25 January 1871. See also *SCA*, 18 September 1868, 1 February 1871; *Nashville Christian Advocate*, 9 March 1872; 6 December 1879; Harrison, *Gospel among the Slaves*, 384; Savage, *Life of Lane*, 154–55; Clary, "Founding of Paine College," 37. Historians have pointed out the contradiction between Southern Methodism's nonpolitical pronouncements and its support for the Confederacy. See Lewis M. Purifoy, "The Southern Methodist Church and the Proslavery Argument," *Journal of Southern History* 32 (August 1966): 333, 341. Northern missionaries also charged the southerners with being hypocritical about being nonpolitical.

29   The white pastor was Rev. William Shepherd. *Nashville Christian Advocate*, 7 September 1872.

30   Holsey quotation from Cade, *Holsey*, 84. See also Lakey, *History*, 259–60; Graham, "Patterns of Intergroup Relations," 56, 58; Lane, *Autobiography*, 81–82; and Savage, *Life of Lane*, 92–94.

31   Lane quotation from Lane, *Autobiography*, 98. See also ibid., 97–103; Lakey, *History*, 262, 449–51; Savage, *Life of Lane*, 123–26, 130.

32   Holsey quotations from Holsey, *Autobiography*, 23–24, also appearing in Holsey, "The Colored Methodist Episcopal Church," 217. See also Clary, "Founding of Paine College," 48; Eskew, "Black Elitism," 651; Cade, *Holsey*, 23–24; and Michael L. Thurmond, *A Story Untold: Black Men and Women in Athens History* (Athens, Ga.: Clarke Country School District, 1978), 126.

33   Graham, "Patterns of Intergroup Relations," 76.

34   In 1903, the president of Paine College wrote: "I welcome the type of education being given at Hampton and Tuskegee . . . but it simply happens that Paine College is working in another field." Graham, "Patterns of Intergroup Relations," 123. See also Clary, "Founding of Paine College," 85–110, esp. 113–14.

35   All quotations from Cade, *Holsey*, 85. See also Graham, "Patterns of Intergroup Relations," 59–62.

36   Graham, "Patterns of Intergroup Relations," 64–66; Cade, *Holsey*, 83–84.

37   Lakey, *History*, 262–63, 446–67; Clary, "Founding of Paine College," 7–9, 66, 91, statistics from 95, 127–28, 130, 132; Cade, *Holsey*, 83–84; Savage, *Life of Lane*, 133–34; Harold W. Mann, *Atticus Greene Haygood: Methodist Bishop, Editor and Educator* (Athens: University of Georgia Press, 1965), 190; Eskew, "Black Elitism," 649. The hardening of racial attitudes among white Evangelicals is discussed in Bailey, "Racial Separations in Southern Protestantism," 471–73.

38   Clary, "Founding of Paine College," 40.

39   Cade, *Holsey*, 102.

40   Lakey, *History*, 448; Graham, "Patterns of Intergroup Relations," 116, 125 (trustee ratios) 128; Clary, "Founding of Paine College," 81, 82, 112–13, quotation from 136–37. The

first black faculty member was John Wesley Gilbert who also earned a degree from Brown University. The white teacher who resigned in protest was C. H. Carson Jr. The second black faculty member was Charles A. Dryscoll who had studied at the New England Conservatory of Music. Enrollment figures appear in Lakey, *History,* 265.

41   For the best portrayal of the career of B. T. Washington, see Louis R. Harlan, *Booker T. Washington: The Making of a Black Leader, 1856–1901* (New York: Oxford University Press, 1972), and Harlan, *Booker T. Washington: The Wizard of Tuskegee, 1901–1915* (New York: Oxford University Press, 1983). I make this allusion to B. T. Washington to help illustrate the dynamics of the new paternalism, but I do not mean to suggest that there is a clear historical or analytical connection between Colored Methodism and Washington's accommodationism. The similarities between the two are obvious and interesting, but those approaches to race advancement had significant differences (see note 34 for one example). They were products of different time periods, and they developed in response to very different circumstances.

3   AFRICAN METHODISTS SEEK THEIR BRETHREN

1   *Minutes of the South Carolina Annual Conference of the African Methodist Episcopal Church, 1865,* reprinted in Charles Spencer Smith, *A History of the African Methodist Episcopal Church* (Philadelphia: Book Concern of the A.M.E. Church, 1922; reprint, New York: Johnson Reprint Corporation, 1968), 505–6; *Christian Recorder* (Philadelphia) [hereafter referred to as *CR*], 3 June 1865; Theophilus Gould Steward, *From 1864 to 1914: Fifty Years in the Gospel Ministry* (Philadelphia: A.M.E. Book Concern [1921]), 31–33.

2   Daniel A. Payne, *Recollections of Seventy Years* (Nashville: A.M.E. Sunday School Union, 1888; reprint, New York: Arno Press, 1969), 11–40, quotation on 39. See also Josephus Roosevelt Coan, *Daniel Alexander Payne: Christian Educator* (Philadelphia: A.M.E. Book Concern, 1935), 9–20; Richard R. Wright Jr., *The Bishops of the African Methodist Episcopal Church* (Nashville: A.M.E. Sunday School Union, 1963), 266–79; South Carolina Conference, *Minutes of the South Carolina Annual Conference of the African Methodist Episcopal Church: Twelfth Session, 1876* (Charleston, S.C.: Walker, Evans and Cogswell, 1876), 9; Harry V. Richardson, *Dark Salvation: The Story of Methodism as It Developed among Blacks in America* (Garden City, N.Y.: Doubleday, 1976), 89–90.

3   Quotation from Payne, *Recollections,* 162. See also William E. Montgomery, *Under Their Own Vine and Fig Tree: The African-American Church in the South, 1865–1900* (Baton Rouge: Louisiana State University Press, 1993), 61 (re Cain) 67–69; Clarence E. Walker, *A Rock in a Weary Land: The African Methodist Episcopal Church during the Civil War and Reconstruction* (Baton Rouge: Louisiana State University Press, 1982), 49. Both Montgomery and Walker mention that Lynch's father purchased his mother's freedom; neither suggests that James's freedom had to be purchased or won in some other way, so I am assuming that the boy was born free after his mother was freed. Both Montgomery and Walker based their accounts on Smith, *History,* 46 (re Cain) 505.

4   A copy of the *Charleston News and Courier*'s account of the proceedings of the South Carolina Conference was forwarded to the *Christian Recorder* (Philadelphia) by James Lynch and reprinted in that paper on 3 June 1865. It is probable that the account was orginally written by either James A. Handy or by Lynch himself.

5   *CR*, 3 June 1865; Montgomery, *Their Own Vine and Fig Tree*, 71.

6   Quotation was reprinted in *CR*, 3 June 1865. For reference to the title of Major Delany's lecture, see Steward, *Gospel Ministry*, 31. See also Victor Ullman, *Martin R. Delany: The Beginnings of Black Nationalism* (Boston: Beacon Press, 1971); Cyril E. Griffith, *The African Dream: Martin R. Delany and the Emergence of Pan-African Thought* (University Park: Pennsylvania State University Press, 1975); and James Theodore Holly, "In Memoriam," A.M.E. *Church Review* 3 (October 1886): 117–25.

7   Richard Allen, *The Life Experience and Gospel Labors of the Rt. Rev. Richard Allen* (Philadelphia: n.p., 1833; reprint, New York: Abingdon Press, 1960), 23–36; Charles H. Wesley, *Richard Allen: Apostle of Freedom* (Washington, D.C.: Associated Publishers, 1935), 124–52; Carol V. R. George, *Segregated Sabbaths: Richard Allen and the Emergence of Independent Black Churches, 1760–1840* (New York: Oxford University Press, 1973), 49–88.

8   Allen, *Life Experiences*, 15–36; Wesley, *Allen*, 124–57; Reginald F. Hildebrand, "Methodist Episcopal Policy on the Ordination of Black Ministers, 1784–1864," *Methodist History* 20 (April 1982): 124–25.

9   Wesley, *Allen*, 244–48; Smith, *History*, 13–47; Montgomery, *Their Own Vine and Fig Tree*, 29. For a sketch of the history and purpose of the *Repository*, see John M. Brown, "A Word to Our Subscribers and Friends," *Repository of Religion and Literature* 3 (April 1861): 49–52; Payne, *Recollections*, 56–64, 72–81, 93–94, 109–10.

10   *CR*, 28 February 1863, 14 March 1863; Stephen Ward Angell, *Bishop Henry McNeal Turner and African-American Religion in the South* (Knoxville: University of Tennessee Press, 1992), 39–40.

11   *CR*—Payne's announcement of the purchase of Wilberforce 28 March 1863; first quotation and Payne's announcement of postponement of Baltimore Conference 4 April 1863; second quotation 6 June 1863; final quotation 9 May 1863.

12   *CR*, 2 May 1863, 9 May 1863; Coan, *Payne*, 109. Turner also turned his church in Washington into a recruiting station for a regiment of colored troops. See Angell, *Turner*, 51–53, and Montgomery, *Their Own Vine and Fig Tree*, 57.

13   *CR*, quotation from 4 April 1863, 2 May 1863, 9 May 1863; Smith, *History*, 51–52; Coan, *Payne*, 109.

14   *CR*, 30 May 1863.

15   Quotations from *CR*, 30 May 1863. See also ibid., 6 June 1863; Coan, *Payne*, 109; Montgomery, *Their Own Vine and Fig Tree*, 63.

16   Walker, *Rock in a Weary Land*, 50. Rev. Rue's career as a missionary is documented in *Minutes of the New England Annual Conference of the African Methodist Episcopal Church: 1862* (New Bedford: Evening Standard Steam Printing, 1862), 9, 12, 21, and *CR*, 19 July 1862, 9 August 1862, 13 September 1862, 1 November 1862; 8 April 1865, 29 July 1865; 5 January 1867, 2 February 1867. See also Alexander W. Wayman, *Cyclopedia of African Methodism* (Baltimore: Methodist Episcopal Book Depository, 1882), 110, and Montgomery, *Their Own Vine and Fig Tree*, 59. I am indebted to Dennis C. Dickerson, the Historiographer of the A.M.E. Church, for supplying me with a copy of the minutes of the New England Conference.

17   L. S. Burkhead, "History of the Difficulties of the Pastorate of the Front Street Methodist Church, Wilmington, N.C., for the Year 1865," in *An Annual Publication of Historical*

Papers Published by the Historical Society of Trinity College, Durham, N.C., Series 8 (1908–9), 42.

18 Ibid.

19 Ibid.

20 Ibid., 98–99. Hunter's claim on the church was soon successfully contested by Rev. J. W. Hood of the A.M.E. Zion denomination. See Stephen Ward Angell, "Henry McNeal Turner and Black Religion in the South, 1865–1900" (Ph.D. diss., Vanderbilt University, 1988), 143.

21 First quotation from *CR*, 25 June 1864; second quotation from 27 May 1865.

22 Quotation from *CR*, 25 February 1865. See also ibid., 11 February 1865, 4 March 1865. For a sketch of Turner's life and career in the A.M.E. Church, see Wright, *Bishops*, 329–41. The best biography of Turner is Angell, esp. pp. 33–59; see also M. M. Ponton, *Life and Times of Henry M. Turner: The Antecedent and Preliminary History of the Life and Times of Bishop H. M. Turner* (Atlanta: A. B. Caldwell Publishing, 1917; reprint, New York: Negro Universities Press, 1970), and Montgomery, *Their Own Vine and Fig Tree*, 60.

23 The editor of the *Christian Recorder* was Rev. Elisha Weaver; the editor's quotations are from *CR*, 6 May 1865. In an article of his own that appeared in the same issue of the *Recorder,* Turner gave the details of his conquest in Raleigh. Turner quotation from *CR*, 20 January 1866; Walker, *Rock in a Weary Land*, 71–72.

24 Montgomery, *Their Own Vine and Fig Tree*, 62; Walker, *Rock in a Weary Land*, 66–67; Smith, *History*, 59.

25 William Seraile, *Voice of Dissent: Theophilus Gould Steward (1843–1924) and Black America* (Brooklyn: Carlson Publishing, 1991), 7–13; Wayman, *Encyclopedia*, 155–56; Steward, *Gospel Ministry*, (quotation) 25, 26, 339. The two other ministers who accompanied Bishop Payne to South Carolina were Reverends James A. Handy and James H. A. Johnson, both members of the Baltimore Conference. Smith, *History*, 506.

26 Seraile, *Voice of Dissent*, 13; Steward, *Gospel Ministry*, 41.

27 Steward, *Gospel Ministry*, 43.

28 Ibid., 44.

29 Ibid., 44–45.

30 First quotation from *CR*, 23 March 1867; final quotation from Steward, *Gospel Ministry*, 153. See also Seraile, *Voice of Dissent*, 13–41; Steward, *Gospel Ministry*, 39–40, 90–91. The American Missionary Association was a strongly antislavery and nominally nonsectarian evangelical organization founded in 1846; it became closely associated with the Congregational denomination. See note 39.

31 Quotation from *CR*, 20 June 1863. See also Steward, *Gospel Ministry*, 72–73; Smith, *History*, 57; Angell, *Turner*, 69; Wayman, *Encyclopedia*, 11–12; Wright, *Bishops*, 119, and *CR*, 30 May 1863. For examples of Cain's activities on behalf of the freedpeople before he left the North, see *CR*, 13 February 1864, 20 February 1864, 18 March 1864, 2 April 1864 (Cain is referred to here as "Superintendent of Missions in South Carolina"), 1 June 1867; W. B. Derrick and James C. Embry, "The Late Bishop Cain," *A.M.E. Church Review* 3 (April 1887): 337–50.

32 Quotation from *CR*, 14 October 1865. For Rev. Adams's subsequent observations on Emanuel, see 28 April 1866; Wilbert Lee Jenkins, "Chaos, Conflict and Control: The

Responses of the Newly-Freed Slaves in Charleston, South Carolina to Emancipation and Reconstruction, 1865–1877" (Ph.D. diss., Michigan State University, 1993), 283; Joel Williamson, *After Slavery: The Negro in South Carolina during Reconstruction, 1861–1877* (New York: W. W. Norton, 1965), 190; Montgomery, *Their Own Vine and Fig Tree*, 95; Steward, *Gospel Ministry*, 73, 86. On more than one occasion Steward was involved in adamant disagreements with his senior colleague and supervisor, see Seraile, *Voice of Dissent*, 20–22.

33 Quotation from *CR*, 29 September 1866. See also ibid., 13 October 1866, 1 June 1867, 12 June 1869; *South Carolina Leader*, 14 July 1866. In the 1870s, Cain edited another newspaper called the *Missionary Record*, see same 5 July 1877.

34 The minutes of the first session of the Louisiana Conference are reprinted in Smith, *History*, 548–49; quotation from ibid., 71. For a roll call and review of the accomplishments of other A.M.E. "trailblazers," see ibid., 51–73. And see John Wesley Gaines, *African Methodism in the South, or Twenty Five Years of Freedom* (Atlanta: Franklin Publishing, 1890); Revels A. Adams, *Cyclopedia of African Methodism in Mississippi* (n.p., 1902); Israel L. Butt, *History of African Methodism in Virginia or Four Decades in the Old Dominion* (Norfolk: Hampton Institute Press, 1908); Charles Sumner Long, *History of the A.M.E. Church in Florida* (Philadelphia: A.M.E. Book Concern, 1934); H. T. Kealing, *History of African Methodism in Texas* (Waco, Texas: C. F. Blanks, 1885). See also Nancy V. Ashmore, "The Development of the African Methodist Episcopal Church in South Carolina, 1865–1965" (Ph.D. diss., University of South Carolina, 1969).

35 Kealing, *African Methodism in Texas*, 132.

36 A. Weston, "How African Methodism Was Introduced in the Up Country," in *Proceedings of the Quarto-Centennial Conference of the African Methodist Episcopal Church of South Carolina, . . . , 1889*, ed. Benjamin W. Arnett (n.p., 1890), 70.

37 Ibid., 71. The names of the women were Caroline Brown and Winnie Simmons.

38 For the constitution of the Parent Home and Foreign Missionary Society as adopted by the General Conference of 1860, see "Minutes of the Twelfth General Conference of the African Methodist Episcopal Church, 1860," as reprinted in Smith, *History*, 460–61. For a sketch of the history of the Missionary Society, see ibid., 342–43. See also *CR*, 12 November 1864 and 10 June 1865, and Donald Franklin Roth, " 'Grace Not Race': Southern Negro Church Leaders, Black Identity, and Missions to West Africa, 1865–1919" (Ph.D. diss., University of Texas at Austin, 1975), 70, 80.

39 Although officially nonsectarian, the A.M.A. became closely associated with the Congregational Church. Joe M. Richardson, "The Failure of the American Missionary Association to Expand Congregationalism among Southern Blacks," *Southern Studies* 18 (Spring 1979): 52–55; Richardson, *Christian Reconstruction: The American Missionary Association and Southern Blacks, 1861–1890* (Athens: University of Georgia Press, 1986), vii–viii, 71–72; Payne, *Recollections*, 161; Seraile, *Voice of Dissent*, 9–10, 14–15; Smith, *History*, 60; Coan, *Payne*, 109; Walker, *Rock in a Weary Land*, 88–89.

40 William B. Gravely, "The Social, Political and Religious Significance of the Formation of the Colored Methodist Episcopal Church (1870)," *Methodist History* 18 (October 1979): 12–19; Katherine L. Dvorak, *An African-American Exodus: The Segregation of the Southern Churches* (Brooklyn: Carlson Publishing, 1991), 100, 137; Walker, *Rock in a Weary Land*, 95–97; Montgomery, *Their Own Vine and Fig Tree*, 120–21; Seraile, *Voice of Dissent*, 12, 39; William L. Graham, "Patterns of Intergroup Relations in the

Cooperative Establishment, Control, and Administration of Paine College (Georgia) by Southern Negro and White People: A Study of Intergroup Process" (Ph.D. diss., New York University, 1955), 48–49.

41 Quotation from *Minutes of the New England Annual Conference of the African Methodist Episcopal Church: 1866* (New Bedford: Evening Standard Steam Printing, 1862), 9. See also *CR*, 10 June 1865; Payne, *Recollection*, 153–54, 165. I am indebted to Dennis C. Dickerson, the Historiographer of the A.M.E. Church, for supplying me with a copy of the minutes of the New England Conference.

42 Quotations from *CR*, 28 April 1866; *Minutes of the New England Annual Conference . . . : 1866, 9.*

43 Brown quotation from *CR*, 21 November 1868; Cain quotation from ibid., 6 February 1866. Rev. E. J. Adams estimated that the congregation of Emanuel had raised nearly $6,000 in about nine months and that about $12,000 would be needed to pay for the church. Ibid., 28 April 1866.

44 Carr quotation from *CR*, 30 October 1869; Steward quotation from *ibid.*, 23 March 1867. See also Wayman, *Encyclopedia*, 32; Jenkins, "Chaos, Conflict and Control," 274; Steward, *Gospel Ministry*, 33–34. Seven ordained ministers were members of the inaugural South Carolina Conference in 1865; nine preachers were "admitted on trial." Two years later at the Third Annual Session of the S.C. Conference, fifty-three ordained ministers answered the roll. On the second day of the conference, forty-six preachers were admitted on trial; on the third day of the conference, thirty additional names were listed as being admitted on trial. According to Clarence Walker, a total of only seventy-seven Northern A.M.E. missionaries were active in all of the South. Clearly, most of the new ministers in the South Carolina Conference were not coming from the North. "Minutes of the South Carolina Annual Conferences," as reprinted in Smith, *History,* 505–6, 509–10; Walker, *Rock in a Weary Land,* 50; Montgomery, *Their Own Vine and Fig Tree,* 99.

45 Angell, *Turner,* 146. For information concerning Emperor Williams, see *New Orleans Advocate,* 12 December 1868, and *Southwestern Christian Advocate,* 10 September 1896. For a disparaging characterization of Williams based on A.M.E. sources, see Walker, *Rock in a Weary Land,* 76.

46 Cain quotations from *CR*, 24 February 1866. See also Angell, *Turner,* 101–2, 107, 138, 144, 148, 152–53, 174–75; Montgomery, *Their Own Vine and Fig Tree,* 206, 210; Roth, " 'Grace Not Race,' " 69–70.

47 William J. Walls, *The African Methodist Episcopal Zion Church: Reality of the Black Church* (Charlotte, N.C.: A.M.E. Zion Publishing, 1974), 185–202; *CR*, 24 June, 30 December 1865; Montgomery, *Their Own Vine and Fig Tree,* 64–65. For a sketch of the life and career of Hood, see Sandy Dwayne Martin, "Black Churches and the Civil War: Theological and Ecclesiastical Significance of Black Methodist Involvement, 1861–1865," *Methodist History* 32 (April 1994): 179–82, and D. W. Culp, ed., *Twentieth Century Negro Literature or a Cyclopedia of Thought* (Atlanta: J. L. Nichols, 1902), 51.

48 First quotation from *CR*, 24 June 1865; second quotation from ibid., 30 December 1865. See also Angell, *Turner,* pp. 64–66. For a brief history of the official measures that were taken in an effort to bring about union, see Smith, *History,* 56, 370–79. For accounts of the A.M.E. Zion mission to the South, see James Walker Hood, *One Hundred Years of the African Methodist Episcopal Zion Church; or, the Centennial of African Method-*

ism (New York: A.M.E. Zion Book Concern, 1895), 282–382, and Walls, *Reality of the Black Church*, 185–99, 201–20.

49 Kealing, *African Methodism in Texas*, 34; see also 79–81, 111, 165–66.

50 *CR*, 16 June 1866.

51 *CR*, 23 June 1866.

52 *CR*, 12 November 1870.

53 *CR*, 14 May 1874.

54 Richardson, *Christian Reconstruction*, 253; Montgomery, *Their Own Vine and Fig Tree*, 105, 117–18. David Tucker comes to the following conclusion: "But for more than a generation after the Civil War, the C.M.E. still lagged far behind the African Methodist Episcopal denomination which captured the masses with its strong ties to the cause of black liberation." Tucker also points out that after the era of the emancipation generation, Colored Methodism became the largest black Methodist denomination in Memphis, a local development that he attributes to the migration of rural people to the city. David M. Tucker, *Black Pastors and Leaders: Memphis, 1819–1972* (Memphis: Memphis State University Press, 1975), 17, 24.

55 That thesis is thoughtfully developed throughout Dvorak's book. Another interpretation is put forward by David Tucker in his study of the C.M.E. Church in Memphis: he concludes that the members of that denomination valued the "genteel culture of house servants," which they often associated with light complexions. He also found that whites in Memphis characterized Colored Methodist worship as "dignified" and acceptable, in contrast to African Methodist services which they believed were marred by "wild enthusiasm." Tucker, *Black Pastors*, 21.

4 EXEGESIS OF THE GOSPEL OF FREEDOM

1 Quotation from *Christian Recorder* (Philadelphia) [hereafter referred to as *CR*], 3 June 1865. In November 1863, Cain wrote, "I conceive that the present period is the most auspicious which ever dawned upon our Church and people at large." *CR*, 21 November 1863. For other statements by Cain on the significance of the "new era," see *CR*, 7 May 1864 and 21 April 1866.

2 Frederick Cooper, "Elevating the Race: The Social Thought of Black Leaders, 1827–50," *American Quarterly* 24 (December 1972): 604–25; Benjamin Quarles, *Black Abolitionists* (New York: Oxford University Press, 1969), 82–115.

3 First Cain quotations *CR*, 21 April 1866; final quotation from ibid., 7 May 1864. Cain also wrote an essay called "Power of Christianity" in which he put forward the view that "it is impossible to stay the progress of Christianity in its course. Ibid., 6 September 1862. African Methodists often professed their belief that history was moving forward and carrying with it the destiny of their race. As early as November 1861, Henry M. Turner asserted: "However slow the tooth of time may seem to grind . . . we shall rise from our abhorred abasement to ranks of honor and fame." Ibid., 30 November 1861. James Lynch referred to "the inevitable sequence of the uncontrollable course of events." Ibid., 30 January 1864. See also William B. Gravely, "James Lynch and the Black Christian Mission during Reconstruction," in *Black Apostles at Home and Abroad*, ed. David W. Wills and Richard Newman (Boston: G. K. Hall, 1982), 165. Daniel Payne contended that the rise and fall of countries and civilizations were "exhibitions of the retributive justice and providence of God as the almighty Ruler of races, and nations, of

kingdoms and empires." Daniel A. Payne, "Semi-Centennial Sermon," in *Sermons and Addresses, 1853–1891, Bishop Daniel A. Payne*, ed. Charles Killian (New York: Arno Press, 1972), 79.

4   Turner quotation from *CR*, 25 February 1865; first Cain quotation from ibid., 29 June 1867; second Cain quotation from ibid., 12 August 1880.

5   Payne quotations from Daniel A. Payne, *Recollections of Seventy Years* (Nashville: A.M.E. Sunday School Union, 1888; reprint, New York: Arno Press, 1969), 137; Turner quotation from Henry M. Turner, *Celebration of the First Anniversary of Freedom, Held in Springfield Baptist Church, January 1st, 1866, and Containing an Outline of an Oration Delivered on the Occasion by Chaplain Henry M. Turner* (Augusta, Ga.: Loyal Georgian, 1866), 12; Cain quotation from *CR*, 7 May 1864. James Walker Hood went so far as to state that at the time of emancipation the freedpeople were a "mass of sin and ignorance." James Walker Hood, *One Hundred Years of the African Methodist Episcopal Zion Church; or the Centennial of African Methodism* (New York: A.M.E. Zion Book Concern, 1895), 15–16.

6   Hood quotation from James W. Hood, *Speech of Rev. James W. Hood, of Cumberland County Court on the Question of Suffrage, Delivered in the Constitutional Convention of North Carolina, February 12th, 1868* (Raleigh: W. W. Holden and Son, 1868), 9; Turner quotation from *CR*, 5 August 1865; Payne quotation from Daniel A. Payne, "Welcome to the Ransomed: or Duties of the Colored Inhabitants of the District of Columbia," in *Sermons and Addresses*, 6.

7   Turner quotation from *CR*, 6 December 1862; Lynch quotation from ibid., 27 June 1863. See also 12 October 1861.

8   First Turner quotation from *CR*, 1 November 1862; second from ibid., 5 August 1865; Cain quotation from ibid., 7 January 1865; final Turner quotations from ibid., 20 January 1866.

9   *CR*, 18 March 1865.

10 Hood quotation from Hood, *One Hundred Years*, 20. (Hood also wrote: "A race is judged by its distinguished men, but where there is no opportunity for distinction, it is impossible to judge a race by that method." Ibid., 21–22.) First Cain quotations from *CR*, 23 June 1866 (Cain used the pen name "Leo"); Turner quotation from ibid., 1 November 1862; second Cain quotation from ibid., 7 January 1865; Payne quotation from Daniel A. Payne, *The African M.E. Church in Its Relation to the Freedmen* (Xenia, Ohio: Torchlight, 1868), 4. See also Clarence E. Walker, *A Rock in a Weary Land: The African Methodist Episcopal Church during the Civil War and Reconstruction* (Baton Rouge: Louisiana State University Press, 1982), 52.

11 H. T. Kealing, *History of African Methodism in Texas* (Waco, Texas: C. F. Blanks, 1885), 121–24.

12 Ibid.

13 The quotation regarding Hood was written by Rev. William H. Day and can be found in the introduction to Hood, *One Hundred Years*, vii; Lynch quotation from *CR*, 27 January 1866; Cain quotation from ibid., 29 September 1866. For a discussion of the founding of the A.M.E. denomination, see Richard Allen, *The Life Experience and Gospel Labors of the Rt. Rev. Richard Allen* (Philadelphia: n.p., 1833, reprint, New York: Abingdon Press, 1960), 23–41; Carol V. R. George, *Segregated Sabbaths: Richard Allen and the Emergence of Independent Black Churches, 1760–1840* (New York: Oxford Univer-

sity Press, 1973), 49–89; Reginald F. Hildebrand, "Methodist Episcopal Policy on the Ordination of Black Ministers, 1784–1864," *Methodist History* 20 (April 1982): 124–26; Daniel A. Payne, *History of the African Methodist Episcopal Church,* ed. Charles S. Smith (Nashville: A.M.E. Sunday School Union, 1890; reprint, New York: Johnson Reprint Corp., 1968), 3–18; George A. Singleton, *The Romance of African Methodism: A Study of the African Methodist Episcopal Church* (New York: Exposition, 1952), 1–24; and Charles H. Wesley, *Richard Allen: Apostle of Freedom* (Washington: Associated Publishers, 1935), 74–157. For a discussion of the founding of the A.M.E. Zion denomination, see David H. Bradley, *A History of the A.M.E. Zion Church Part I, 1796–1872* (Nashville: Parthenon Press, 1956), 42–95; Hildebrand, "Methodist Episcopal Policy," 127–29; Hood, *One Hundred Years,* 56–64; Christopher Rush, *A Short History of the Rise and Progress of the African M.E. Church in America* (n.p., 1843; reprint, New York: J. J. Zuille, 1866), 48–78; William J. Walls, *The African Methodist Episcopal Zion Church: Reality of the Black Church* (Charlotte, N.C.: A.M.E. Zion Publishing, 1974), 43–83.

14   Kealing, *African Methodism in Texas,* 162–63.

15   Bernard Lewis, *History Remembered, Recovered, Invented* (Princeton, N.J.: Princeton University Press, 1975), 66; Hood quotation from Hood, *Speech of Rev. James W. Hood,* 11, see also 10–14; Turner, *Celebration of the First Anniversary of Freedom,* 10.

16   William H. Heard, *From Slavery to the Bishopric in the A.M.E. Church: An Autobiography* (Philadelphia: A.M.E. Book Concern, 1924), 90. See also Stephen Ward Angell, *Bishop Henry McNeal Turner and African-American Religion in the South* (Knoxville: University of Tennessee Press, 1992), 158.

17   U.S. Congress, House of Representatives, *Congressional Record* (24 January 1874), vol. 2, part 1, 901.

18   Turner quotation from Turner, *Celebration of the First Anniversary of Freedom,* 10; Cain quotation from U.S. Congress, House of Representatives, *Congressional Record* (24 January 1874) vol. 2, part 1, 901. In 1861, Lynch resolved to record the exploits of blacks in the Union army so that "our virtues, bravery, and fidelity shall not bloom in obscurity." See Gravely, "James Lynch," 164.

19   Payne quotation from Payne, "Semi-Centennial Sermon," in *Sermons and Addresses,* 84. Lynch described Cain as a man who "looks the world squarely in the face, preferring to destroy the obstacles lying in his way, than fruitlessly spend time in begging or waiting for them to move." *CR,* 16 July 1864. Cain quotations from ibid., 12 August 1880. Cain gave an early indication of his belief in the malleability of culture in a letter he wrote to the *Christian Recorder* in December 1861 while still pastor of an A.M.E. church in Brooklyn. Drawing an object lesson from a concert given by the children of his church, Cain concluded his letter with the following observation: "If the sweet music which these children, by a few week's training produced is an exhibition of what the human voice can be made to perform in a state so imperfect as this, what might not be accomplished by the right kind of training in all departments of human relations?" *CR,* 11 January 1862.

20   Kealing, *African Methodism in Texas,* 113–14.

21   First quotations from T. G. Steward, "Inaugural Sermon, Beaufort, S.C., June 18, 1865," in *From 1864 to 1914: Fifty Years in the Gospel Ministry* (Philadelphia: A.M.E. Book Concern, [1921]), 44; Cain quotation from *CR,* 30 April 1864; Lynch quotation from

ibid., 27 February 1864; Turner quotation from ibid., 5 August 1866. For criticisms and skepticism concerning white missionaries, see *CR*, 4 April 1863, 7 May 1864, 5 August 1865. See also Walker, *Rock in a Weary Land*, 52.

22   Cain quotation from *CR*, 30 May 1863; Payne quotation from ibid., 24 February 1866.

23   First quotation from M. M. Ponton, *The Life and Times of Henry M. Turner: The Antecedent and Preliminary History of the Life and Times of Bishop H. M. Turner* (Atlanta: A. B. Caldwell Publishing, 1917; reprint, New York: Negro Universities Press, 1970), 55; Turner quotation from *CR*, 4 March 1865; Payne quotation from Payne, *The African M.E. Church*, 7–8. For additional information about Turner's southern background and his early connection with the Southern Methodist Church, see William P. Harrison, ed., *The Gospel among the Slaves: A Short Account of Missionary Operations among the African Slaves of the Southern States* (Nashville: Publishing House of the M.E. Church, South, 1893), 379–80.

24   Cain quotation from U.S. Congress, House of Representatives, *Congressional Record* (24 January 1874) vol. 2, part 1, 901. For Cain's criticisms of the North, see *CR*, 7 January 1865; for Hood's criticisms of the North, see Hood, *Speech of James W. Hood*, 11–12. Turner remained skeptical of the North even after the Emancipation Proclamation was issued. "But you ask me what am I grumbling about," he wrote in November 1862. "Has not the President issued his Emancipation Proclamation? The President has, but the country has not." *CR*, 6 December 1862; see also ibid., 18 April 1863. For discussion of proscriptions against black voting in the antebellum North, see Leon F. Litwack, *North of Slavery: The Negro in the Free States, 1760–1860* (Chicago: University of Chicago Press, 1961), 74–79.

25   Cain quotation from *CR*, 16 August 1862; Steward quotation from Steward, "The Centre of Power in the Work of Social Reform," in *From 1864 to 1914*, 100. For Cain's views on the same subject, see U.S. Congress, House of Representatives, *Congressional Record* (3 February 1875) vol. 3, part 2, 957. See also Eric Foner, *Free Soil, Free Labor, Free Men: The Ideology of the Republican Party before the Civil War* (New York: Oxford University Press, 1970), and Jonathan A. Glickstein, *Concepts of Free Labor in Antebellum America* (New Haven, Conn.: Yale University Press, 1991).

26   Cain quotation from *CR*, 9 July 1864; Turner quotation from ibid., 18 April 1863; Payne quotation from Payne, *Recollections*, 106.

27   Tanner quotation from *CR*, 19 March 1870; Cain quotation from ibid., 9 July 1864; Turner quotation from Turner, *Celebration of the First Anniversary*, 12.

28   Robert F. Engs, *Freedom's First Generation: Black Hampton, Virginia, 1861–1890* (Philadelphia: University of Pennsylvania Press, 1979), 144–50. See also Louis R. Harlan, *Booker T. Washington: The Making of a Black Leader, 1856–1901* (New York: Oxford University Press, 1972), 109–56.

29   *CR*, 2 May 1878.

30   Turner quotations from *CR*, 2 May 1878; Tanner quotation from ibid., 19 October 1876. In 1853 the A.M.E. denomination tried to establish a school on the "Manual Labor Plan." The school was called Union Seminary Institute and was located about fourteen miles from Columbus, Ohio. According to Payne, Union was not a success. Payne, *History*, 399. For a more favorable estimation of the Union project, see a letter on the subject by Edward D. Davis, *CR*, 6 April 1863.

31   Israel L. Butt, *The History of African Methodism in Virginia or Four Decades in the*

Old Dominion (Norfolk: Hampton Institute Press, 1908), 81–82. The "pastor" referred to here was a Rev. Mr. Dennison.

32 Turner quotation from Turner, *Celebration of the First Anniversary,* 12; Payne quotation from Payne, *Recollections,* 106.

33 Cain quotation from *Missionary Record* (Charleston), 1 April 1876; Payne quotations from Payne, *The African M.E. Church,* 7.

34 Joyce D. Clayton, "Education, Politics and Statesmanship: The Story of James Walker Hood in North Carolina, 1864–1890" (M.A. Thesis, North Carolina Central University, 1978), 33.

35 *CR,* 29 June 1867.

36 Payne quotation from "Semi-Centennial Sermon," in *Sermons and Addresses,* 84; Cain quotation from *CR,* 12 August 1880. See also Payne, *Recollections,* 137.

37 Turner quotation from *CR,* 18 April 1863; first Cain quotation from ibid., 21 November 1863; second Cain quotation from ibid., 12 August 1880; Lynch quotation from ibid., 9 September 1865. See also Payne, *Recollections,* 75–76; Payne, *The Semi-Centenary and the Retrospection of the African Methodist Episcopal Church in the United States of America* (Baltimore: Sherwood, 1866; reprint, Freeport, N.Y.: Books for Libraries Press, 1972), 60–61; Harry V. Richardson, *Dark Salvation: The Story of Methodism as It Developed among Blacks in America* (Garden City, N.Y.: Doubleday, 1976), 199; Angell, *Turner,* 113.

38 Quotation from Payne, *The African M.E. Church,* 15; see also Payne, "Annual Report and Retrospection of the First Decade of Wilberforce University, June 18, 1873," in *Sermons and Addresses,* 4, 11; Payne, *History,* 428–38; Payne, *Recollections,* 152–53, 230; Arthur P. Stokes, "Daniel Alexander Payne: Churchman and Educator" (Ph.D. diss., Ohio State University, 1973), 143–45; Richard R. Wright Jr., *Centennial Encyclopedia of the African Methodist Episcopal Church* (Philadelphia: Book Concern of the A.M.E. Church, 1916), 371–74.

39 First Cain quotation from *CR,* 21 November 1863; Turner quotation from ibid., 29 August 1863; second and third quotations are from Cain's article, "The Necessity of Wilberforce University for Our Youth—The Demands for Such an Institution." Cain insisted that education and scholarship, like other aspects of the Gospel of Freedom, be dynamic. A faculty that merely taught old knowledge was not sufficient. According to Cain, an acceptable faculty had to be about the business of "elaborating systems, and theories of scientific investigation, producing something new, improving research on old systems." *CR,* 26 November 1864. See also Payne, *The African M.E. Church,* 6; Stokes, "Payne," 156; and Wright, *Bishops,* 119.

40 Payne, *Recollections,* 231; Angell, *Turner,* 160–62; Grace Naomi Perry, "The Educational Work of the African Methodist Episcopal Church prior to 1900," (M.A. thesis, Howard University, 1948), 39–56; Walls, *Reality of the Black Church,* 305–16. Zion Wesley Institute was originally located in Concord, North Carolina.

41 The first quotation is by James Lynch and is from *CR,* 10 March 1866; Cain quotation from ibid., 21 April 1866. Like Lynch, Cain foresaw an era of unlimited economic opportunity. In the same article from which the quotation was taken, he wrote: "Now that freedom has dawned upon the nation these [the freedpeople] are prepared to enter every avenue and engage in every department of business." In 1869, when Turner was a member of the Georgia State Legislature, he convened a meeting of his fellow black solons

to discuss the plight of black workers in the state. The meeting proposed the formation of a workers association. Edmund L. Drago, *Black Politicians and Reconstruction in Georgia: A Splendid Failure* (Baton Rouge: Louisiana State University Press, 1982), 87.

42 Lynch quotation from *CR*, 22 September 1866; Turner quotation from Turner, *Celebration of the First Anniversary*, 12. See also *CR*, 19 May 1866.

43 Payne quotation from Payne, *The African M.E. Church*, 4; Lynch quotation from *CR*, 10 March 1866; Lynch quotation on "dress . . . and . . . pleasure," from ibid., 19 May 1866; Turner quotation from ibid., 5 August 1865. See also Payne, *Recollections*, 107–8. In 1862, Payne exhorted the contrabands in Washington to "Work, work, work! Shun no work that will bring you an honest penny." Payne, "Welcome to the Ransomed," in *The African M.E. Church*, 9. The year before he went South, Cain wrote that black youth should be taught that "honest industry will bring its reward." *CR*, 16 July 1864. Turner preached a similar message to the freedpeople in Georgia. Turner, *Celebration of the First Anniversary*, 13.

44 First Cain quotation from *South Carolina Leader*, 8 December 1866; second Cain quotation from *Proceedings of the Constitutional Convention of South Carolina* [hereafter, *Proceedings of the Constitutional Convention S.C.*] (Charleston: Denny and Perry, 1868), 138; all other Cain quotations from *CR*, 21 April 1866; final quotation is from an article by B. T. Tanner in *CR*, 16 July 1874. See also *CR*, 14 October 1865; Thomas C. Holt, *Black over White: Negro Political Leadership in South Carolina during Reconstruction* (Urbana: University of Illinois Press, 1977), 165.

45 Cain quotation from *CR*, 16 July 1864; Lynch quotation from ibid., 19 May 1866.

46 All Turner quotations from *CR*, 25 March 1866; Cain quotation from *South Carolina Leader*, 25 August 1866. While visiting Goldsboro, N.C., in 1878, Turner was very moved by the poverty of blacks in that area. "Hard-hearted as I am," he wrote, "I had to cry like a child at the statements made to me about the condition of our people." *CR*, 1 August 1878. For examples of Turner's activism on behalf of black workers, see Drago, *Black Politicians and Reconstruction*, 87. *Proceedings of the Constitutional Convention S.C.*, 196, 379. See also Walker, *Rock in a Weary Land*, 56.

47 Cain quotations from *Proceedings of the Constitutional Convention S.C.*, 196, 281, 379, 380, 419.

48 First Cain quotations from *CR*, 16 July 1864; second Cain quotation from *Proceedings of the National Convention of Colored Men, Held in the City of Syracuse, N.Y.* (Boston: J. S. Rock and Geo. L. Ruffin, 1864; reprinted in *Minutes of the Proceedings of the National Negro Conventions 1830–1864*, ed. Howard Holman Bell, New York: Arno Press, 1969), 26, see also 34. Final quotation from *South Carolina Leader*, 8 December 1866.

49 First quotation from *Proceedings of the Constitutional Convention S.C.*, 166–67; second Cain quotation from Carol K. R. Bleser, *The Promised Land: The History of the South Carolina Land Commission, 1869–1890* (Columbia: University of South Carolina Press, 1969), 76–77. See also Holt, *Black over White*, 131; *Journal of the Senate of the General Assembly of the State of South Carolina . . . : 1869*, 49; ibid., *1870*, 217, 225, 237. Cain originally proposed the issuance of two million dollars in state bonds, but later he dropped the figure to one million. Claude F. Oubre, *Forty Acres and a Mule: The Freedmen's Bureau and Black Land Ownership* (Baton Rouge: Louisiana State University Press, 1978), 174–77. For a brief discussion of the Lincolnville project, see Joel

Williamson, *After Slavery: The Negro in South Carolina during Reconstruction* (New York: W. W. Norton, 1975), 207. It may have been Cain's mishandling of Lincolnville that prompted Payne to characterize him in the following manner: "But while full of energy, tact and pluck, Richard Harvey Cain was greatly lacking in moral conscience. He seemed to be perfectly oblivious of the moral significance of a promise—so much so that in financial dealings with his acquaintances and friends he was a miserable failure." Payne, *Recollections*, 332.

50 Quotation from *Proceedings of the Constitutional Convention S.C.*, 381. Cain did support efforts to shape tax and debtor relief legislation in ways that would have forced landowners to sell some of their holdings. See Richard L. Hume, "Negro Delegates to the State Constitutional Conventions of 1867–69," in *Southern Black Leaders of the Reconstruction Era*, ed. Howard N. Rabinowitz (Urbana: University of Illinois Press, 1982), 142.

51 *CR,* 9 September 1865.

52 Payne quotations from Payne, *The African M.E. Church,* 5–6, and Butt, *History of African Methodism,* 95; Hood quotation from Hood, *One Hundred Years,* 18–19. In his *History of the A.M.E. Church,* published in 1891, Payne wrote that by becoming a politician Cain had "damaged his usefulness as an embassador [*sic*] of the Cross." Payne, the historian, believed that an "apology" was required for minister/politicians. He explained that they were "forced" into politics because of the need that existed for their "intelligence and organizing power." Payne's position on ministerial involvement in politics in 1891 was strikingly different from the position he expressed in 1868. It should be noted that Hood's ambivalence about political involvement was expressed in a book published in 1895, almost two decades after the end of Reconstruction. See also William E. Montgomery, *Under Their Own Vine and Fig Tree: The African-American Church in the South, 1865–1900* (Baton Rouge: Louisiana State University Press, 1993), 178–80, 182–84; Angell, *Turner,* 82.

53 Turner quotations from Wright, *Bishops,* 334–35. See Edwin S. Redkey, *Black Exodus: Black Nationalist and Back-to-Africa Movements, 1890–1910* (New Haven, Conn.: Yale University Press, 1969), 27. Concerning Turner's service in the Georgia legislature, Payne wrote: "The majority cast from the legislature were members of the A.M.E. Church. The heroic leader of the movements against the Democrats, is Rev. H. M. Turner, one of its Presiding Elders. A braver patriot does not tread the soil of the Republic." Payne, *The African M.E. Church,* 6. See also E. Merton Coulter, *Negro Legislators in Georgia during the Reconstruction* (Athens: Georgia Historical Quarterly, 1968), 13. Turner also served as a Washington lobbyist for the Georgia Equal Rights Association. *CR,* 9 June 1866. See also Angell, *Turner,* 82–99, 115–16. Eric Foner, *Freedom's Lawmakers: A Directory of Black Officeholders during Reconstruction* (New York: Oxford University Press, 1993), 215–16. The positions of postmaster and custom collector were appointed through political patronage, not elected.

54 Williamson, *After Slavery,* 206–7; Cain quotation from U.S. Congress, House of Representatives, *Congressional Record* (10 February 1875) vol. 3, part 2, 1153. For references to Hood, see Clayton, "Story of Hood," 23, 28.

55 *Proceedings of the Constitutional Convention S.C.*, 83.

56 Hood, *Speech of James W. Hood,* 3–4.

57 *Proceedings of the Constitutional Convention S.C.*, 830; *New York Times,* 17 June 1865;

U.S. Congress, House of Representatives, *Congressional Record* (14 January 1878) vol. 7, part 1, 322; Coulter, *Negro Legislators*, 16; Angell, *Turner*, 98. It should be noted that Hood did not share the views of Cain and Turner on the issue of women's suffrage. His position was as follows: "When a race of men are enfranchised, the women and children of that race are enfranchised through these male representatives, who are the guardians of their rights and the protectors of their liberties." Hood, *Speech of James W. Hood*, 8.

58   Weaver quotation from *CR*, 1 July 1865; H. M. Turner to Capt. J. E. Bryant, 13 April 1865, John Emory Bryant Papers, Manuscript Department, Perkins Library, Duke University, Durham, North Carolina.

59   Tanner quotation from *CR*, 9 April 1870; Turner quotation from William J. Simmons, *Men of Mark: Eminent, Progressive and Rising* (Cleveland: G. M. Rewell, 1887), 62.

60   Quotation from U.S. Congress, House of Representatives, *Congressional Record* (10 January 1874) vol. 2, part 1, 565. Peggy Lamson, *The Glorious Failure: Black Congressman Robert Brown Elliot and the Reconstruction in South Carolina* (New York: W. W. Norton, 1972), 121. While serving as a state senator in 1868, Cain downplayed civil rights legislation. His reasoning remains unclear. See William C. Hine, "Dr. Benjamin A. Boseman, Jr.: Charleston's Black Physician-Politician," in *Southern Black Leaders of the Reconstruction Era*, ed. Howard N. Rabinowitz (Urbana: University of Illinois Press), 342. For some additional thoughts on why some black Reconstructionists "did not push more vigorously for racial equality," see Hume, "Negro Delegates," 143–44. For a clear and concise explanation of the distinction African Methodists made between access to public accommodations and social equality, see Singleton T. Jones, "The Church: Its Work, Its Future Glory," in *Sermons and Addresses of the Late Rev. Bishop Singleton T. Jones, D.D. of the African M.E. Zion Church*, ed. J. W. Smith (York, Pa.: Anstart and Sons, 1892), 283.

61   *CR*, 17 August 1867. In his biography of Payne, Charles Killian concluded that the bishop rated Methodism itself only "slightly above the Republican Party." Charles Killian, "Bishop Daniel A. Payne: Black Spokesman for Reform" (Ph.D. diss., Indiana University, 1971), 98.

62   *CR*, 31 August 1878.

63   First Tanner quotation from *CR*, 6 January 1876; second quotation from ibid., 11 November 1875. See also Drago, *Black Politicians*, 63, 72.

64   *CR*, 11 November 1875.

65   *CR*, 26 April 1877.

66   Quotation from *CR*, 10 May 1877; Angell, *Turner*, 127–30, 133.

67   For the best account of the venture of the Liberian Exodus Co., see George B. Tindall, "The Liberian Exodus of 1878," *South Carolina Historical Magazine* 53 (July 1952): 133–45. See also Tindall, *South Carolina Negroes, 1877–1900* (Columbia: University of South Carolina Press, 1952), 153–68. Twenty-three of the passengers died during the voyage, and the others arrived in West Africa without many of the supplies and resources necessary for making a successful beginning in a new land. Tindall concluded: "the Liberian Exodus Joint Stock Steamship Company must be put down as a failure" largely due to the "natural error of inexperienced persons." Ibid., 167. See also Nell Irvin Painter, *Exodusters: Black Migration to Kansas after Reconstruction* (New York: Alfred A. Knopf, 1977), 138–40.

68   Tindall, "Liberian Exodus," 134–39; Tindall, *South Carolina Negroes*, 156; Brown quo-

tation is from an account of the consecration ceremony that originally appeared in the *Charleston News and Courier* on 22 March 1878, see reprint of the article in *CR,* 4 April 1878. See also *CR,* 18 April 1878; Angell, *Turner,* 135; Donald Franklin Roth, " 'Grace not Race': Southern Negro Church Leaders, Black Identity, and Missions to West Africa, 1865–1919" (Ph.D. diss., University of Texas at Austin, 1975), 75–76.

69   *CR,* 4 April 1878.

70   Both quotations are by Turner and are from *CR,* 18 April 1878 and 1 August 1878. See also ibid., 20 December 1877. For examples of A.M.E. opposition to emigration, see *CR,* 29 March 1862, 6 September 1862; 3 January 1878, and 17 January 1878. Both Cain and Turner had been criticized for their emigrationist sympathies in the early 1860s, before either of them had begun missionary work in the South. See *CR,* 14 December 1861, 30 August 1862, 30 May 1863. Delany was the most prominent black emigrationist during the 1850s. See Victor Ullman, *Martin R. Delany: The Beginnings of Black Nationalism* (Boston: Beacon Press, 1971), 141–267. In reference to the *Azor* expedition, Benjamin T. Tanner wrote: "It is well known that we have never been one of those who favored the wholesale manner in which our South Carolina friends went into this affair." *CR* 4 April 1878.

71   Quotation from John Wesley Gaines, *African Methodism in the South, or Twenty Five Years of Freedom* (Atlanta: Franklin Publishing, 1890), 188. See also Turner, *Respect Black: The Writings and Speeches of Henry McNeal Turner,* ed. Edwin S. Redkey (New York: Arno Press, 1971), and *CR,* 30 September 1880.

5   THE METHODIST EPISCOPAL CHURCH: A MISSION TAKES SHAPE

1   *Christian Advocate and Journal* (New York) [hereafter referred to as *NYCA*], 20 July 1865.

2   *NYCA,* 20 July 1865; Harry V. Richardson, *Dark Salvation: The Story of Methodism as It Developed among Blacks in America* (Garden City, N.Y.: Doubleday, 1976), 62–75; Reginald F. Hildebrand, "Methodist Episcopal Policy on the Ordination of Black Ministers, 1784–1864," *Methodist History* 20 (April 1982): 124–27.

3   Lewis V. Baldwin, *"Invisible" Strands in African Methodism: A History of the African Union Methodist Protestant and Union American Methodist Episcopal Churches, 1805–1980* (Metuchen, N.J.: Scarecrow Press, 1983), 37–51; Baldwin, *The Mark of a Man: Peter Spencer and the African Union Methodist Tradition: The Man, the Movement, the Message and the Legacy* (New York: University Press of America, 1987); Carol V. R. George, *Segregated Sabbaths: Richard Allen and the Emergence of Independent Black Churches, 1760–1840* (New York: Oxford University Press, 1973), 72–90; Richardson, *Dark Salvation,* 76–84, 117–31; Lewis M. Hagood, *The Colored Man in the Methodist Episcopal Church* (Cincinnati: Cranston and Stowe, 1890; reprint, Westport, Conn.: Negro Universities Press, 1970), 79–103, 137–44; Hildebrand, "Policy on Ordination," 125–40.

4   *Journal of the General Conference of the Methodist Episcopal Church: 1864* (New York: Carlton and Porter, 1864), 380, 278.

5   First quotation from ibid., 278; final quotation from *Annual Report of the Missionary Society of the Methodist Episcopal Church: Forty-Sixth, 1874* (New York: Printed for the Society, 1865), 102–3. See also Donald G. Mathews, *Slavery and Methodism: A Chapter in American Morality, 1780–1845* (Princeton, N.J.: Princeton University

Press, 1965), 246–82; Ralph E. Morrow, *Northern Methodism and Reconstruction* (East Lansing: Michigan State University Press, 1956), 50–51.

6 *Journal of the General Conference . . . : 1864,* 486.

7 Quotations from ibid., 279, 486–47. See also Hildebrand, "Policy on Ordination," 126–38.

8 First quotation from *Journal of the General Conference . . . : 1864,* 253; final quotation from *NYCA,* 2 June 1864. See also *Journal of the General Conference . . . : 1864,* 252–53, 263, 487–88. The Washington Conference embraced "Western Maryland, the District of Columbia, Virginia, and the territory South." The Delaware Conference included "the territory north and east of the Washington Conference." See *NYCA,* 2 June 1864; Hildebrand, "Policy on Ordination," 141–42; see also *Minutes and Journal of Proceedings of the Washington Annual Conference: First Session, October 27–31, 1864,* reprint (n.p., n.d.); and William C. Jason Jr., "The Delaware Annual Conference of the Methodist Church, 1864–1965," *Methodist History* 4 (July 1966): 26, 30–32. For accounts of the first session of the Delaware Conference, see also *NYCA,* 11 August 1864, and *Christian Recorder* (Philadelphia), 6 August 1864 and 20 August 1864. The establishment of these conferences was not without controversy. When the New England Annual Conference met in April 1865, it passed a strongly worded resolution that deplored "colored conferences" because "they only tend to separate brethren in the ministry, and to foster prejudices that are contrary to the word of God." *NYCA,* 27 April 1865.

9 *Zion's Herald and Wesleyan Journal* (Boston), 11 February 1863; *NYCA,* 3 March 1864.

10 John Emory Bryant, Augusta, Georgia, to [Emma Bryant], ALS, 29 May 1865, John Emory Bryant Papers, Manuscripts Department, Perkins Library, Duke University, Durham, North Carolina.

11 *Journal of the General Conference . . . : 1864,* 441; *NYCA,* 13 April 1865. It should be noted that Moore also made a very interesting proposal that self-governing colonies of freedmen be established under the protection of black veterans. Moore contended that under such an arrangement black power would deter white depredations and the "freedmen would pass promptly from the military to industrial, social, civil and religious life, and would have neither time nor space to relapse into habits of idleness or of vagabondism; they would enjoy protection in all their interests and rights."

12 Quotation from *Annual Report of the Missionary Society . . . : Forty-Eighth, 1866,* 116. See also *NYCA,* 10 March 1864, 23 November 1865; Eric Foner, *Nothing but Freedom: Emancipation and Its Legacy* (Baton Rouge: Louisiana State University Press, 1983); *Annual Report of the Freedmen's Aid Society of the Methodist Episcopal Church: Fifth, 1873,* 33; ibid., *Eighth, 1875,* 6, 8, 10, 20; ibid., *Ninth, 1876,* 8, 40, 44,; ibid., *Eleventh, 1878,* 9.

13 Donald G. Jones, *The Sectional Crisis and Northern Methodism: A Study in Piety, Political Ethics and Civil Religion* (Metuchen, N.J.: Scarecrow Press, 1979), 282–83; *Journal of the General Conference . . . : 1864,* 440–41; *NYCA,* 14 January 1864 and 21 April 1864.

14 First quotation from *Zion's Herald and Wesleyan Journal,* 25 March 1863; final quotation from ibid., 8 July 1863. See also *NYCA,* 3 March 1864.

15 Quotation from Robert N. Scott, ed., *War of the Rebellion: A Compilation of the Official Records of the Union and Confederate Armies,* series 1, vol. 34, part 2 (Washington, D.C.: Government Printing Office, 1891), 311. See also Frank Kenneth Pool, "The South-

ern Negro in the Methodist Episcopal Church" (Ph.D. diss., Duke University, 1939), 33; Morrow, *Northern Methodism*, 33, 42.

16   Quotation from *Zion's Herald and Wesleyan Journal*, 18 March 1863. See also Pool, "Southern Negro," 27–33; Morrow, *Northern Methodism*, 43–45.

17   Wheatley quotation from *NYCA*, 4 February 1864; Gilbert quotation from ibid., 27 April 1865; Moore quotation from ibid., 31 August 1865. See also ibid., 11 May 1865.

18   Quotation from Nathan Brown, New York, to Rev. D. Brown, ALS, 3 March 1862, Nathan Brown Papers, South Caroliniana Library, University of South Carolina, Columbia, South Carolina. See also A. M. French, *Slavery in South Carolina and the Ex-Slaves; or The Port Royal Mission*. 1862. Reprint, New York: Negro Universities Press, 1969, xii, 27–29. The best account of the Port Royal mission is Willie Lee Rose, *Rehearsal for Reconstruction: The Port Royal Experiment* (New York: Oxford University Press, 1964); see also Elizabeth Ware Pearson, ed., *Letters from Port Royal* (Boston: W. B. Clarke, 1905; reprint, New York: Arno Press, 1969); *NYCA*, 27 March 1862 and 21 April 1864.

19   *Journal of the General Conference . . . : 1864*, 440–42, quotation from page 442; *NYCA*, 22 October 1863. For resolutions endorsing the National Freedmen's Association from the New York East Conference and from the New York Conference, see *NYCA*, 21 April 1864 and 5 May 1864. Charles C Leigh, New York, N.Y., to Rev. Mathew [*sic*] Simpson D.D. [Philadelphia], ALS, 11 March 1864, Matthew Simpson Papers, Library of Congress, Washington, D.C.; Pool, "Southern Negro," 75–76; James E. Kirby, "The Ecclesiastical and Social Thought of Matthew Simpson" (Ph.D. diss., Duke University, 1963), 216–17; Morrow, *Northern Methodism*, 155.

20   *Reports of the Freedmen's Aid Society of the Methodist Episcopal Church, 1866–1875*, 3–13, quotation from 3; *Report of the Freedmen's Aid Society, 1868*, 3–7; Morrow, *Northern Methodism*, 155–60.

21   *Reports of the Freedmen's Aid Society . . . , 1866–1875*, 3–13; Morrow, *Northern Methodism*, 156–60; Pool, "Southern Negro," 80–81, 83–86; Walter W. Benjamin, "The Era of Reconstruction: The Freedmen's Aid Society," in *The History of American Methodism*, vol. 2, ed. Emory Stevens Bucke (New York: Abingdon Press, 1964), 360–64; for the endorsement of the Board of Bishops, see *Report of the Freedmen's Aid Society, 1868*, inside cover; *Journal of the General Conference . . . : 1868*, 332. The names of the persons present at the inaugural meeting of the F.A.S. were as follows: Bishop D. W. Clark, Revs. Adam Poe, J. M. Reid, R. S. Rust, J. M. Walden, J. R. Stillwell, and Mr. J. F. Larkin of Cincinnati; Rev. Luke Hitchcock and Mr. Grant Goodrich of Chicago; Rev. B. F. Crary of St. Louis, Missouri; and Rev. Robert Allyn of Lebanon, Illinois. Rev. T. M. Eddy of Chicago arrived on the second day of the meeting.

22   The first article referred to is from *NYCA*, 1 June 1865. See also *NYCA*, for "Reconstruction of the Church," 27 April 1865; "Methodism in the South," 11 May 1865; "Church Reconstruction," 25 May 1865; and "Reconstruction," 15 June 1865. Morrow, *Northern Methodism*, 63–64. The next to last quotation is from an editorial also entitled "Reconstruction," *NYCA*, 22 June 1865; final quotation from ibid., 8 June 1865.

23   All quotations from *NYCA*, 22 June 1865. See also William W. Sweet, "The Methodist Episcopal Church and Reconstruction," *Journal of the Illinois State Historical Society* 7 (October 1914): 149–50, and Morrow, *Northern Methodism*, 66–68.

24   *NYCA*, 8 June 1865 and 31 August 1865; Morrow, *Northern Methodism*, 68–70.

25   First quotation from W. B. Hesseltine, "Methodism and Reconstruction in East Tennessee," *East Tennessee Historical Society Publications* (1931): 46; last quotation is by
     Thomas H. Pearne and can be found in Morrow, *Northern Methodism*, 104. For an
     account of Rev. John H. Caldwell's censure and subsequent decision to switch from
     Southern to Northern Methodism, see John H. Caldwell, *Reminiscences of the Reconstruction of Church and State in Georgia* (Wilmington, Del.: J. Miller Thomas, 1895),
     5–7; Edmund Jordan Hammond, *The Methodist Episcopal Church in Georgia, being
     a Brief History of the Two Georgia Conferences of the Methodist Episcopal Church
     together with a Summary of the Causes of Major Methodist Divisions in the United
     States and of the Problems Confronting Methodist Union* (Atlanta: n.p., 1935), 106–8;
     and Daniel W. Stowell, " 'We Have Sinned, and God Has Smitten Us!' John H. Caldwell
     and the Religious Meaning of Confederate Defeat," *Georgia Historical Quarterly* 78
     (Spring 1994): 33–38. See also E. Merton Coulter, *William G. Brownlow: Fighting Parson of the Southern Highlands* (Chapel Hill: University of North Carolina Press, 1937),
     294–98.

26   Caldwell, *Reminiscences*, 8; Pool, "Southern Negro," 39–40; Donald G. Jones, "The
     Moral, Social and Political Ideas of the Methodist Episcopal Church from the Closing
     Years of the Civil War through Reconstruction, 1864–1876," Ph.D. diss., Drew University, 1969, 317–19; Morrow, *Northern Methodism*, 70–71.

27   Gilbert quotation from *NYCA*, 20 July 1985; Hawkins quotation from ibid., 10 August
     1865.

28   *NYCA*, 8 June 1865, 31 August 1865, quotation from 7 September 1865; *New Orleans
     Advocate*, 20 January 1866; Morrow, *Northern Methodism*, 98–99, 106–7.

29   First quotation from *NYCA*, 28 January 1864; last quotation from *NYCA*, 31 August
     1865. For another reference to the Good Samaritan, see *Annual Report of the Freedmen's Aid Society . . . : Seventh, 1874*, 6. See also Jones, *Sectional Crisis*, 251, 259–60;
     Annual Report of the Freedmen's Aid Society . . . : Third, 1872, 14–15; Pool, "Southern
     Negro," 42.

30   *New Orleans Advocate*, 20 January 1866; *Annual Report of the Freedmen's Aid Society . . . : Third, 1872*, 14–16.

31   Morrow, *Northern Methodism*, 134–35; Clarence E. Walker, *A Rock in a Weary Land:
     The African Methodist Episcopal Church during the Civil War and Reconstruction*
     (Baton Rouge: Louisiana State University Press, 1982), 83–84; *NYCA*, 14 April 1864,
     quotation from ibid., 20 July 1865.

32   *NYCA*, 14 April 1864, 25 May 1865, 20 July 1865; first and second quotations from ibid.,
     10 August 1865; Morrow, *Northern Methodism*, 135–37.

33   Quotation from *NYCA*, 17 November 1864. See also William B. Gravely, *Gilbert Haven,
     Methodist Abolitionist: A Study in Race, Religion, and Reform, 1850–1880* (New York:
     Abingdon Press, 1973); Morrow, *Northern Methodism*, 181–85; Jones, *Sectional Conflict*, 287.

34   John L. Thomas, "Romantic Reform in America, 1815–1865," *American Quarterly* 17
     (Winter 1965): quotation from 656 (Thomas himself is quoting T. E. Hulme), 658–59,
     662. See also Anne C. Loveland, "Evangelicalism and 'Immediate Emancipation' in
     American Antislavery Thought," *Journal of Southern History* 32 (May 1966): 174, 177–
     79, 181; David Brion Davis, "The Emergence of Immediatism in British and American
     Antislavery Thought," *Mississippi Valley Historical Review* 49 (September 1962): 212–

13, 228. McPherson's thesis is put forward in two works that deal with postbellum "abolitionism"—*The Struggle for Equality: Abolitionists and the Negro in the Civil War and Reconstruction* (Princeton, N.J.: Princeton University Press, 1964), and *The Abolitionist Legacy: From Reconstruction to the NAACP* (Princeton, N.J.: Princeton University Press, 1975).

35   Quotations by Taylor from *NYCA,* 22 June 1865; French quotation from ibid., 13 July 1865. Taylor and French contended that the example set by the church would exert great influence on the way the nation treated the freedpeople.

36   First quotation from *NYCA,* 27 April 1865; final quotation from an editorial entitled "Reconstruction," ibid., 25 May 1865. See also ibid., 17 November 1864.

6   THE APPEAL OF NORTHERN METHODISM

1   W. H. Lawrence, *The Centenary Souvenir: Containing a History of Centenary Church, Charleston, and an Account of the Life and Labors of Rev. R. V. Lawrence, Father of the Pastor of Centenary Church* (Charleston: n.p., 1885), ix. See also John W. Curry, *Passionate Journey: History of the 1866 South Carolina Annual Conference* (St. Matthews, S.C.: State Printing, 1980), 3; Warren M. Jenkins, *Steps along the Way: The Origin and Development of the South Carolina Conference of the Central Jurisdiction of the Methodist Church* (Columbia, S.C.: State Printing, 1967), 5; Ralph E. Morrow, *Northern Methodism and Reconstruction* (East Lansing: Michigan State University Press, 1956), 130.

2   Quotation from *New Orleans Advocate,* 24 March 1866. See also ibid., 20 January 1866; Lawrence, *Centenary Souvenir,* ix; Morrow, *Northern Methodism,* 129–30.

3   Quotation from *New Orleans Advocate,* 24 March 1866. See also Morrow, *Northern Methodism,* 131.

4   *Annual Report of the Missionary Society of the Methodist Episcopal Church: Forty-Seventh, 1865,* 137; *New York Christian Advocate and Journal* (New York) [hereafter *NYCA*], 23 November 1865, 11 April 1867, 25 July 1867; *Zion's Herald and Wesleyan Journal* (Boston), 15 November 1865; William E. Montgomery, *Under Their Own Vine and Fig Tree: The African-American Church in the South, 1865–1900* (Baton Rouge: Louisiana State University Press, 1993), 89; Morrow, *Northern Methodism,* 33–41; *New Orleans Advocate,* 27 January 1866, 3 February 1866.

5   Quotation from *Zion's Herald and Wesleyan Journal,* 29 August 1866. See also ibid., 23 August 1865, 6 December 1865, 14 May 1868; *NYCA,* 8 March 1866; *Annual Report of the Church Extension Society of the Methodist Episcopal Church: Fourth, 1869,* 5; ibid., *Fifth, 1870,* 33, 37; ibid., *Sixth, 1871,* 46, 70; *New Orleans Advocate,* 3 March 1866; Jenkins, *Steps along the Way,* 6; Wilbert Lee Jenkins, "Chaos, Conflict and Control: The Responses of the Newly-Freed Slaves in Charleston, South Carolina to Emancipation and Reconstruction, 1865–1877" (Ph.D. diss., Michigan State University, 1993), 283–86.

6   The four departments were as follows: (1) Mississippi, which included Mississippi, Louisiana, and Texas, under the supervision of Bishop Thompson; (2) Middle, which included Alabama and Western Georgia, under the supervision of Bishop Clark; (3) Southern, which included Florida, Eastern Georgia, and South Carolina, under the supervision of Bishop Baker; and (4) Northern, which included Eastern North Carolina "and so much of Virginia as is not included in the Baltimore Conference," under the supervision of Bishop Scott. *Annual Report of the Missionary Society . . . : Forty-Seventh, 1865,* 136.

7   Frank Kenneth Pool, "The Southern Negro in the Methodist Episcopal Church" (Ph.D. diss., Duke University, 1939), 46–47; *Annual Report of the Missionary Society . . . : Forty-Seventh, 1865,* 150.

8   Both quotations from *Proceedings of the Mississippi Mission Conference Organized in New Orleans by Bishop Thompson: First Session, December 25th, 1865* (n.p., n.d.), 4. See also *Annual Report of the Missionary Society . . . : Forty-Seventh, 1865,* 140; James W. May, "The War Years," in *The History of American Methodism,* vol. 2, ed. Emory Stevens Bucke (New York: Abingdon Press, 1964), 250; William W. Sweet, "The Methodist Episcopal Church and Reconstruction," *Journal of the Illinois State Historical Society* 7 (October 1914): 153.

9   *Proceedings of the Mississippi Mission Conference, First Session,* 3–4; Pool, "Southern Negro," 201–2; Morrow, *Northern Methodism,* 55. Morrow is in error when he indicates that the *New Orleans Advocate* began publication on 30 December 1865; the first issue appeared 6 January 1866. See also Sweet, "Reconstruction," 152–53.

10 NYCA, 31 March 1864, 23 November 1865, 31 March 1866; *Methodist Advocate* (Atlanta), 19 January 1870; *Journal of the General Conference . . . : 1864,* 486.

11 Pierre Landry, "Autobiographical Sketch," TMs, Dunn-Landry Papers, Amistad Research Center, Tulane University, New Orleans, Louisiana, Montgomery, *Their Own Vine and Fig Tree,* 101–3.

12 *Annual Report of the Missionary Society . . . : 1865,* 137–38.

13 All Round quotations from NYCA, 31 March 1864, 4 August 1864, 22 October 1868; Lewis quotations from *Annual Report of the Missionary Society . . . : 1865,* 157. See also NYCA, 8 July 1863; *New Orleans Advocate,* 3 March 1866, 31 March 1866, 2 June 1866; Pool, "Southern Negro," 151–53.

14 For information on Henry Green, see *Minutes of the Annual Conferences of the Methodist Episcopal Church, Spring Conference: 1889* (New York: Hunt and Eaton, 1889), 97. For information on Anthony Ross, see ibid., *1893* (New York: Hunt and Eaton, 1893), 114, and Matthew Simpson, ed., *Cyclopaedia of Methodism Embracing Sketches of Its Rise, Progress, and Present Condition, with Biographical Notices and Numerous Illustrations,* 4th ed. (Philadelphia: Louis H. Everts, 1881), 767; *Proceedings of the Mississippi Mission Conference . . . : First Session, 1865,* 12, 3–4; Pool, "Southern Negro," 151. A Southern Methodist journalist derisively referred to the newly ordained Revs. Chinn, Green, and Ross as "our old colored preachers" in an article that appeared in the 20 January issue of the *New Orleans Christian Advocate* of the M.E. Church, South, and reprinted in the *New Orleans Advocate* of the M.E. Church, 27 January 1866. For information on Sasportas, see Lawrence C. Bryant, ed., *Negro Senators and Representatives in the South Carolina Legislature, 1868–1902* (Orangeburg, S.C.: Dr. Lawrence C. Bryant, Publisher, 1968), 61; Curry, *Passionate Journey,* 14. For information on Cardoza, see ibid., 17–18; Thomas Holt, *Black over White: Negro Political Leadership in South Carolina during Reconstruction* (Urbana: University of Illinois Press, 1977), 65. For information on the formation of the Washington and Delaware Conferences by the General Conference of 1864, see p. 77 in this volume. On Dardis, see *Annual Report of the Church Extension Society, Now the Board of Church Extension of the Methodist Episcopal Church: Seventh, 1872,* 85–86. On Fisher, see ibid., *Sixth, 1871,* 47–48. On Revels, see William B. Gravely, "Hiram Revels Protests Racial Separation in the Methodist Episcopal Church (1876)," *Methodist History* 8 (April 1970): 13–14. On Lynch, see

Gravely, "A Black Methodist on Reconstruction in Mississippi: Three Letters by James Lynch in 1868–1869," *Methodist History* 11 (July 1973): 5–7. On Randolph, see *Minutes of the South Carolina Annual Conference of the Methodist Episcopal Church, Held at Camden, S.C.: Fourth Session, February 11th, 1869* (Charleston, S.C.: Republican Job Office, 1869), 6–7.

15 Quotation from *Methodist Advocate*, 29 March 1876. See also Morrow, *Northern Methodism*, 130. The obituary of Rev. Thomas Evans of the S.C. Conference noted that immediately after emancipation he joined the A.M.E. denomination, "but when he found an opportunity to connect himself with the M.E. Church, he gladly came within this fold, feeling that here all of the rights of his manhood were duly respected, and all the blessings of Christian fellowship and labor freely extended without invidious distinction, on the account of race or previous condition." *Minutes of the South Carolina Conference of the Methodist Episcopal Church, held at Camden, S.C.: Tenth Session, January 14–18, 1875* (Charleston, S.C.: Edward Perry, 1875), 18.

16 Smith quotation from *Methodist Advocate*, 29 March 1876; the second minister quoted is Rev. J. C. Tate, ibid., 26 April 1876.

17 First quotation from *Annual Report of the Missionary Society . . . : Forty-Seventh, 1865,* 143, cf. 144–45; second quotation from *New Orleans Advocate*, 27 January 1866. See also *Annual Report of the Missionary Society . . . : Forty-Eighth, 1866,* 119–22, 138–39; *Annual Report of the Freedmen's Aid Society of the Methodist Episcopal Church: Third, 1878,* 10; Curry, *Passionate Journey,* 21. For a roll call of the early graduates of the Baker Institute, see Jenkins, *Steps along the Way,* 8; Pool, "Southern Negro," 153–57.

18 Smith quotation from *Methodist Advocate*, 29 March 1876; Tate quotation from *Methodist Advocate,* 26 April 1876. The bishop referred to here was Singleton T. Jones. See also Pool, "Southern Negro," 91–124; *Annual Report of the Freedmen's Aid Society . . . : Eighth, 1875,* 14–41; and Jay S. Stowell, *Methodist Adventures in Negro Education* (New York: Methodist Book Concern, 1922), 18–25.

19 Quotation from Gravely, "Hiram Revels Protests," 14. See also *Annual Report of the Missionary Society . . . : Forty Seventh, 1865,* 139; Morrow, *Northern Methodism*, 131. In 1868 a black presiding elder in Louisiana named Emperor Williams reported that one of the ministers on his district had only received $100 from the Missionary Society and the shortfall in expected income had made it "hard for him to get along." *New Orleans Advocate,* 12 December 1868.

20 Thomas Holt found that of the black ministers who served in the "radical" S.C. legislature, twelve were Northern Methodists, nine–twelve were African Methodists, six were Baptists, two were Presbyterians, and one was Congregational. Holt, *Black over White,* 81.

21 First quotation from *New Orleans Advocate*, 20 January 1866; all other quotations from ibid., 14 November 1868, 10 April 1869. See also ibid., 5 May 1866, 15 June 1867, 11 April 1868. For assassination of Randolph, see *Minutes of the South Carolina Annual Conference . . . : Fourth Session, 1869,* 5–7. See also *Minutes of the South Carolina Annual Conference . . . : Sixth Session, 1870,* 12; *Proceedings of the Mississippi Mission Conference: Second Session [December 13–19, 1866],* 9, 20; *Annual Report of the Church Extension Society . . . : Fifth, 1870,* 32–33; *Zion's Herald and Wesleyan Journal* (Boston), 15 April 1869, 22 April 1869. Morrow suggests that the reports of violence were probably exaggerated. See Morrow, *Northern Methodism,* 241–42.

22 Gravely, "A Black Methodist on Reconstruction," 3–5; Charles Spencer Smith, *A History of the African Methodist Episcopal Church* (Philadelphia: Book Concern of the A.M.E. Church, 1922; reprint, New York: Johnson Reprint Corporation, 1968), 51–52. For a sketch of Lynch's life through 1867, see *New Orleans Advocate,* 10 August 1867.

23 All quotations from *CR,* 27 August 1864. See also William B. Gravely, "James Lynch and the Black Christian Mission during Reconstruction," in *Black Apostles at Home and Abroad,* ed. David W. Wills and Richard Newman (Boston, G. K. Hall, 1982), 166–70; *CR,* 4 April 1863.

24 *Minutes of the South Carolina Annual Conference of the African Methodist Episcopal Church* [May 1865]," reprinted in Smith, *History,* 505. See also Gravely, "James Lynch," 162, 170–74.

25 James Lynch, Philadelphia, to Bishop M. Simpson, Philadelphia, 29 March 1867, printed in full in Gravely, "The Decision of A.M.E. Leader, James Lynch, to Join the Methodist Episcopal Church: New Evidence at Old St. George's Church, Philadelphia," *Methodist History* 15 (July 1977): 265–66.

26 Ibid.

27 Ibid., 265.

28 Ibid. First quotation from *New Orleans Advocate,* 10 August 1867; Lynch quotation from ibid., 2 November 1867. Lynch quickly established himself as one of the leading figures in his new denomination and as a major force in Mississippi politics. He served as secretary of state and declined nominations to run for lieutenant governor and U.S. senator. He also founded and edited a newspaper in Jackson called *The Colored Citizen's Monthly.* A white Mississippian remembered Lynch as a speaker without peer: "fluent and graceful, he stirred his great audiences as no other man did or could do." William Harris Hardy, "Recollections of Reconstruction in East and Southeast Mississippi," in *Publications of the Mississippi Historical Society* (Oxford, Miss., 1901) vol. 4, ed. Franklin L. Riley, 126. Lynch died on 18 December 1872 of a bronchial infection and Bright's disease. See Gravely, "James Lynch," 162, 175–80; *NYCA,* 5 November 1868; *Zion's Herald and Wesleyan Journal,* 5 November 1868. The prolific Rev. Lynch wrote many articles detailing his activities in the South. Citations for some of them follow: *New Orleans Advocate,* 7 December 1867, 1 February 1868, 29 February 1868, 2 May 1868, 3 April 1869; *Methodist Advocate,* 19 April 1869; *Zion's Herald and Wesleyan Journal,* 25 March 1869, 11 January 1872.

7 REPUBLICANISM AND THE RISE AND FALL OF ANTICASTE RADICALISM

1 *Forty-Seventh Annual Report of the Missionary Society . . . 1865,* 138; second quotation from *New Orleans Advocate,* 2 January 1869. See also *Proceedings of the Second Session of the Mississippi Mission Conference [December 13–19, 1866],* 21. In the issue of the *Methodist Advocate* for 27 October 1869 an article entitled "A Word to Colored Men" issued the following advice: "It is said that next to Godliness is cleanliness, but certainly next to cleanliness is prudence and economy in the affairs of life." The article also told its black readers that "Prudence and economy can do much . . . , perhaps more than any legislative enactment in relieving the colored people of the South of their disabilities."

2 French quotation from *Christian Advocate and Journal* (New York) [hereafter *NYCA*], 21 April 1864; Moore quotation from 13 April 1865. At the time they made their proposals, French was in Beaufort, South Carolina, and Moore was in Jacksonville, Florida.

3   *NYCA*, 22 June 1865.

4   *NYCA*, 10 March 1864; *New Orleans Advocate*, 23 June 1866, quotation 28 July 1866. The minister referred to here is identified only as "B," but is probably Rev. N. L. Brakeman; *Proceedings of the Mississippi Mission Conference: Second Session [December 13–19, 1866]*, 21. The editors and the minister cited here are white; most of the ministers in the Mississippi Conference were black. I have not been able to discern a distinctive black critique of the "mainstream" economic discourse described here, although one may have existed.

5   Quotation by Rev. P. Landry, *Southwestern Christian Advocate* (New Orleans), 25 October 1877. For reports of destitution, see *NYCA*, 23 November 1865; *Zion's Herald and Wesleyan Journal*, 2 January 1868, 23 July 1868; *New Orleans Advocate*, 25 January 1868.

6   Quotation from *NYCA*, 1 November 1866. See also Donald G. Jones, *The Sectional Crisis and Northern Methodism: A Study in Piety, Political Ethics and Civil Religion* (Metuchen, N.J.: Scarecrow Press, 1979), 293; Ralph E. Morrow, *Northern Methodism and Reconstruction* (East Lansing: Michigan State University Press, 1956), 204; *NYCA*, 18 May 1865, 4 October 1866; *New Orleans Advocate*, 23 June 1866; *Proceedings of the Mississippi Mission Conference . . . : Second Session [December 13–19, 1866]*, 20. As a new member of the Mississippi Conference, James Lynch authored a resolution calling for the restoration of the South to the Union on a basis that would ensure "civil and political equality without regard to race or color." *Minutes of the Mississippi Mission Conference of the Methodist Episcopal Church: Third Session, 1867*, 13; *Zion's Herald and Wesleyan Journal*, 23 April 1868.

7   First quotation from *New Orleans Advocate*, 11 May 1867; second quotation from ibid., 18 May 1867. See also *Methodist Advocate*, 3 June 1874. The editor of the *New Orleans Advocate* was John P. Newman. The editor of the *Methodist Advocate*, E. Q. Fuller, was taken to task for his opposition to the Civil Rights Bill by his A.M.E. counterpart, B. T. Tanner, editor of the *Christian Recorder* [hereafter, *CR*]: "Dr. E. Q. Fuller is determined in his opposition to the Civil Rights Bill. . . . Are our brethren of the South, those in connection with the M.E. Church, satisfied with their organ and its editor?" *CR*, 1 October 1874.

8   Quotation from *Methodist Advocate*, 30 April 1873. See also Frank Kenneth Pool, "The Southern Negro in the Methodist Episcopal Church" (Ph.D. diss., Duke University, 1939), 266–67; *New Orleans Advocate*, 23 June 1866.

9   First quotation from *Raleigh Christian Advocate*, 19 November 1873; see also 18 March 1874; 15 December 1875; second and third quotations appear in William B. Gravely's excellent biography, *Gilbert Haven, Methodist Abolitionist: A Study in Race, Religion, and Reform, 1850–1880* (New York: Abingdon Press, 1973), 220; last quotation from William G. Matton, "Memoir," Chapter 10, 1, AMs, n.d., Manuscripts Department, Perkins Library, Duke University, Durham, North Carolina. See also Jones, *Sectional Crisis*, 296; *Raleigh Christian Advocate*, 17 September 1873, 18 March 1874, 15 December 1875; William Haven Daniels, ed. *Memorials of Gilbert Haven, Bishop of the Methodist Episcopal Church* (Boston: B. B. Russell, 1880); and George Prentice, *The Life of Gilbert Haven, Bishop of the Methodist Episcopal Church* (New York: Phillips and Hunt, 1883).

10   *Methodist Advocate*, 19 March 1873, quotations from 22 April 1874; Gravely, *Gilbert Haven*, 227.

11   Quotation from *Raleigh Christian Advocate*, 21 May 1979. See also ibid., 15 December 1875; 17 December 1879, 11 February 1880; *North Carolina Christian Advocate* (Raleigh), 6 May 1863; *Nashville Christian Advocate*, 9 March 1872, 15 November 1879.

12   Although Hiram Revels joined the M.E. Church in 1868, he did not seek "ministerial membership" until after he was out of politics. See William B. Gravely, "Hiram Revels Protests Racial Separation in the Methodist Episcopal Church (1876)," *Methodist History* 8 (April 1970): 14. An article in the *Methodist Advocate* entitled "Non-Political," took the following position: "This is not a political paper. . . . Still, we wish it distinctly understood that, in our opinion, political matters are not so sacred as to be entirely outside the scope of religious journalism." *Methodist Advocate*, 6 January 1869. Morrow, *Northern Methodism*, 209–10; all Lynch quotations from James Lynch, Meridian [Mississippi], to Rev. M. Simpson D.D. [Philadelphia, Pennsylvania], 6 October 1869, printed in full in Gravely, "A Black Methodist on Reconstruction in Mississippi: Three Letters by James Lynch in 1868–1869," *Methodist History* 11 (July 1973): 15–16. The *Methodist Advocate* took the following position on Lynch's election to office: "We have never known an instance, nor can we conceive of one in which a minister could be more clearly justified in taking active part in politics, but still express regrets that the entire thoughts, time and interest of Brother Lynch cannot be given to the one work. The whole South needs him as a Christian minister." *Methodist Advocate*, 16 February 1870. For the best account of Lynch's political career, see William C. Harris, "James Lynch: Black Leader in Southern Reconstruction," *Historian* 34 (November 1971): 40–61. Final quotation from *Register of the Georgian Annual Conference of the Methodist Episcopal Church: Second Session, 1868*, 4.

13   Lynch quotation from James Lynch, Meridian [Mississippi], to Rev. M. Simpson D.D. [Philadelphia, Pennsylvania], 6 October 1869, in Gravely, "A Black Methodist on Reconstruction," 16; second quotation from *NYCA*, 10 August 1865.

14   Edward D. Jervey, "Motives and Methods of the Methodist Episcopal Church in the Period of Reconstruction," *Methodist History* 4 (July 1966): 17–25; Donald G. Jones, "The Moral, Social and Political Ideas of the Methodist Episcopal Church from the Closing Years of the Civil War through Reconstruction, 1864–1876" (Ph.D. diss., Drew University, 1969), 316–17; Pool, "Southern Negro," 37–39; Morrow, *Northern Methodism*, 203–29; William W. Sweet, "The Methodist Episcopal Church and Reconstruction," *Journal of the Illinois State Historical Society* 7 (October 1914): 153–56, 159–65. For an exploration of the political involvement of evangelical religion in general, see Victor B. Howard, *Religion and the Radical Republican Movement, 1860–1870* (Lexington: University Press of Kentucky, 1990).

15   *Minutes of the South Carolina Annual Conference . . . : Sixth Session [December 22–26, 1870]* (Charleston, S.C.: Republican Book and Job Office, 1871), first quotation from 11, second quotation from back cover. By way of contrast, the minutes of the 1868 session of the Georgia Annual Conference were published by the Western Methodist Book Concern in Cincinnati.

16   Pool, "Southern Negro," 33; Morrow, *Northern Methodism*, 33, 216–18; *New Orleans Advocate*, 9 January 1868; quotation from *Journal of the General Conference of the*

Methodist Episcopal Church: 1868, 151; Sweet, "Reconstruction," 148, 164–65; Eric Foner, *Reconstruction: America's Unfinished Revolution, 1863–1877* (New York: Harper and Row, 1988), 352.

17   For statements of the Northern Methodist interpretation of the American dichotomy, see *Zion's Herald and Wesleyan Journal,* 27 November 1861, 14 January 1863, 27 February 1868; *NYCA,* 25 May 1865, 22 February 1866, 23 June 1870; and *Annual Report of the Freedmen's Aid Society . . . : Eleventh, 1878,* 54–57. Rev. John H. Caldwell was a white southerner who joined the M.E. Church and claimed to be the originator of the term "New South," a concept for which he labored "heart and soul." John H. Caldwell, *Reminiscences of the Reconstruction of the Church and State in Georgia* (Wilmington, Del.: J. Miller Thomas, 1895), 11. For a sharp southern rejoinder to the Northern Methodist dichotomy, see *Raleigh Christian Advocate,* 15 December 1875.

18   Haven quotation from G. Haven, Atlanta, Georgia, to My dear [unclear], [n.p.] [This is a very brief general letter of introduction and probably was not sent to a specific person], 1 June 1877, ALS, Bryant Papers; Bryant quotation on the American dichotomy from Bryant, "The South: The Opportunity for Christian Work, The Mission of the Methodist Episcopal Church in the Southern States [10 June 1880]," AMs, 2, Bryant Papers. See also Bryant, "The Southern Advance Association: The South, the Condition, the Cause, the Remedy, 1880," AMs, John Emory Bryant Papers, Manuscripts Department, Perkins Library, Duke University, Durham, North Carolina, and Bryant's essay, "Why Is our Church in the South?" in *Church Extension Annual, including the Annual Report of the Board of Church Extension: Fourteenth, 1879,* 25–26; Ruth Currie-McDaniel, *Carpetbagger of Conscience: A Biography of John Emory Bryant* (Athens: University of Georgia Press, 1987), 157–59. Concern about the influence of the Southern Historical Society was also expressed in a speech to the Freedmen's Aid Society by Rev. C. H. Fowler. See *Annual Report of the Freedmen's Aid Society . . . : Eleventh, 1878,* 56; E. Merton Coulter, *The South during Reconstruction, 1865–1877* (Baton Rouge: Louisiana State University Press, 1947), 182–83; E. Q. Fuller, Atlanta, Georgia, to The Friends of National Ideas, [n.p.], 7 February 1881, ALS, Bryant Papers.

19   Tourgee quotation from Albion W. Tourgee, *A Fool's Errand, by One of the Fools: A Novel of the South during Reconstruction* (New York: Harper and Row, [1879] 1966), 168; Bryant quotations from J. E. Bryant, to My Darling Wife [Emma Bryant], Philadelphia, 1 February 1880, ALS, Bryant Papers. See also Currie-McDaniel, *Carpetbagger of Conscience,* 156–57; Otto H. Olson, *Carpetbagger's Crusade: The Life of Albion Winegar Tourgee* (Baltimore: John Hopkins University Press, 1965), esp. 5, 49, 321.

20   Quotation from *Methodist Advocate,* 20 March 1872. See also ibid., 3 April 1872, 26 June 1872. Fuller became an opponent of Gilbert Haven's anticaste positions as soon as he assumed the editorship of the *Methodist Advocate.* See Gravely, *Gilbert Haven,* 188–89, 202.

21   Pool, "Southern Negro," 43; Morrow, *Northern Methodism,* 186. For the best assessment of the continuity of the ethos of abolition into the Reconstruction period and through the early twentieth century, see James M. McPherson, *The Abolitionist Legacy: From Reconstruction to the NAACP* (Princeton, N.J.: Princeton University Press, 1975), esp. 227–38.

22   *NYCA,* 7 September 1865.

23   All quotations from *NYCA,* 28 July 1864. See also Pool, "Southern Negro," 218–20;

Morrow, *Northern Methodism,* 187–88. The segregation of Ames Chapel became a very controversial issue. Gilbert Haven editorialized against Newman's policies in *Zion's Herald and Wesleyan Journal,* 12 March 1868. In response, Newman offered to "say some plain things about him [Haven] and his notions." *New Orleans Advocate,* 2 May 1868. See also McPherson, *Abolitionist Legacy,* 229. Gravely, *Gilbert Haven,* 229.

24 Quotation from Matton, "Memoir," AMs, chap. 13, pp. 1–2. See also McPherson, *Abolitionist Legacy,* 230. In an article entitled "Mixed or Separate Conferences," E. Q. Fuller put forward the view that M.E. Conferences could be divided into five different classes. The fourth class included de facto colored conferences that claimed to be integrated because they had a token white membership. According to Fuller, the following conferences fell into the fourth class: South Carolina, Florida, Mississippi, Louisiana, Texas, and West Texas. Fuller wrote: "In all of these conferences, with an aggregate of 80,000 members, there are probably not 500 of them white. I do not know any one [*sic*] who thinks it best to attempt to separate the races in these conferences. What is there to separate?" *Methodist Advocate,* 14 May 1873.

25 Pool, "Southern Negro," 66–67.

26 *Methodist Advocate,* 20 March 1872, 3 April 1872, 26 June 1872, 14 May 1873; Edmund Jordan Hammond, *The Methodist Episcopal Church in Georgia . . .* (Atlanta: n.p., 1935), 119–21.

27 *Methodist Advocate,* 3 April 1872.

28 Morrow, *Northern Methodism,* 120; *Methodist Advocate,* 13 May 1874, 12 January 1876.

29 Quotation from a letter from an M.E. minister that appeared under the heading "The Other Side," *Methodist Advocate,* 5 April 1876. See also ibid., 20 March 1872, 3 April 1872, 11 June 1873, 26 June 1972, 13 May 1874, 2 June 1875, 8 March 1876, 22 March 1876, 12 April 1876.

30 All quotations from *Methodist Advocate,* 1 May 1872. Following the notice that appeared in the *Methodist Advocate* announcing the colored convention, editor E. Q. Fuller assured his readers that the delegates would "keep in mind the fact that there is no disposition on the part of their white brethren to push them out of the Conference, or in any way trammel their action." Ibid., 13 March 1872. See also McPherson, *Abolitionist Legacy,* 230–32.

31 The first quotation is by "C. P." of Lebanon, Tennessee, *Methodist Advocate,* 29 September 1875; second quotation is by Rev. J. C. Tate, in ibid., 1 March 1876.

32 Revels quotation from, Hiram Revels, "We Ought Not to Separate," in *New Orleans Southwestern Advocate,* 4 May 1876, printed in full in Gravely, "Hiram Revels Protests Racial Separation," 19–20. In 1868, Lynch and the ministers and members of his district in Mississippi sent a petition to the General Conference opposing the creation of separate conferences. *Journal of the General Conference . . . : 1868,* 186. *Zion's Herald and Wesleyan Journal,* 25 March 1869. Second quotation by Rev. Amos Hays, *Methodist Advocate,* 9 July 1873. See also ibid., 29 September 1875, 29 March 1876; Pool, "Southern Negro," 227–28.

33 Morrow, *Northern Methodism,* 183–84, 192; Gravely, *Gilbert Haven,* 197n; *Methodist Advocate,* 3 April 1872. During his time of troubles in the 1830s, Matlack received succor and support from black Methodists. He recalled: "Then it was, when the white man thrust me out, the freedman [*sic*] took me in. Their houses and their pulpits were open, and I became their frequent, always welcome guest." *Annual Report of the Freedmen's*

Aid Society . . . : *Tenth, 1877*, 70–71. During a fight against caste in 1876, Matlack wrote: "For twenty five years I was an anti-slavery seceder from the M.E. Church. Every day of those years I was one of the Wesleyan Con. of America, whose constitution forbids all distinctions of the kind now deprecated." *CR*, 6 July 1876. See also Richard M. Cameron, "Orange Scott and the Organization of the Wesleyan Methodists," in *The History of American Methodism*, vol. 2, ed. Emory Stevens Bucke (New York: Abingdon Press, 1964), 39–44 and Matlack, *The History of American Slavery and Methodism from 1780–1849* (New York: #5 Spruce Street, 1849).

34 Lansing quotation from *Methodist Advocate*, 8 March 1876; Franklin quotation from ibid., 12 April 1876. See also ibid., 5 April 1876.

35 Quotation from *Journal of the General Conference* . . . : *1872*, 90. See also ibid., 34–35, 37, 92–94, 109, 116, 120, 167, 197, 417; Gravely, *Gilbert Haven*, 199.

36 Pool, "Southern Negro," 226; McPherson, *Abolitionist Legacy*, 232; Morrow, *Northern Methodism*, 192; Gravely, *Gilbert Haven*, 162, 202. Gravely correctly points out that the General Conference of 1872 was not controlled by anticaste radicals; two conservative opponents of Haven were also elected bishops. Ibid., 198.

37 Gravely, "James Lynch and the Black Christian Mission during Reconstruction," in *Black Apostles at Home and Abroad*, ed. David W. Wills and Richard Newman (Boston: G. K. Hall, 1982), 162, 180–81. A member of the Mississippi delegation asked the General Conference to help Lynch's widow meet a financial obligation she had incurred trying to help the state of Mississippi erect a monument to the memory of the young preacher. *Journal of the General Conference* . . . : *1876*, 242. Gravely, *Gilbert Haven*, 212; for an example of the anti-Haven backlash, see *Journal of the General Conference* . . . : *1876*, 177; McPherson, *Abolitionist Legacy*, 232.

38 Quotation from *Journal of the General Conference* . . . : *1876*, 188. See also ibid., 113, 130, 164, 170, 189, 245; Pool, "Southern Negro," 230.

39 All Matlack quotations from *CR*, 6 July 1876; editor's quotation from ibid., 15 June 1876. See also Gravely, *Gilbert Haven*, 236–37; *Journal of the General Conference* . . . : *1876*, 329–31; Pool, "Southern Negro," 232.

40 Gravely, *Gilbert Haven*, 238.

41 Quotation from *Journal of the General Conference* . . . : *1876*, 274, 278. See also Gravely, *Gilbert Haven*, 238; see also Hammond, *Methodist Episcopal Church in Georgia*, 141. The Commission met in Cape May, New Jersey, in August 1876. William W. Sweet, *Methodism in American History* (New York: Abingdon Press, 1953), 328–29, 399.

42 Quotation appeared in the *Raleigh Christian Advocate*, 19 February 1879. See also Gravely, *Gilbert Haven*, 246.

43 McPherson, *Abolitionist Legacy*, 234; Morrow, *Northern Methodism*, 196–97; Gravely, *Gilbert Haven*, 252–53.

44 *CR*, 8 January 1880.

45 *Journal of the General Conference* . . . : *1868*, 220–21; ibid., *1872*, 91, 93, 128, 253; ibid., *1876*, 158, 159, 177, 188, 195, 244; ibid., *1880*, 157, 167, 173, 199, 252–53, 281–82; *CR*, 30 March 1872; *Methodist Advocate*, 6 March 1872, 20 March 1872, 1 May, 19 June 1872; McPherson, *Abolitionist Legacy*, 264–68; Pool, "Southern Negro," 240–45; Donald Franklin Roth, " 'Grace not Race': Southern Negro Church Leaders, Black Identity, and Missions to West Africa, 1865–1919" (Ph.D. diss., University of Texas at Austin, 1975), 135–36. The first black M.E. bishops elected to preside over black con-

ferences in the United States were Matthew W. Clair Sr. and Robert E. Jones. Harry V. Richardson, *Dark Salvation: The Story of Methodism as It Developed among Blacks in America* (Garden City, N.Y.: Doubleday, 1976), 271–72.

46   In their study of the black church, C. Eric Lincoln and Lawrence H. Mamiya give the Methodist membership figures as of 1896: Colored Methodist, 130,000; Northern Methodist, 250,000; A.M.E. Zion, 350,000; A.M.E. 450,000. C. Eric Lincoln and Lawrence H. Mamiya, *The Black Church in the African American Experience* (Durham, N.C.: Duke University Press, 1990), 65. For histories of the educational mission, see Henry M. Johnson, "The Methodist Episcopal Church and the Education of Southern Negroes, 1862–1900" (Ph.D. diss., Yale University, 1939), 380–90, 407–30, 437–45, and Jay S. Stowell, *Methodist Adventures in Negro Education* (New York: Methodist Book Concern, 1972). The best general studies of the education of the freedpeople are James D. Anderson, *The Education of Blacks in the South, 1860–1935* (Chapel Hill: University of North Carolina Press, 1988); Robert C. Morris, *Reading, 'Riting, and Reconstruction: The Education of Freedmen in the South, 1861–1870* (Chicago: University of Chicago Press, 1976); and McPherson, *Abolitionist Legacy*, 143–295.

47   Jones, *Sectional Crisis*, 297–301.

CONCLUSION

1   Holsey quotation appears in Michael L. Thurmond, *A Story Untold: Black Men and Women in Athens History* (Athens, Ga.: Clarke County School District, 1978), 129. See also Glenn T. Eskew, "Black Elitism and the Failure of Paternalism in Postbellum Georgia: The Case of Bishop Lucius Henry Holsey," *Journal of Southern History* 58 (November 1992): 655–66.

2   C. Eric Lincoln and Lawrence H. Mamiya, *The Black Church in the African American Experience* (Durham, N.C.: Duke University Press, 1990), 50–68; Julius E. Del Pino, "Blacks in the United Methodist Church from Its Beginning to 1968," *Methodist History* 19 (October 1980): 17–18; J. H. Graham, *Black United Methodists: Retrospect and Prospect* (New York: Vantage Press, 1979), 100–7; Othal H. Lakey, *The History of the C.M.E. Church* (Memphis: C.M.E. Publishing, 1985), 538–42; Harry V. Richardson, *Dark Salvation: The Story of Methodism as It Developed among Blacks in America* (Garden City, N.Y.: Doubleday, 1976), 267, 272–88.

3   For a very brief but instructive discussion of the relationship between class and denominational affiliation in Charleston, see Wilbert Lee Jenkins, "Chaos, Conflict and Control: The Responses of the Newly-Freed Slaves in Charleston, South Carolina to Emancipation and Reconstruction, 1865–1877" (Ph.D. diss., Michigan State University, 1993), 293–96. Jualynne Dodson, "Nineteenth-Century A.M.E. Preaching Women: Cutting Edge of Women's Inclusion in Church Polity," in *Women in New Worlds*, ed. Rosemary Skinner Keller and Hilah F. Thomas (Nashville: Abingdon Press, 1981), 276–89; Evelyn Brooks Higginbotham, *Righteous Discontent: The Women's Movement in the Black Baptist Church, 1880–1920* (Cambridge, Mass.: Harvard University Press, 1993); Kathleen C. Berkeley, " 'Colored Ladies Also Contributed': Black Women's Activities from Benevolence to Social Welfare, 1866–1896," in *The Web of Southern Social Relations: Women, Family, and Education*, ed. Walter J. Fraser Jr., R. Frank Saunders Jr. and Jon L. Wakelyn (Athens: University of Georgia Press, 1985), 181–203. See also the autobiographies of Jarena Lee and Julia A. J. Foote in William L. Andrews, ed., *Sisters of the Spirit: Three*

Black Women's Autobiographies of the Nineteenth Century (Bloomington: Indiana University Press, 1986), and David W. Wills, "Womanhood and Domesticity in the A.M.E. Tradition: The Influence of Daniel Alexander Payne," in *Black Apostles at Home and Abroad*, ed. Richard Newman and David W. Wills (Boston: G. K. Hall, 1982), 133–46. Sara J. Duncan, *Progressive Missions in the South and Addresses with Illustrations and Sketches of Missionary Workers and Ministers and Bishops' Wives* (Atlanta: Franklin Printing and Publishing, 1906), 244.

4   Unless Methodists are very atypical, it would appear that the "ideology" of paternalism has had a much stronger hold on the thinking of historians than it ever had on the main portion of the southern black population. For a discussion of the theory of "paternalistic hegemony" and how it impacted slave religion and emancipation, see Eugene D. Genovese, *Roll, Jordan, Roll: The World the Slaves Made* (New York: Vintage Books, 1976), esp. 5, 124, 126–28, 137, 140–48. For a thoughtful and incisive critique of the Genovese thesis, see James D. Anderson, "Aunt Jemima in Dialectics: Genovese on Slave Culture," *Journal of Negro History* 41 (January 1976): 99–114. See also Reginald F. Hildebrand, "Some Persistent Doubts about Paternalistic Hegemony: *Roll, Jordan, Roll* Twenty Years Later," *Contention* 3 (Fall 1993): 67–86.

5   H. Richard Niebuhr, *The Social Sources of Denominationalism* (New York: New American Library, 1975), 275.

BIBLIOGRAPHY

PRIMARY SOURCES

Manuscripts
Amistad Research Center, Tulane University, New Orleans, Louisiana
    Dunn-Landry Papers. Pierre Landry. "Autobiographical Sketch" TMs.
Library of Congress, Washington, D.C.
    Matthew Simpson Papers
Perkins Library, Duke University, Durham, North Carolina
    John Emory Bryant Papers
    Crum, Mason. "What Became of the Negro membership?" [n.d.] TMs.
    William G. Matton Papers. "Memoir" AMs. [n.d.]
    "Minutes of the Salisbury, N.C. District Conference, 1868–1877." AD [Bound Hw.]
    "[North Carolina Annual Conference] Conference Journal, 1867–1873." AD [Bound Hw.]
    "[North Carolina Annual Conference] Conference Journal, 1874–1881." AD [Bound Hw.]
South Caroliniana Library, University of South Carolina, Columbia, South Carolina
    Nathan Brown Papers
    Mood, Francis Asbury. "Autobiography" TMs. [n.d.]

Periodicals

A. African Methodist Episcopal
A.M.E. Church Review
Christian Recorder [CR] (Philadelphia), 1862–1880
Missionary Record (Charleston), R. H. Cain, ed., 1877
South Carolina Leader (Charleston), R. H. Cain, ed., 1866

B. Methodist Episcopal
Christian Advocate and Journal [NYCA] (New York)
Methodist Advocate (Atlanta)
New Orleans Advocate, 1868
Southwestern Christian Advocate (New Orleans), 1896
Zion's Herald and Wesleyan Journal (Boston)

C. Methodist Episcopal, South
Episcopal Methodist (Raleigh), 1868–1871
Nashville Christian Advocate, 1872, 1979
New Orleans Christian Advocate, 1866
North Carolina Christian Advocate (Raleigh), 1863
Raleigh Christian Advocate, 1863–1879
Southern Christian Advocate [SCA] (Charleston), 1859–1871
Texas Christian Advocate (Galveston), 1872

D. Secular Newspapers
New York Times, 1865
Weekly Message (Greensboro, N.C.), 1860

Journals, Minutes, Proceedings, and Reports

A. African Methodist Episcopal

Minutes of the New England Annual Conference of the African Methodist Episcopal Church:
1862; 1866 [separate volumes]. New Bedford: Evening Standard Steam Printing, 1862;
1866.

Minutes of the South Carolina Annual Conference of the African Methodist Episcopal
Church: 1865–1867 [separate volumes]; May 1865 minutes reprinted in Charles Spencer
Smith, *A History of the African Methodist Episcopal Church*

Minutes of the South Carolina Annual Conference of the African Methodist Episcopal
Church: Twelfth Session, 1876. Charleston, S.C.: Walker, Evans and Cogswell, 1876.

Proceedings of the Quarto-Centennial Conference of the African Methodist Episcopal Church
of South Carolina, at Charleston, S.C., May 15, 16, and 17, 1889. Edited by Benjamin W.
Arnett. N.p., 1890.

B. Methodist Episcopal

Annual Report of the Church Extension Society of the Methodist Episcopal Church: Fourth,
1869; Fifth, 1870; Sixth, 1871 [separate volumes]

Annual Report of the Church Extension Society, Now the Board of Church Extension of the
Methodist Episcopal Church: Seventh, 1872

Annual Report of the Freedmen's Aid Society of the Methodist Episcopal Church: Third,
1872; Fifth, 1873; Seventh, 1874; Eighth, 1875; Ninth, 1876; Tenth, 1877; Eleventh,
1878 [separate volumes]

Annual Report of the Missionary Society of the Methodist Episcopal Church: Forty-Sixth,
1864; Forty-Seventh, 1865; Forty-Eighth, 1866 [separate volumes]. New York: Printed
for the Society, 1864; 1865; 1866.

Church Extension Annual, including the Annual Report of the Board of Church Extension:
Fourteenth, 1879

Journal of the General Conference of the Methodist Episcopal Church: 1864; 1868; 1872;
1876; 1880 [separate volumes]. New York: Carlton and Porter.

Minutes and Journal of Proceedings of the Washington Annual Conference: First Session,
October 27–31, 1864. Reprint. N.p., n.d.

Minutes of the Annual Conferences of the Methodist Episcopal Church, Spring Conference:
1889; 1893 [separate volumes]. New York: Hunt and Eaton, 1889; 1893.

Minutes of the Mississippi Mission Conference of the Methodist Episcopal Church: Third
Session, 1867

Minutes of the South Carolina Annual Conference of the Methodist Episcopal Church, Held
at Camden, S.C.: Fourth Session, February 11th, 1869; Sixth Session, Dec. 22–26, 1870;
Tenth Session, January 14–18, 1875 [separate volumes]. Charleston, S.C.: Republican
Job Office, 1869, 1871; Edward Perry, 1875.

Proceedings of the Mississippi Mission Conference Organized in New Orleans by Bishop
Thompson: First Session, December 25th, 1865; Second Session, [December 13–19,
1866] [separate volumes]. N.p., n.d.

Register of the Georgian Annual Conference of the Methodist Episcopal Church: Second
Session, 1868

Reports of the Freedman's Aid Society of the Methodist Episcopal Church, 1866–1875

C. Methodist Episcopal, South

Annual Report of the Board of Missions of the Methodist Episcopal Church, South, June 1, 1876. Nashville: Southern Methodist Publishing, 1876.

Annual Report of the Missionary Society of the South Carolina Conference, December 14, 1861

Minutes of the Annual Conferences of the Methodist Episcopal Church, South: 1871; 1880 [separate volumes]. Nashville: Southern Methodist Publishing, 1872; 1881.

Minutes of the South Carolina Annual Conference of the Methodist Episcopal Church, South, 1865

D. Secular Minutes

Journal of the Senate of the General Assembly of South Carolina being the Regular Session, Commencing November 23, 1869; November 22, 1870. Columbia, S.C.: John W. Denny, Printer to the State, 1869; 1870.

Proceedings of the Constitutional Convention of South Carolina. Charleston, S.C.: Denny and Perry, 1868.

Proceedings of the National Convention of Colored Men, Held in the City of Syracuse, N.Y. Boston: J. S. Rock and George L. Ruffin, 1864. Reprinted in *Minutes of the Proceedings of the National Negro Conventions, 1830–1864.* Ed. Howard Holman Bell. New York: Arno Press, 1969.

U.S. Congress, House of Representatives. *Congressional Record* (10 January 1874), vol. 2, part 1, 565; (24 January 1874), vol. 2, part 1, 901; (10 February 1875), vol. 3, part 2, 1153; (14 January 1878), vol. 7, part 1, 322.

Memoirs, Sermons, and Speeches

A. African Methodist Episcopal

Allen, Richard. *The Life Experience and Gospel Labors of the Rt. Rev. Richard Allen.* Philadelphia: n.p., 1833; reprint, New York: Abingdon Press, 1960.

Brown, John M. "A Word to Our Subscribers and Friends," *Repository of Religion and Literature* 3 (April 1861): 49–52.

Gaines, John Wesley. *African Methodism in the South, or Twenty Five Years of Freedom.* Atlanta: Franklin Publishing, 1890.

Heard, William H. *From Slavery to the Bishopric in the A.M.E. Church: An Autobiography.* Philadelphia: A.M.E. Book Concern, 1924.

Kealing, H. T. *History of African Methodism in Texas.* Waco, Texas: C. F. Blanks, 1885.

Payne, Daniel A. *The African M.E. Church in Its Relation to the Freedmen.* Xenia, Ohio: Torchlight, 1868.

———. *History of the African Methodist Episcopal Church.* Edited by Charles S. Smith. Nashville: A.M.E. Sunday School Union, 1891; reprint, New York: Johnson Reprint Corp., 1968.

———. *Recollections of Seventy Years.* Nashville: A.M.E. Sunday School Union, 1888; reprint, New York: Arno Press, 1969.

———. *The Semi-Centenary and the Retrospection of the African Methodist Episcopal Church in the United States of America.* Baltimore: Sherwood, 1866; reprint, Freeport, N.Y.: Books for Libraries Press, 1972.

———. *Sermons and Addresses, 1853–1891, Bishop Daniel A. Payne.* Edited by Charles Killian. New York: Arno Press, 1972.

Steward, Theophilus Gould. *From 1864 to 1914: Fifty Years in the Gospel Ministry.* Philadelphia: A.M.E. Book Concern, [1921].

Turner, Henry M. *Celebration of the First Anniversary of Freedom, Held in Springfield Baptist Church, January 1st, 1866, and Containing an Outline of an Oration Delivered on the Occasion by Chaplain Henry M. Turner.* Augusta, Ga.: Loyal Georgian, 1866.

———. *Respect Black: The Writings and Speeches of Henry McNeal Turner.* Ed. Edwin S. Redkey. New York: Arno Press, 1971.

Wayman, Alexander W. *Cyclopedia of African Methodism.* Baltimore: Methodist Episcopal Book Depository, 1882.

Weston, A. "How African Methodism Was Introduced in the Up Country." In *Proceedings of the Quarto-Centennial Conference of the African Methodist Episcopal Church of South Carolina, at Charleston, S.C., May 15, 16, and 17, 1889,* 70–72. Ed. Benjamin W. Arnett. n.p., 1890.

B. African Methodist Episcopal Zion

Hood, James Walker. *One Hundred Years of the African Methodist Episcopal Zion Church; or the Centennial of African Methodism.* New York: A.M.E. Zion Book Concern, 1895.

———. *Speech of Rev. James W. Hood, of Cumberland County Court on the Question of Suffrage, Delivered in the Constitutional Convention of North Carolina, February 12th, 1868.* Raleigh: W. W. Holden and Son, 1868.

Jones, Singleton T. *Sermons and Addresses of the Late Rev. Bishop Singleton T. Jones, D.D. of the African M.E. Zion Church.* Edited by J. W. Smith. York, Pa.: Anstart and Sons, 1892.

C. Colored Methodist Episcopal

Holsey, Lucius H. *Autobiography, Sermons, Addresses and Essays of Bishop L. H. Holsey, D.D.* Atlanta: Franklin Printing and Publishing, 1898.

Lane, Isaac. *The Autobiography of Bishop Isaac Lane, LL.D., with a Short History of the C.M.E. Church in America and of Methodism.* Nashville: Publishing House of the M.E. Church, South, 1916.

Phillips, Charles H. *From the Farm to the Bishopric: An Autobiography.* Nashville: Parthenon Press, 1932.

D. Methodist Episcopal

Caldwell, John H. *Reminiscences of the Reconstruction of Church and State in Georgia.* Wilmington, Del.: J. Miller Thomas, 1895.

Daniels, William Haven, ed. *Memorials of Gilbert Haven, Bishop of the Methodist Episcopal Church.* Boston: B. B. Russell, 1880.

French, A. M. *Slavery in South Carolina and the Ex-Slaves; or The Port Royal Mission.* 1862. Reprint, New York: Negro Universities Press, 1969.

Hagood, Lewis M. *The Colored Man in the Methodist Episcopal Church.* Cincinnati: Cranston and Stowe, 1890; reprint, Westport, Conn.: Negro Universities Press, 1970.

Lawrence, W. H. *The Centenary Souvenir: Containing a History of Centenary Church,*

Charleston, and an Account of the Life and Labors of Rev. R. V. Lawrence, Father of the Pastor of Centenary Church. Charleston: N.p., 1885.

Matlack, Lucius C. *The History of American Slavery and Methodism from 1780–1849.* New York: #5 Spruce Street, 1849.

Simpson, Matthew. *Cyclopaedia of Methodism Embracing Sketches of Its Rise, Progress, and Present Condition, with Biographical Notices and Numerous Illustrations.* 4th ed. Philadelphia: Louis H. Everts, 1881.

E. Methodist Episcopal, South

Burkhead, L. S. "History of the Difficulties of the Pastorate of the Front Street Methodist Church, Wilmington, N.C., for the Year 1865." In *An Annual Publication of Historical Papers Published by the Historical Society of Trinity College, Durham, N.C.* Series 8 (1908–9), 35–118.

Harrison, William P., ed. *The Gospel among the Slaves: A Short Account of Missionary Operations among the African Slaves of the Southern States.* Nashville: Publishing House of the M.E. Church, South, 1893.

Mood, Francis Asbury. *Methodism in Charleston: A Narrative of the Chief Events relating to the Rise and Progress of the Methodist Episcopal Church in Charleston, S.C.* Nashville: E. Stevenson and J. E. Evans, 1856.

Redford, A. H. *History of the Organization of the Methodist Episcopal Church, South.* Nashville: Published by A. H. Redford, Agent for the M.E. Church, South, 1871.

Wightman, William M. *Life of William Capers, D.D., One of the Bishops of the Methodist Episcopal Church, South, Including an Autobiography.* Nashville: Southern Methodist Publishing, 1858.

Willson, John O. *Sketch of the Methodist Church in Charleston, S.C., 1787–1887.* Charleston, 1888.

York, Brantley. *The Autobiography of Brantley York.* Durham, N.C.: Seeman Printery, 1910.

F. Secular Memoirs and Records

Berlin, Ira, Barbara J. Fields, Thavolia Glymph, Joseph P. Reidy, and Leslie S. Rowland, eds. *Freedom: A Documentary History of Emancipation, 1861–1867.* Vol. 1, Series 1: *The Destruction of Slavery.* Cambridge, U.K.: Cambridge University Press, 1985.

Hardy, William Harris. "Recollections of Reconstruction in East and Southeast Mississippi." In *Publications of the Mississippi Historical Society (1901),* vol. 4. Edited by Franklin L. Riley, 105–32. Oxford, Miss., 1901.

Pearson, Elizabeth Ware, ed. *Letters from Port Royal.* Boston: W. B. Clarke, 1905; reprint, New York: Arno Press, 1969.

Rawick, George P., ed. *The American Slave: A Composite Autobiography.* Vol. 10, Supplement, Series 1, Part 5: *Mississippi Narratives.* Westport, Conn.: Greenwood Press, 1977.

Scott, Robert N., ed. *War of the Rebellion: A Compilation of the Official Records of the Union and Confederate Armies.* Series 1, vol. 34, part 3. Washington, D.C.: Government Printing Office, 1891.

SECONDARY SOURCES

Books and Periodicals

Adams, Revels A. *Cyclopedia of African Methodism in Mississippi.* N.p., 1902.

Anderson, James D. "Aunt Jemima in Dialectics: Genovese on Slave Culture." *Journal of Negro History* 41 (January 1976): 99–114.

———. *The Education of Blacks in the South, 1860–1935.* Chapel Hill: University of North Carolina Press, 1988.

Andrews, William L., ed. *Sisters of the Spirit: Three Black Women's Autobiographies of the Nineteenth Century.* Bloomington: Indiana University Press, 1986.

Angell, Stephen Ward. *Bishop Henry McNeal Turner and African-American Religion in the South.* Knoxville: University of Tennessee Press, 1992.

Bailey, Kenneth K. "The Post Civil War Racial Separations in Southern Protestantism: Another Look." *Church History* 46 (December 1977): 453–73.

Baldwin, Lewis V. *"Invisible" Strands in African Methodism: A History of the African Union Methodist Protestant and Union American Methodist Episcopal Churches, 1805–1980.* Metuchen, N.J.: Scarecrow Press, 1983.

———. *The Mark of a Man: Peter Spencer and the African Union Methodist Tradition: The Man, the Movement, the Message and the Legacy.* New York: University Press of America, 1987.

Bassett, John Spencer. "North Carolina Methodism and Slavery." *An Annual Publication of Historical Papers Published by the Historical Society of Trinity College, Durham, N.C.* Series 4 (1900): 1–11.

Benjamin, Walter W. "The Era of Reconstruction: The Freedmen's Aid Society." In *The History of American Methodism,* vol. 2, 360–80. Ed. Emory Stevens Bucke. New York: Abingdon Press, 1964.

Berkeley, Kathleen C. "'Colored Ladies Also Contributed': Black Women's Activities from Benevolence to Social Welfare, 1866–1896." In *The Web of Southern Social Relations: Women, Family, and Education,* 181–203. Ed. Walter J. Fraser Jr., R. Frank Saunders Jr., and Jon L Wakelyn. Athens: University of Georgia Press, 1985.

Berlin, Ira. *Slaves without Masters: The Free Negro in the Antebellum South.* New York: Oxford University Press, 1974.

Berlin, Ira, Barbara J. Fields, Steven F. Miller, Joseph P. Reidy, and Leslie S. Rowland. *Slaves No More: Three Essays on Emancipation and the Civil War.* Cambridge, U.K.: Cambridge University Press, 1992.

Bleser, Carol K. R. *The Promised Land: The History of the South Carolina Land Commission, 1869–1890.* Columbia: University of South Carolina Press, 1969.

Bradley, David H. *A History of the A.M.E. Zion Church Part I, 1796–1872.* Nashville: Parthenon Press, 1956.

Bryant, Lawrence C., ed. *Negro Senators and Representatives in the South Carolina Legislature, 1868–1902.* Orangeburg, S.C.: Dr. Lawrence C. Bryant, Publisher, 1968.

Butt, Israel L. *History of African Methodism in Virginia or Four Decades in the Old Dominion.* Norfolk: Hampton Institute Press, 1908.

Cade, John B. *Holsey: The Incomparable.* New York: Pagent Press, 1964.

Coan, Josephus Roosevelt. *Daniel Alexander Payne: Christian Educator.* Philadelphia: A.M.E. Book Concern, 1935.

Cohen, William. *At Freedom's Edge: Black Mobility and the Southern White Quest for Racial Control, 1861–1915.* Baton Rouge: Louisiana State University Press, 1991.

Cooper, Frederick. "Elevating the Race: The Social Thought of Black Leaders, 1827–1850." *American Quarterly* 24 (December 1972): 604–25.

Coulter, E. Merton. *Negro Legislators in Georgia during the Reconstruction.* Athens: Georgia Historical Quarterly, 1968.

———. *The South during Reconstruction, 1865–1877.* Baton Rouge: Louisiana State University Press, 1947.

———. *William G. Brownlow: Fighting Parson of the Southern Highlands.* Chapel Hill: University of North Carolina Press, 1937.

Cromwell, John W. "The Aftermath of Nat Turner's Insurrection." *Methodist History* 5 (April 1920): 208–34.

Culp, D. W., ed. *Twentieth Century Negro Literature or a Cyclopedia of Thought.* Atlanta: J. L. Nichols, 1902.

Currie-McDaniel, Ruth. *Carpetbagger of Conscience: A Biography of John Emory Bryant.* Athens: University of Georgia Press, 1987.

Curry, John W. *Passionate Journey: History of the 1866 South Carolina Annual Conference.* St. Matthews, S.C.: State Printing, 1980.

Davis, David Brion. "The Emergence of Immediatism in British and American Antislavery Thought." *Mississippi Valley Historical Review* 49 (September 1962): 209–30.

Delany, Martin R. *The Condition, Elevation, Emigration and Destiny of the Colored People of the United States.*; reprint, New York: Arno Press, 1968.

Del Pino, Julius E. "Blacks in the United Methodist Church from Its Beginning to 1968." *Methodist History* 19 (October 1980): 3–20.

Derrick, W. B., and James C. Embry. "The Late Bishop Cain." *A.M.E. Church Review* 3 (April 1887): 337–50.

Dodson, Jualynne. "Nineteenth Century A.M.E. Preaching Women: Cutting Edge of Women's Inclusion in Church Polity." In *Women in New Worlds,* 276–89. Ed. Rosemary Skinner Keller and Hilah F. Thomas. Nashville: Abingdon Press, 1981.

Drago, Edmund L. *Black Politicians and Reconstruction in Georgia: A Splendid Failure.* Baton Rouge: Louisiana State University Press, 1982.

Drescher, Seymour, and Frank McGlynn, eds. *The Meaning of Freedom: Economics, Politics, and Culture after Slavery.* Pittsburgh, Pa.: University of Pittsburgh Press, 1992.

Du Bois, W. E. B. *Black Reconstruction in America: An Essay toward a History of the Part which Black Folk Played in the Attempt to Reconstruct Democracy in America, 1860–1880.* 1935. Reprint, New York: Atheneum, 1977.

———. *The Souls of Black Folk.* 1903. Reprint, New York: Penguin, 1989.

Duncan, Russell. *Freedom's Shore: Tunis Campbell and the Georgia Freedmen.* Athens: University of Georgia Press, 1986.

Duncan, Sara J. *Progressive Missions in the South and Addresses with Illustrations and Sketches of Missionary Workers and Ministers and Bishops' Wives.* Atlanta: Franklin Printing and Publishing, 1906.

Dvorak, Katherine L. *An African-American Exodus: The Segregation of Southern Churches.* Brooklyn: Carlson Publishing, 1991.

Engs, Robert F. *Freedom's First Generation: Black Hampton, Virginia, 1861–1890.* Philadelphia: University of Pennsylvania Press, 1979.

Eskew, Glenn T. "Black Elitism and the Failure of Paternalism in Postbellum Georgia: The Case of Bishop Lucius Henry Holsey." *Journal of Southern History* 58 (November 1992): 637–66.

Farish, Hunter D. *The Circuit Rider Dismounts: A Social History of Southern Methodism, 1865–1900.* Richmond: Dietz Press, 1938; reprint, New York: Da Capo Press, 1969.

Fields, Barbara Jeanne. *Slavery and Freedom on the Middle Ground: Maryland during the Nineteenth Century.* New Haven, Conn.: Yale University Press, 1985.

Foner, Eric. *Freedom's Lawmakers: A Directory of Black Officeholders during Reconstruction.* New York: Oxford University Press, 1993.

———. *Free Soil, Free Labor, Free Men: The Ideology of the Republican Party before the Civil War.* New York: Oxford University Press, 1970.

———. *Nothing but Freedom: Emancipation and Its Legacy.* Baton Rouge: Louisiana State University Press, 1983.

———. *Reconstruction: America's Unfinished Revolution, 1863–1877.* New York: Harper and Row, 1988.

Foner, Philip S. *History of Black Americans: From Africa to the Emergence of the Cotton Kingdom.* Westport, Conn.: Greenwood Press, 1975.

Franklin, John Hope. *The Emancipation Proclamation.* Garden City, N.Y.: Doubleday, 1963.

———. *Reconstruction after the Civil War.* Chicago: University of Chicago Press, 1961.

Fraser, Walter J. Jr., R. Frank Saunders Jr., and Jon L. Wakelyn, eds. *The Web of Southern Social Relations: Women, Family, and Education.* Athens: University of Georgia Press, 1985.

Frazier, E. Franklin. *The Negro Church in America.* New York: Schocken Books, 1963.

Frederickson, George M. *The Black Image in the White Mind: The Debate on Afro-American Character and Destiny, 1817–1914.* New York: Harper and Row, 1971.

Genovese, Eugene D. *Roll, Jordan, Roll: The World the Slaves Made.* New York: Vintage Books, 1974.

George, Carol V. R. *Segregated Sabbaths: Richard Allen and the Emergence of Independent Black Churches, 1760–1840.* New York: Oxford University Press, 1973.

Glickstein, Jonathan A. *Concepts of Free Labor in Antebellum America.* New Haven, Conn.: Yale University Press, 1991.

Goen, C. C. *Broken Churches, Broken Nation: Denominational Schisms and the Coming of the American Civil War.* Macon, Ga.: Mercer University Press, 1985.

Graham, J. H. *Black United Methodists: Retrospect and Prospect.* New York: Vantage Press, 1979.

Gravely, William B. "A Black Methodist on Reconstruction in Mississippi: Three Letters by James Lynch in 1868–1869." *Methodist History* 11 (July 1973): 3–18.

———. "The Decision of A.M.E. Leader, James Lynch, to Join the Methodist Episcopal Church: New Evidence at Old St. George's Church, Philadelphia." *Methodist History* 15 (July 1977): 263–69.

———. *Gilbert Haven, Methodist Abolitionist: A Study in Race, Religion, and Reform, 1850–1880.* New York: Abingdon Press, 1973.

———. "Hiram Revels Protests Racial Separation in the Methodist Episcopal Church (1876)." *Methodist History* 8 (April 1970): 13–20.

———. "James Lynch and the Black Christian Mission during Reconstruction." In *Black*

Apostles at Home and Abroad, 161–88. Eds. David W. Wills and Richard Newman. Boston: G. K. Hall, 1982.

———. "The Social, Political and Religious Significance of the Formation of the Colored Methodist Episcopal Church (1870)." *Methodist History* 18 (October 1979): 3–25.

Griffith, Cyril E. *The African Dream: Martin R. Delany and the Emergence of Pan-African Thought*. University Park: Pennsylvania State University Press, 1975.

Hall, Robert L. " 'Yonder Come Day': Religious Dimensions of the Transition from Slavery to Freedom in Florida." *Florida Historical Quarterly* 65 (April 1987): 411–20.

Hammond, Edmund Jordan. *The Methodist Episcopal Church in Georgia, being a Brief History of the Two Georgia Conferences of the Methodist Episcopal Church together with a Summary of the Causes of Major Methodist Divisions in the United States and of the Problems Confronting Methodist Union*. Atlanta: N.p., 1935.

Harlan, Louis R. *Booker T. Washington: The Making of a Black Leader, 1856–1901*. New York: Oxford University Press, 1972.

———. *Booker T. Washington: The Wizard of Tuskegee, 1901–1915*. New York: Oxford University Press, 1983.

Harris, William C. "James Lynch: Black Leader in Southern Reconstruction." *Historian* 34 (November 1971): 40–61.

Hayden, J. Carleton. "After the War: The Mission and Growth of the Episcopal Church among Blacks in the South, 1865–1877." *Historical Magazine of the Protestant Episcopal Church* 42 (December 1973): 403–27.

Hesseltine, W. B. "Methodism and Reconstruction in East Tennessee." *East Tennessee Historical Society Publications* Number 3 (1931), 42–61.

Higginbotham, Evelyn Brooks. *Righteous Discontent: The Women's Movement in the Black Baptist Church, 1880–1920*. Cambridge, Mass.: Harvard University Press, 1993.

Hildebrand, Reginald F. " 'An Imperious Sense of Duty': Documents Illustrating an Episode in the Methodist Reaction to the Nat Turner Revolt." *Methodist History* 19 (April 1981): 155–74.

———. "Methodist Episcopal Policy on the Ordination of Black Ministers, 1784–1864." *Methodist History* 20 (April 1982): 124–42.

———. "Some Persistent Doubts about Paternalistic Hegemony: *Roll, Jordan, Roll* Twenty Years Later." *Contention* 3 (Fall 1993): 67–86.

Hine, William C. "Dr. Benjamin A. Boseman, Jr.: Charleston's Black Physician-Politician." In *Southern Black Leaders of the Reconstruction Era*, 335–62. Ed. Howard N. Rabinowitz. Urbana: University of Illinois Press, 1982.

Holly, James Theodore. "In Memoriam." *A.M.E. Church Review* 3 (October 1886): 117–25.

Holt, Thomas C. *Black over White: Negro Political Leadership in South Carolina during Reconstruction*. Urbana: University of Illinois Press, 1977.

———. *The Problem of Freedom: Race, Labor, and Politics in Jamaica and Britain, 1832–1938*. Baltimore: Johns Hopkins University Press, 1992.

Howard, Victor B. *Religion and the Radical Republican Movement, 1860–1870*. Lexington: University Press of Kentucky, 1990.

Hume, Richard L. "Negro Delegates to the State Constitutional Conventions of 1867–69." In *Southern Black Leaders of the Reconstruction Era*, 129–53. Ed. Howard N. Rabinowitz. Urbana: University of Illinois Press, 1982.

Jason, William C. Jr. "The Delaware Annual Conference of the Methodist Church, 1864–1965." *Methodist History* 4 (July 1966): 26–40.

Jenkins, Warren M. *Steps along the Way: The Origin and Development of the South Carolina Conference of the Central Jurisdiction of the Methodist Church.* Columbia, S.C.: State Printing, 1967.

Jervey, Edward D. "Motives and Methods of the Methodist Episcopal Church in the Period of Reconstruction." *Methodist History* 4 (July 1966): 17–25.

Jones, Donald G. *The Sectional Crisis and Northern Methodism: A Study in Piety, Political Ethics and Civil Religion.* Metuchen, N.J.: Scarecrow Press, 1979.

Kolchin, Peter. *First Freedom: The Responses of Alabama's Blacks to Emancipation and Reconstruction.* Westport, Conn.: Greenwood Press, 1972.

Lakey, Othal H. *The History of the c.m.e. Church.* Memphis: c.m.e. Publishing, 1985.

———. *The Rise of "Colored Methodism": A Study of the Background and the Beginnings of the Christian Methodist Episcopal Church.* Dallas: Crescendo Book Publications, 1972.

Lamson, Peggy. *The Glorious Failure: Black Congressman Robert Brown Elliot and the Reconstruction in South Carolina.* New York: W. W. Norton, 1972.

Lewis, Bernard. *History Remembered, Recovered, Invented.* Princeton, N.J.: Princeton University Press, 1975.

Lincoln, C. Eric, and Lawrence H. Mamiya. *The Black Church in the African American Experience.* Durham, N.C.: Duke University Press, 1990.

Litwack, Leon F. *Been in the Storm So Long: The Aftermath of Slavery.* New York: Alfred A. Knopf, 1979.

———. *North of Slavery: The Negro in the Free States, 1760–1860.* Chicago: University of Chicago Press, 1961.

Long, Charles Sumner. *History of the a.m.e. Church in Florida.* Philadelphia: a.m.e. Book Concern, 1939.

Loveland, Anne C. "Evangelicalism and 'Immediate Emancipation' in American Antislavery Thought." *Journal of Southern History* 32 (May 1966): 172–88.

Magdol, Edward. *A Right to the Land.* Westport, Conn.: Greenwood Press, 1977.

Mandle, Jay R. *Not Slave, Not Free: The African American Economic Experience since the Civil War.* Durham, N.C.: Duke University Press, 1992.

Mann, Harold W. *Atticus Greene Haygood: Methodist Bishop, Editor and Educator.* Athens: University of Georgia Press, 1965.

Martin, Sandy Dwayne. "Black Churches and the Civil War: Theological and Ecclesiastical Significance of Black Methodist Involvement, 1861–1865." *Methodist History* 32 (April 1994): 174–86.

Mathews, Donald G. "The Methodist Mission to the Slaves, 1829–1844." *Journal of American History* 51 (March 1965): 615–31.

———. *Religion in the Old South.* Chicago: University of Chicago Press, 1977.

———. *Slavery and Methodism: A Chapter in American Morality, 1780–1845.* Princeton, N.J.: Princeton University Press, 1965.

May, James W. "The War Years." In *The History of American Methodism,* vol. 2, 206–56. Ed. Emory Stevens Bucke. New York: Abingdon Press, 1964.

McPherson, James M. *The Abolitionist Legacy: From Reconstruction to the NAACP.* Princeton, N.J.: Princeton University Press, 1975.

————. *The Struggle for Equality: Abolitionists and the Negro in the Civil War and Reconstruction*. Princeton, N.J.: Princeton University Press, 1964.

Mixon, W. H. *History of the African Methodist Episcopal Church in Alabama*. Nashville: A.M.E. Sunday School Union, 1902.

Mohr, Clarence L. *On the Threshold of Freedom: Masters and Slaves in Civil War Georgia*. Athens: University of Georgia Press, 1986.

Montgomery, William E. *Under Their Own Vine and Fig Tree: The African-American Church in the South, 1865–1900*. Baton Rouge: Louisiana State University Press, 1993.

Moore, David O. "The Withdrawal of Blacks from Southern Baptist Churches following Emancipation." *Baptist History and Heritage* (July 1981): 12–18.

Morris, Robert C. *Reading, 'Riting, and Reconstruction: The Education of Freedmen in the South, 1861–1870*. Chicago: University of Chicago Press, 1976.

Morrow, Ralph E. *Northern Methodism and Reconstruction*. East Lansing: Michigan State University Press, 1956.

Niebuhr, H. Richard. *The Social Sources of Denominationalism*. New York: New American Library, 1975.

Olson, Otto H. *Carpetbagger's Crusade: The Life of Albion Winegar Tourgee*. Baltimore: Johns Hopkins University Press, 1965.

Oubre, Claude F. *Forty Acres and a Mule: The Freedmen's Bureau and Black Land Ownership*. Baton Rouge: Louisiana State University Press, 1978.

Painter, Nell Irvin. *Exodusters: Black Migration to Kansas after Reconstruction*. New York: Alfred A. Knopf, 1977.

Perman, Michael. *Emancipation and Reconstruction, 1862–1879*. Arlington Heights, Ill.: Harlan Davidson, 1987.

Phillips, Charles H. *The History of the Colored Methodist Episcopal Church in America*. Jackson, Tenn.: Publishing House of the C.M.E. Church, 1900.

Ponton, M. M. *Life and Times of Henry M. Turner: The Antecedent and Preliminary History of the Life and Times of Bishop H. M. Turner*. Atlanta: A. B. Caldwell Publishing, 1917; reprint, New York: Negro Universities Press, 1970.

Prentice, George. *The Life of Gilbert Haven, Bishop of the Methodist Episcopal Church*. New York: Phillips and Hunt, 1883.

Purifoy, Lewis M. "The Southern Methodist Church and the Proslavery Argument." *Journal of Southern History* 32 (August 1966): 325–41.

Quarles, Benjamin. *Black Abolitionists*. New York: Oxford University Press, 1969.

Raboteau, Albert J. *Slave Religion: The "Invisible Institution" in the Antebellum South*. New York: Oxford University Press, 1978.

Ransom, Roger L., and Richard Sutch. *One Kind of Freedom: The Economic Consequences of Emancipation*. Cambridge: Cambridge University Press, 1977.

Redkey, Edwin S. *Black Exodus: Black Nationalist and Back-to-Africa Movements, 1890–1910*. New Haven, Conn.: Yale University Press, 1969.

Richardson, Harry V. *Dark Salvation: The Story of Methodism as It Developed among Blacks in America*. Garden City, N.Y.: Doubleday, 1976.

Richardson, Joe M. *Christian Reconstruction: The American Missionary Association and Southern Blacks, 1861–1890*. Athens: University of Georgia Press, 1986.

————. "The Failure of the American Missionary Association to Expand Congregationalism among Southern Blacks." *Southern Studies* 18 (Spring 1979): 51–73.

Rose, Willie Lee. *Rehearsal for Reconstruction: The Port Royal Experiment*. New York: Oxford University Press, 1964.

Rush, Christopher. *A Short History of the Rise and Progress of the African M.E. Church in America*. N.p., 1843; reprint, New York: J. J. Zuille, 1866.

Savage, Horace C. *Life and Times of Bishop Isaac Lane*. Nashville: National Publication Company, 1958.

Scott, Rebecca J. *Slave Emancipation in Cuba: The Transition to Free Labor, 1860–1899*. Princeton, N.J.: Princeton University Press, 1985.

Seraile, William. *Voice of Dissent: Theophilus Gould Steward (1843–1924) and Black America*. Brooklyn: Carlson Publishing, 1991.

Sernett, Milton C. *Black Religion and American Evangelicalism: White Protestants, Plantation Missions, and the Flowering of Negro Christianity, 1787–1865*. Metuchen, N.J.: Scarecrow Press, 1975.

Shipp, Albert M. *History of Methodism in South Carolina*. Nashville: Southern Methodist Publishing, 1884.

Simmons, William J. *Men of Mark: Eminent, Progressive and Rising*. Cleveland: G. M. Rewell, 1887.

Singleton, George A. *The Romance of African Methodism: A Study of the African Methodist Episcopal Church*. New York: Exposition, 1952.

Smith, Charles Spencer. *A History of the African Methodist Episcopal Church*. Philadelphia: Book Concern of the A.M.E. Church, 1922; reprint, New York: Johnson Reprint Corporation, 1968.

Smith, George G. *The Life and Times of George Foster Pierce, D.D. LL.D. Bishop of the Methodist Episcopal Church, South*. Sparta, Ga.: Hancock Publishing, 1888.

Smith, John David. *An Old Creed for the New South: Proslavery Ideology and Historiography, 1865–1918*. Westport, Conn.: Greenwood Press, 1985.

Smoot, Thomas A. "Early Methodism on the Lower Cape Fear." In *Historical Papers of the North Carolina Conference Historical Society and the Western North Carolina Conference Historical Society, 1925*. Greensboro: North Carolina Christian Advocate, 1925.

Southall, Eugene P. "The Attitude of the Methodist Episcopal Church, South toward the Negro from 1844 to 1870." *Journal of Negro History* 16 (October 1931): 359–70.

Stowell, Daniel W. " 'We Have Sinned, and God Has Smitten Us!' John H. Caldwell and the Religious Meaning of Confederate Defeat." *Georgia Historical Quarterly* 78 (Spring 1994): 1–38.

Stowell, Jay S. *Methodist Adventures in Negro Education*. New York: Methodist Book Concern, 1922.

Sweet, William W. "The Methodist Episcopal Church and Reconstruction." *Journal of the Illinois State Historical Society* 7 (October 1914): 147–65.

Taylor, Alrutheus A. *The Negro in the Reconstruction of Virginia*. Washington, D.C.: Association for the Study of Negro Life and History, 1926.

Thomas, John L. "Romantic Reform in America, 1815–1865." *American Quarterly* 17 (Winter 1965): 656–81.

Thornbrough, Emma Lou, ed. *Black Reconstructionists*. Englewood Cliffs, N.J.: Prentice-Hall, 1972.

Thurmond, Michael L. *A Story Untold: Black Men and Women in Athens History*. Athens, Ga.: Clarke County School District, 1978.

Tindall, George B. "The Liberian Exodus of 1878." *South Carolina Historical Magazine* 53 (July 1952): 133–45.

———. *South Carolina Negroes, 1877–1900.* Columbia: University of South Carolina Press, 1952.

Tourgee, Albion W. *A Fool's Errand, by One of the Fools: A Novel of the South during Reconstruction.* New York: Harper and Row, [originally published 1879] 1966.

Tucker, David M. *Black Pastors and Leaders: Memphis, 1819–1972.* Memphis: Memphis State University Press, 1975.

Ullman, Victor. *Martin R. Delany: The Beginnings of Black Nationalism.* Boston: Beacon Press, 1971.

Walker, Clarence E. *A Rock in a Weary Land: The African Methodist Episcopal Church during the Civil War and Reconstruction.* Baton Rouge: Louisiana State University Press, 1982.

Walls, William J. *The African Methodist Episcopal Zion Church: Reality of the Black Church.* Charlotte, N.C.: A.M.E. Zion Publishing, 1974.

Washington, James M. *Frustrated Fellowship: The Black Baptist Quest for Social Power.* Macon, Ga.: Mercer University Press, 1986.

Wesley, Charles H. *Richard Allen: Apostle of Freedom.* Washington, D.C.: Associated Publishers, 1935.

Wharton, Vernon L. *The Negro in Mississippi, 1865–1890.* Chapel Hill: University of North Carolina Press, 1947.

Williamson, Joel. *After Slavery: The Negro in South Carolina during Reconstruction, 1861–1877.* New York: W. W. Norton, 1975.

———. *The Crucible of Race: Black-White Relations in the American South since Emancipation.* New York: Oxford University Press, 1984.

Wills, David W. "Womanhood and Domesticity in the A.M.E. Tradition: The Influence of Daniel Alexander Payne." In *Black Apostles at Home and Abroad,* 133–46. Edited by Richard Newman and David W. Wills. Boston: G. K. Hall, 1982.

Woodson, Carter G. *The History of the Negro Church.* 3rd ed. Washington, D.C.: Associated Publishers, 1972.

Woodward, C. Vann. *The Strange Career of Jim Crow.* 3rd ed. New York: Oxford University Press, 1974.

Wright, Richard R. Jr. *The Bishops of the African Methodist Episcopal Church.* Nashville: A.M.E. Sunday School Union, 1963.

———. *Centennial Encyclopedia of the African Methodist Episcopal Church.* Philadelphia: Book Concern of the A.M.E. Church, 1916.

Dissertations and Theses

Angell, Stephen Ward. "Henry McNeal Turner and Black Religion in the South, 1865–1900." Ph.D. diss., Vanderbilt University, 1988.

Ashmore, Nancy Vance. "The Development of the African Methodist Episcopal Church in South Carolina, 1865–1965." Masters' thesis, University of South Carolina, 1969.

Clary Jr., George Esmond. "The Founding of Paine College: A Unique Venture in Interracial Cooperation in the New South, 1882–1903." Ed.D. diss., University of Georgia, 1965.

Clayton, Joyce D. "Education, Politics and Statesmanship: The Story of James Walker Hood in North Carolina, 1864–1890." M.A. thesis, North Carolina Central University, 1978.

Graham, William L. "Patterns of Intergroup Relations in the Cooperative Establishment, Control, and Administration of Paine College (Georgia) by Southern Negro and White People: A Study of Intergroup Process." Ph.D. diss., New York University, 1955.

Griffin, Paul R. "Black Founders of Reconstruction Era Methodist Colleges: Daniel A. Payne, Joseph C. Price and Isaac Lane, 1863–1890." Ph.D. diss., Emory University, 1983.

Jenkins, Wilbert Lee. "Chaos, Conflict and Control: The Responses of the Newly-Freed Slaves in Charleston, South Carolina to Emancipation and Reconstruction, 1865–1877." Ph.D. diss., Michigan State University, 1993.

Johnson, Henry M. "The Methodist Episcopal Church and the Education of Southern Negroes, 1862–1900." Ph.D. diss., Yale University, 1939.

Jones, Donald G. "The Moral, Social and Political Ideas of the Methodist Episcopal Church from the Closing Years of the Civil War through Reconstruction, 1864–1876." Ph.D. diss., Drew University, 1969.

Killian, Charles. "Bishop Daniel A. Payne: Black Spokesman for Reform." Ph.D. diss., Indiana University, 1971.

Kirby, James E. "The Ecclesiastical and Social Thought of Matthew Simpson." Ph.D. diss., Duke University, 1963.

Perry, Grace Naomi. "The Educational Work of the African Methodist Episcopal Church prior to 1900." M.A. thesis, Howard University, 1948.

Pool, Frank Kenneth. "The Southern Negro in the Methodist Episcopal Church." Ph.D. diss., Duke University, 1939.

Roth, Donald Franklin. " 'Grace not Race': Southern Negro Church Leaders, Black Identity, and Missions to West Africa, 1865–1919." Ph.D. diss., University of Texas at Austin, 1975.

Stokes, Arthur P. "Daniel Alexander Payne: Churchman and Educator." Ph.D. diss., Ohio State University, 1973.

INDEX

Holsey, Lucius H., 15, 16, 20, 22, 23, 119; conversion and call to preach, 19; disillusionment with new paternalism, 121; on education, 24–27; opposition to political involvement, 23
Honour, John, 6
Hood, James Walker, 46, 52, 55, 56, 58; political career, 68; on merger between African Methodisms, 46; on politics, 67
Hunter, William H., 35, 36–38, 40

Johnson, Andrew, xvi, 91, 106
Johnson, Griffin, 48
Johnston, Richard M., 16

Kealing, H. T., 42, 54, 55, 57
Ku Klux Klan, xvi, 23, 48

Laity: role in recruiting ministers, 42, 93; sparsity of information concerning, xxi, 48, 122; women, 42, 122–23
Landry, Pierre, 93–94
Lane College, 24
Lane, Cullen, 17
Lane, Isaac, 16–17, 20; conversion and call to preach, 18–19
Lansing, Issac J., 113
Leigh, C. C., 35
Lewis, Bernard, 55–56
Lewis, T. W., 79, 82, 89–90, 94, 109
Liberian Exodus Joint Steamship Company, 71
Lincolnville, 66
Litwack, Leon, xvi
Long, Charles Sumner, 42
Lynch, James, xix, 32, 35, 52, 57, 95, 108, 112–13, 114; death, 115; on economics, 64, 65; on education, 33; joins M.E. Church, 98–100

McPherson, James M., 87
McTyeire, Holland, 13, 14
Martin, William, 4
Mathews, Donald G., xxi, 5
Matlack, Lucius C., 113, 114, 115–16
Matton, W. G., 110

Membership statistics: A.M.E., 48; A.M.E. Zion, 48; C.M.E., 3, 14, 48; M.E., 92, 93, 117; M.E. Church, South, 7; unreliability of, 48
Methodist, 83
Methodist Advocate, 107
Methodist Episcopal Church (M.E.), xvii, xviii, xxiii; Central Jurisdiction, 122; Church Extension Society, 76, 82, 88, 91; on civil rights, 103–4; competition with A.M.E., 43, 85–86; Delaware Conference, 77, 87, 88; on economics, 102–3; education and Freedmen's Aid Society, 81–82, 88, 89, 92, 96–97, 117; General Conference of 1864, 75–77, 78, 87, 108, 117; General Conference of 1868, 82, 100, 110; General Conference of 1872, 114; General Conference of 1876, 114–16, 117; General Conference of 1880, 117; mission to whites, 84–85, 111, 113; Missionary Society, 78, 82, 88, 91; object of violence, 97–98; on political involvement, 105–8; on social equality, 104; Washington Conference, 77, 87, 88. *See also* anticaste radicalism; preachers: M.E.
Methodist Episcopal Church, South (M.E. Church, South), xvii, xviii, xxiii; on Colored Methodism, 11–14; on education for blacks, 9–10, 24, 25–27; founding, xxiv, 90; General Conference of 1866, 10–11, 84; loss of black membership, 7; mission to slaves, 4–6; on political noninvolvement, 105; relationship with A.M.E., 12–13, 43; separation from Northern Methodism, 4, 76; supports subordination of blacks, 9
Methodist Quarterly Review, 83
Middleton, James B., 114
Miles, Mary, 17
Miles, William A., 14, 16, 17, 20; conversion and call to preach, 19; opposition to political involvement, 23; on education, 24
Miller, Simon, 42
Montgomery, William, xvi
Mood, Francis Asbury, 6

Reginald F. Hildebrand is Associate Professor of Afro-
American Studies and History at the University of North Carolina
at Chapel Hill.

Library of Congress Cataloging-in-Publication Data
Hildebrand, Reginald Francis.
The times were strange and stirring : Methodist preachers
and the crisis of emancipation / Reginald F. Hildebrand.
Includes bibliographical references and index.
ISBN 0-8223-1627-7. — ISBN 0-8223-1639-0 (pbk.)
1. Methodist Church—Southern States—History—
19th century.   2. Afro-American Methodists—Southern
States—History—19th century.   3. Southern States—Church history—
19th century.   I. Title.
BX8435.H55   1995
287'.875'09034—dc20   94-46758 CIP